community psychology
and
community mental health

introductory readings

community psychology
and
community mental health

introductory readings

patrick e. cook, editor

florida state university

HOLDEN-DAY

san francisco

community psychology and
community mental health

4567890 BL 80798765

to dorothy, ellen, and eddie

preface

Rather than being a smorgasbord for the reader, I hope this book will be an aperitif that whets the reader's appetite for a new and exciting approach to human problems. The articles collected here represent a distillation of many of the more important concepts, issues, and thinking in community psychology and community mental health. In spite of its title, the book is intended to be of interest and value to others in addition to psychologists. Many of the authors of the articles reprinted here are from fields other than psychology. The book is for people who are concerned about the human condition, community psychology, community mental health, and the potential contribution of community psychology and community mental health to the solution of human problems. It should be of value to students at the advanced undergraduate and graduate level and professionals who are interested in an introduction to community psychology and community mental health.

During the past decade, the social sciences and mental health professions have become increasingly concerned with community approaches to the understanding and remediation of human problems. The formation of a new division within the American Psychological Association, the Division of Community Psychology, is one indicant of the upsurge of interest. Increased attention is being given to community psychology and community mental health training in such related disciplines as psychology, psychiatry, social work, nursing, sociology, and urban and regional planning. Course offerings and formal specialty programs are proliferating at a rapid rate. The literature in the area, however, is just beginning to reflect this dramatic growth. This book was planned to present a brief, yet representative, collection of articles. The articles in themselves are broadly conceived, conceptually stimulating, basic to the general subject matter, and furnish a meaningful introduction to community psychology and community mental health.

The collection includes several position papers and reviews. Articles that can be considered "classic" or fundamental and articles that are especially thought-provoking or demonstrate particularly significant concepts have been selected, rather than those primarily focused on specific community programs. The book is organized into seven sections, each one a substantive area felt to be central to community psychology and community mental health. The articles in Section one present some important thinking in community psychology and community mental health from a conceptual viewpoint. Section two is comprised of a review of the areas of prevention and crisis intervention. Mental health consultation is the subject of the articles in Section three. Section four deals with planned change. Community psychologists, in addition to being consultants and change agents, need to be concerned with mental health manpower and training and the two articles in Section five are representative of the thinking in these areas. The importance of program evaluation and systems analysis for the community specialist is discussed in Section six, and the brief articles in Section seven touch on issues related to the future of community psychology and community mental health. Introductory comments have been written for each section. The selection of articles reflects my bias in favor of a systems approach to community work. This includes a preference for systems intervention within established community structure whenever possible. In order to bring about change, the community specialist should first attempt to work within the framework of those agencies and organizations which are already charged with the delivery of services to the community.

Many disciplines are, or could be, involved in community activities. Psychology is only one of these. There are some unique aspects of community psychology that justify its being a major focus of this book. Some of the concepts and issues involved in community psychology can serve as examples to other professions and disciplines as they, too, attempt to come to terms with pressing social problems. My intent is to demonstrate some ways in which an existing body of knowledge within a discipline, and contributions from other disciplines, can be brought to bear on community problems. Community psychology and community mental health as areas of interest overlap to an extent, but not entirely: Community psychology is something more than psychologists working in community mental health. Community psychology is similar to, yet different from, community psychiatry or community social work. Each profession and discipline brings to the community arena its own orientation, concepts, methodologies, competencies, and biases. Hopefully, the material collected in this volume transcends the boundaries of the various professional groups involved in community programs. A theme of the book is that the community specialist can function most meaningfully as a *participant-conceptualizer* in various community systems. Although I frequently refer to the community psychologist, this should be interpreted to include other "community mental healthers" in addition to the community psychologist.

This book was made possible by a number of people. To the authors of these significant articles and their publishers, for their permission to reprint the articles here, I am most grateful. I also wish to express my appreciation to Dr. Edwin I. Megargee and Dr. Charles D. Spielberger for their consultation; to Elizabeth Byrne for her editorial assistance; to Susan Brown, Glee Coles, Mary Lindquist, and Helen Thomas for their clerical assistance; to my students for their suggestions about articles to exclude from this collection; and to my wife, Dorothy, for her cooperation and encouragement, and to Judith Clancy of Holden-Day for her editorial assistance. Finally, as a community psychologist, I am indebted to Ira Isco and Saul Cooper for what they taught and demonstrated. They each epitomized the "participant-conceptualizer" role of the community psychologist.

Patrick E. Cook
Tallahassee, Florida
April 1970

contents

community psychology
and
community mental health

introductory readings

one   community psychology and
community mental health

Community psychology and community mental health are, more than anything else, attitudes and ideologies. They are orientations toward studying human problems and attempting to do something about them. This book is an introduction to community psychology and community mental health and presents, by means of the original articles, some of the basic concepts, problems, and techniques which presently describe the field.

It is appropriate that books of readings in community psychology and community mental health come at the end of the 1960's and beginning of the 1970's. The past decade was a period during which a great amount of attention was given to the development of programs in community mental health as well as to the development of other social programs. The War on Poverty is one outstanding example of such a program. During this same period the need for new approaches to lingering social problems became increasingly apparent as crises erupted in our urban communities and even in our campus communities. The nation that was able to land men on the moon in 1969 has not yet been able to eliminate or substantially reduce critical social and environmental problems such as mental illness, crime, poverty, discrimination, hunger, and pollution. So, in spite of the increased attention and support that has been marshaled for social programs, much remains to be done. The beginning of this decade marks the time for stock taking and making a new commitment to the improvement of the human condition. Community psychology and community mental health are directed at this improvement.

Probably no one statement or set of statements adequately defines either community psychology or community mental health. In a sense, the material in this book constitutes an attempt at a definition. In essence, the community mental health ideology is based upon the proposition that there must be ways to improve the level of social and emotional functioning of individuals in the community. The traditional ways of helping people have been unsuccessful, or, at best, inefficient. New ways of meeting human needs must be found. It will make the most sense if these new ways are: (1) applicable to groups of people, i.e., populations, and particularly populations "at risk"; (2) in or near the target group's natural habitat, i.e., in the community; (3) designed to articulate community resources in as efficient a way as possible, and in such a way as to insure that there is a residual effect—an increase in the community's ability to bring these resources to bear upon similar problems problems, or, at least providing for early detection of problems so that they may be handled with dispatch. The domain of community mental health includes the following broad areas: development of preventive programs and programs for crisis intervention; articulating the delivery of services, development of new and innovative community interventions, providing consultation to community caregivers (e.g., school teachers, clergy, police, welfare workers, probation and parole officers) and informal caregivers (community leaders, bartenders, scout leaders, and the like); training professionals, subprofessionals, and nonprofessionals in order to increase the mental health manpower pool; intervention in and modification of various social system factors to enhance the mental health of those people upon whose lives those systems impinge; and many other kinds of social and professional activism. In addition, attention is given to research in factors basic to community mental health so that our understanding of the community and its relationship to the well-being of its inhabitants is increased. The evaluation of mental health and social action programs is also given high priority in order to determine their worth.

Iscoe and Spielberger (1970) have reviewed developments in professional psychology leading to community psychology. As it exists today, community psychology shares many of the concerns of community mental health. But community psychology goes beyond community mental health in its concern with non-mental-health problems, e.g., the functioning of individuals within social units, organizations, and communities. Community psychology represents a mixture of mental health, behavioral science, social science, psychology, sociology, and other areas. It is the application of behavioral science principles to the understanding and solution of a variety of problems and community situations, and not just those problems related to mental health and mental illness.

Of course, scholars and practitioners from a variety of disciplines can make contributions to the solutions of problems in the community. The psychologist, however, by virtue of his background in both scholarship and service, is in a special position to function as an agent of change and adaptation in the community. The community psychologist, therefore, functions in community systems as a *participant-conceptualizer*. The notion of the participant-conceptualizer has significant implications above and beyond what has come to be called the "participant-observer." The participant-conceptualizer role implies a more active stance with regard to attempting to understand the data of community transactions. The participant-conceptualizer does not participate solely through observation. The idea of participation-conceptualization is both a general orientation to one's role as a community specialist (as outlined in the first article in this section) and also a specific kind of intervention role (see Section three).

Although the difference between community psychology and community mental health is significant in some respects, the overlap between the two fields may suggest that the differences are primarily semantic. This is not so. Topics such as the prevention of social and emotional problems, early detection of dysfunction, group and population approaches, innovations in services and service delivery, consultation and social system change, manpower training, and community research and program evaluation are common to both areas. Community psychology is predicated on the belief that the behavioral sciences in general, and psychology in particular, can have great impact upon the community and various human systems in a variety of areas, some of which are unrelated to mental health, even when mental health is broadly defined.

Community mental health as an area of interest dates back several decades (Cowen and Zax, 1967). Community psychology, as a specialized area, is relatively more recent, formally dating back to the Boston Conference. In the first article in this section, Chester Bennett has summarized for the American Psychological Association membership some of the major developments at that conference. In the second article, Sylvia Scribner attempts to answer the question "What is community psychology made of?" by describing four different role functions which can characterize the activities of the community psychologist. The third article by Donald Klein delineates a number of community variables of importance for community mental health. The Smith and Hobbs paper "The Community and the Community Mental Health Center" is an official position paper of the American Psychological Association. In the last article in this section, James Kelly discusses ecology and its potential application in the mental health field.

REFERENCES

Cowen, E. L. and Zax, M. The mental health fields today: Issues and problems. E. L. Cowen, E. A. Gardner, and M. Zax, eds., *Emergent approaches to mental health problems.* New York: Appleton-Century-Crofts, 1967.

Iscoe, I. and Spielberger, C. D. The emerging field of community psychology. I. Iscoe and C. D. Spielberger, eds., *Community psychology: Perspectives in training and research.* New York: Appleton-Century-Crofts, 1970.

The concept of community psychology first emerged at the Boston Conference, as Chester Bennett reports in this article. It is important to note that the conference anticipated a major development in the community field —the organization of the American Psychological Association Division of Community Psychology (Division 27). The report makes mention of a number of very important concepts and issues considered at the Conference. Community psychology was conceived to be something more than community mental health. In fact, it was suggested that community psychology be thought of as the most general area, with community mental health being considered a subspecialty within community psychology and clinical psychology a subspecialty of community mental health. The Conference characterized the community psychologist as a participant-conceptualizer, *and the specification of this concept was perhaps one of the most important contributions of the conference. The community psychologist, as a change agent with a service orientation, participates in the community and its subsystems, at the same time bringing with him a scientific attitude, a commitment to research and evaluation, and a desire to conceptualize. Since the Conference was a conference on training, a number of issues were raised with regard to the training of psychologists for work in the community. The issues and questions raised are still very much with us.*

community psychology: impressions of the boston conference on the education of psychologists for community mental health

Chester C. Bennett

The mental health frontier is shifting from the amelioration of illness to preventive intervention at the community level. Traditional methods of patient care are being supplemented by new approaches to interpersonal problems and to the management of group tensions. The community itself is being taught to collaborate in creating health-giving environments. Psychologists, in increasing numbers, are contributing to this endeavor as mental health consultants, mental health educators, human relations counselors, or as community-oriented clinicians. They have achieved a measure of professional identification with an area of service commonly called community mental health. According to Rossi's survey (Rossi, Klein, Von Felsinger, and Plaut, 1961), psychologists devoting substantial time to these activities numbered well over 1,000 in 1960, and the number is certainly increasing. Until recently, however, there has been virtually no systematic training of psychologists for community mental health work. The requisite skills have been learned on the job. Golann's survey (Golann, Wurm, and Magoon, 1964) of university curricula disclosed only one explicit graduate program in community mental health being offered in 1962, although nine other universities were giving "focused attention" to this area.

Increasing awareness of the gap between professional developments and training dictated the planning of a Conference on the Education of Psychologists for Community Mental Health. The Conference was sponsored jointly by Boston University and the South Shore Mental Health Center of Quincy,

Massachusetts, and supported in part by a grant from the National Institute of Mental Health (TI-MH-9505). The meeting was held May 4-8, 1965, at Swampscott, Massachusetts, where the New Ocean House provided a comfortable retreat. The Conference Committee comprised Luleen Anderson, Saul Cooper, Leonard Hassol, Donald C. Klein, Gershen Rosenblum, and the writer as Chairman. Some 30 psychologists who have been active in the development of community mental health programs participated, together with observers from the National Institute of Mental Health, the Administrative Officer, State and Professional Affairs, American Psychological Association, and the Executive Officer of the APA Conference on the Professional Preparation of Clinical Psychologists. Coming from universities, local agencies, state and regional programs, in all sections of the country, conference participants had been associated with innovations in training and with many creative approaches to community service.

An extended report of the Conference proceedings is being made available as a separate publication.[1] By the time this statement is read, preliminary reports will have been hashed by the Conference on the Professional Preparation of Clinical Psychologists and rehashed at the Chicago Convention. Indeed, the year 1964 may well stand in the annals of psychology as the year of professional self-analysis. It is the purpose of this brief report to apprise the APA membership at large of yet another conference and to convey some general impression of its import.

The major work of the Conference was accomplished in uninhibited discussion by three subgroups of participants who spent some 15 hours together, variously around a conference table, on the hotel porch, or out on the rocks talking to the accompaniment of the pounding surf. With limited time to establish communion, it was decided not to rotate group membership. Plenary sessions were held each day to keep the groups in touch with each other's progress. Prepared papers by John C. Glidewell, Robert Reiff, and Louis D. Cohen, to be published in the final report, were read and discussed at evening sessions of the Conference. A polling procedure proved helpful in clarifying some aspects of group consensus.

It became apparent almost immediately that the Conference was interested in emergent roles of psychologists, and areas of participation in community life, identified only in part with the goals of mental health care. Community mental health was viewed as one aspect of a broader spectrum of psychological services which was promptly labeled "community psychology." Reference was made to optimal realization of human potential through planned social action. Community psychologists were characterized as change agents, social systems analysts, consultants in community affairs,

[1]C. C. Bennett, Luleen S. Anderson, S. Cooper, L. Hassol, D. Klein and G. Rosenblum. *Community psychology: A report of the Boston Conference on the education of psychologists for community mental health.* Boston: Boston University and South Shore Mental Health Center, 1966.

and students generally of the whole man in relation to all his environments. For a number of participants this larger concept of psychology's role in community service was the most significant implication of the Conference.

Some of the most soul-searching discussions at the Conference dealt with the issue of activism. In their eagerness to exploit the impact of psychological insight, some participants expressed impatience with the caution and timidity of professional people in not taking command—in not projecting themselves fully into decision-making processes. But, does political activism compromise the professional role? Some participants argued that it does. They saw the professional as providing staff services—consultation, fact finding, and program evaluation—to society's decision-makers. It was not the province of the Conference to write a code of ethics for community psychology, but it was obvious that very subtle issues are at stake in distinguishing between professional expertness and value judgments in this unstructured area of community service.

The applicability of medical concepts and terminology to community psychology was discussed and generally rejected. Certainly it was clear that the potential contributions of psychology to community well-being will not be fully realized under the medical egis. The community psychologist is explicitly committed to furthering normal development. His procedures may have little or nothing to do with disease or disablement. It was recognized, of course, that medicine itself—and psychiatry in particular—is expanding its own conceptions of medical responsibility to encompass preventive and societal intervention. One wonders, however, whether the physician's indoctrination to prescribe with authority is compatible with the psychologist's concern for self-actualization and self-management. In any case, it is not at all clear that the public has given either medicine or psychology a mandate to manage community affairs.

There was considerable agreement that even the community mental health movement has been constrained by its allegiance to the "medical model." The approaching obsolescence of indiscriminate hospitalization of mental patients is long overdue. Psychotherapy is costly, and at best appropriate to certain problems as one method of intervention. Psychologists may well have been more imaginative than physicians in developing other methods. The Conference showed no inclination, however, to arrogate community mental health to psychology. It stressed the importance of interdisciplinary collaboration with the social and political sciences, as well as the psychiatric team. There was some tendency to emphasize the affiliation of community mental health with public health and education rather than psychiatry.

It was felt, with some optimism, that Public Law 88-164 (88th Cong. 1st Sess., Oct. 31, 1963), the Comprehensive Mental Health Centers Construction Act, gives sanction and encouragement to community-oriented services. Broadly interpreted, its provisions can support research and innovation in the mental health field. It was felt, with some concern, however, that the priority given to patient care under medical direction with hospital affiliation, narrowly interpreted, may constrict the development of mental health centers to traditional and limited concepts of medical care, reinforced by the availability of Federal support.

Inevitably the Conference faced the question whether community mental health should be thought of as an area of interest within clinical psychology or as a separate specialization. It is obvious that many community services have emerged as extensions of clinical practice. Most of the Conference participants were converted clinicians. Some were firmly convinced that clinical training, psychotherapy included, will continue to provide the appropriate foundation for community mental health work. For others, the clinician's investment in individual pathology appeared much less relevant. Still others hoped to see a general modification of clinical psychology toward social action and group approaches. Perhaps the temper of the Conference was best reflected in the conclusion of one group that the issue of relations within psychology "is to be resolved empirically by developing several models of training and function, rather than being resolved on an a priori basis at this time."

There was certainly agreement that community psychology is more than a by-product of clinical—that it depends upon and interacts with all the basic areas of psychological knowledge. Particular emphasis was given to the contributions of social psychology, group dynamics, and child development—less, perhaps, to the physiological areas. Indeed, some participants seemed to view community psychology as an integrating focus which enriches the meaning of all psychology. The community was seen as a laboratory, perhaps the ultimate laboratory in which to study the institutionalized behavior of man—the strategies he employs to create a habitat which in turn shapes him.

A recurrent theme of the Conference was its emphasis upon the scientific attitude. The community psychologist was characterized as a "participant-conceptualizer," committed as much to the creation of knowledge as to the promotion of programs. The very newness of the field calls for systematic analyses and evaluation of procedures. There are opportunities for research at every turn. The Conference stressed the need for methodological innovation in dealing with anecdotal information, multivariate interactions, and the assessment of change in midcourse. Psychologists must learn to use some of the techniques of ecology and other social sciences in researching community processes.

It would appear, paradoxically perhaps, that community psychology is applying the scientific method, rather than the scientific findings, of psychology to community problems. Much of our laboratory research has not been relevant. Practitioners search the literature in vain for validated techniques.

They have had to invent their own procedures and courses of action. But the posture of inquiry, the concern for generalized knowledge, and the methods of theory building they learned in graduate school are directly applicable to community psychology. This is the education the Conference would transmit to another generation of students.

In its enthusiastic response to a broader and more venturesome concept of community psychology, the Conference found itself disinclined to spend much time delineating programs of training in community mental health which might soon be discarded as obsolete. On the other hand, participants were explicitly unwilling to cast the preparation of community psychologists in any one mold. Having broken new ground themselves, they were notably receptive to creative pioneering and experimentation with a variety of educational approaches. In tune with the participant who submitted a "No-Position Position Paper," they considered it premature, and perhaps unwise in principle, to formulate a specific curriculum which might inhibit growth and exploration. They were particularly concerned lest a rigid patterning of training might produce a rigid person—a specialized technician rather than a creative generalist.

While no single formula for professional education of community psychologists emerged, the Conference achieved a measure of consensus on directions it might take. There was evident agreement that the field needs people trained at the doctoral level. There was interest in postdoctoral opportunities, but not to the exclusion of doctoral training. Considerable interest was also expressed in potential contributions of people with less than doctoral education, but no real effort was made in the brief Conference to define the functions and training of such groups. There was general acceptance of the PhD as the appropriate degree for community psychology. The establishment of separate professional schools of psychology or of special professional degrees received no support. Nor was there any inclination to commit the education of community psychologists to the medical schools or schools of education. There seemed to be no sense of urgency about establishing numerous PhD programs in community mental health, although some participants were prepared to offer curricula for such programs. By and large, the Conference was willing to make haste slowly—willing to see a variety of educational models tried and evaluated, even as the field itself is testing alternative role models.

The commitment of the Conference to high standards of professional education was unequivocal. This was evident in their concept of a generalist with a basic feeling for principles and versatile skills in practice. It was evident in their emphasis on research competence. Community psychology needs real researchers, not mere "research consumers" unprepared to make their own productive contribution. It was suggested that traditional dissertation requirements might be liberalized to sanction many kinds of knowledge building. There was no inclination to lower standards, however, or to eliminate meaningful training in the scientific method for the participant-conceptualizer.

The appropriateness of field experience as one aspect of the training of community psychologists was never questioned. There was some objection to the term "internship" with its clinical and medical connotations. Certainly there was general agreement that a variety of opportunities for practicum training in community work, other than the clinical internships, needs to be developed. Few clinical programs provide the requisite orientation of experience and supervision in the community setting. There was less clear agreement whether these experiences in community participation should be offered in addition to, in conjunction with, or in place of, clinical training. This question is related, of course, to the ambivalence of the Conference in rejecting its heritage as an outgrowth of clinical psychology. Closure came with the recommendation that many varieties of experience, in many different settings, should be explored before the ideal pattern of practicum training in community service can be specified.

A good deal of sentiment emerged in support of interdisciplinary collaboration in the training of community psychologists. Suggestions were made to involve other professions and other behavioral sciences both in teaching and in supervision of field experiences. A number of participants envisaged integrated student groups representing several disciplines working together. Here again, conceptions of collaboration were by no means limited to the psychiatric team. The Conference emphasized the contributions of anthropology, sociology, and the political sciences. They found common cause with public health practice and education. Biostatistics, law, and city planning were mentioned as cognate disciplines. A strong appeal was voiced for close and continuing cooperation between university faculties and practitioners in the community field. Joint appointments, reciprocal leaves, and frequent consultation were seen as useful linkages in implementing their mutual responsibility for the education of community workers.

As suggested earlier, the Conference was certainly receptive to postdoctoral training programs in community psychology. Reference was also made to in-service training opportunities and retooling of established professionals willing to extend their usefulness in this direction. There seemed to be tacit agreement, however, that the field will not attain professional maturity without the systematic support of predoctoral education and a steady recruitment of dedicated young people to careers in community service.

The Conference did not have time to give adequate consideration to the complex issues of nondoctoral training. By definition, community psychology is committed to sharing its knowledge and skills in the public interest. The Conference was notably lacking in concern for exclusive prerogatives and professional rights. They responded positively to the suggestion that a variety of community services can be rendered by people with less than doctoral education, and were willing to maintain "dialogues" with many interested groups. At the same time, there was no urgent appeal for crash manpower programs. In assessing the critical needs of community psychology at this time, the Conference gave higher priority to careful validation of programs and clarification of conceptual issues than to mere expansion of personnel.

It seems appropriate, as a final note, to report the unanimous recommendation of the Conference that some permanent organizational medium be established, preferably through or affiliated with APA, to facilitate communication among psychologists with vital interest in community psychology.

REFERENCES

Golann, S. E., Wurm, Carolyn A. and Magoon, T. M. Community mental health content of graduate programs in departments of psychology. *Journal of Clinical Psychology*, 1964, **20**, 518-522.

Rossi, A. M., Klein, D. C., Von Felsinger, J. M. and Plaut, T. F. A. A. survey of psychologists in community mental health: Activities and opinions on education needs *Psychological Monographs, 1961,* **74**(4, Whole No. 508).

The next article defines community psychology from a somewhat different vantage point than the Bennett article. Sylvia Scribner looks at community psychology in terms of practice. To answer the question "What is community psychology made of?" she identifies for us four kinds of psychologists that she feels represent different roles for the community psychologist. The social movement psychologist works for change in a political way. The social action psychologist works for change in a professional, apolitical way. A third type, the new clinical psychologist, contributes to change by innovation in clinical service. (Family therapy, new group approaches, and crisis intervention activities are examples of tools that "new clinical" psychologists may use.) The social engineer attempts to bring about change in social systems and social structure that will ultimately touch on the lives of every individual in the community.

As the author points out, these are not pure types and any one community psychologist may fit into more than one category. Also, any one psychologist may move from category to category depending upon the "hat" he wears and the techniques he employs at any given time. The four kinds of community psychologist's roles described by Scribner would seem to describe two major dimensions of community psychology practice. One dimension is that of activism (in the political sense) versus professionalism. A second dimension has to do with intervention and manipulation and ranges from clinical manipulation and intervention to nonclinical, political or systems manipulation and intervention.

The categories suggested by Scribner serve as a useful framework within which to view the various activities of the community psychologist. Case consultation (as described in Section three) most likely would be an activity of the "new clinical" psychologist and perhaps the social action psychologist. Program, administrative, and social system consultation more likely would be in the bailiwick of the social engineer. Advocacy might be associated more often with the activities of the social movement psychologist than any of the other types.

what is community psychology made of?

Sylvia Scribner

"What is community psychology?" appears to have become almost as popular a question among psychologists today as "What is operationism?" some decades ago. This shift in interest certainly testifies to the timeliness of the Boston Conference and the launching of Division 27.

The interest is ripe and the question seems right. But the answer proves troublesome. Attempts to specify the common denominator of community psychology vary widely. Some characterize the motivations and value systems of the individuals attracted to the field ("acceptance of responsibility for problems and issues of society," "humanistic goals"); some point to new work settings (community action programs, Peace Corps, Head Start); some emphasize the employment of new skills and techniques ("social interventionist," "social change agent"). Still others speak of a "common point of view" toward the practical uses of psychological knowledge and methodology. But none of these parameters seems to succeed both in setting the community psychologist apart from other professional colleagues or in uniting him with all those who bear the same label. And often as not the way out has been to present community psychology as all things to all men—a tangled skein of crusading spirit, new techniques of psychotherapy, activism, system theory and God Bless America!

This state of affairs suggests that the question may not be as "right" as it first appears. It is not unusual for other fields in psychology to have a similar difficulty in self-description. What is "social psychology," for example? If we are not content to rely on purely personalistic descriptions but want to characterize the field as it exists in actuality, we usually find ourselves responding to this question by enumerating the kinds of people who are "doing social psychology" and the kinds of problems they are working on.

Reprinted from the American Psychological Association Division of Community Psychology *Newsletter*, 1968, **2**, 4-6, with the permission of the *Newsletter* editor and the author.

This same sort of analytic approach might be a fruitful one for Division 27. If it is the fact—as it appears to be—that community psychology essentially represents the bringing together of various kinds of psychologists who have some concern with the broad question of "man in society" then strictly speaking, *it* isn't anything—neither a homogeneous group, nor a unified body of theory, perhaps not even a single "point of view." We might better ask, "Who are these psychologists? What, if anything, do they have in common?" If we proceed from an analysis of the component "interest groups" in community psychology, we might be in a better position to evaluate the real (as compared to merely hoped-for) potentialities in the Division for new applications of knowledge, for the development of a "participant-conceptualist generalist" or for the generation of new theories.[1]

Of course, there are many ways to carve up interest groups. I have tried my hand at one classification scheme which I offer more to illustrate how we might go about clarifying the different approaches to community psychology than to furnish an accurate analysis.

In what follows, I will be talking about four different kinds of community psychologists to whom I have given labels of convenience: "social movement" psychologist, "social action" psychologist, "new clinical" psychologist, and "social engineer." These labels are not meant to imply that we are necessarily referring to different people—a social actionist and a clinician may certainly be one and the same. We are using these as aids in delineating points of view, not for the purpose of characterizing individuals.

I. SOCIAL MOVEMENT PSYCHOLOGISTS

By this phrase I mean to refer to psychologists who identify themselves with the aims and aspirations of political and social movements working for major change. It is their conviction that fundamental changes in society will only come about through the organized political struggle of sections of the population, and they have committed themselves to support the aggressive political action groups of today—(students, the civil rights or black power movements, peace groups, left or independent political groupings of one kind or another). As psychologists, they are involved in working for social change in a *political* way. They may be actively engaged in local actions and community organization but these activities are viewed within a larger context. Their interest is not only in making progress on some specific social issue but, over and above that, in the gains and growth of the national protest movements which they see as crucial levers for social change.

[1]R. Reiff. Social intervention and the problem of psychological analysis. Presidential address to the Division of Community Psychology (27), American Psychological Association, Washington, D.C., September 1967.

Even within this subgrouping there are substantial differences in ideology between those who are concerned with political action as a strategy for making social gains within the existing social system, and the radicals who are interested, not in preserving and reforming, but in profoundly altering the basic economic, political and social structure of our society which they consider a precondition for creating healthy communities.

We are interested here in how these political views and objectives bear on the professional role. Some of these psychologists may be interested in putting their professional skills and talents to work on behalf of national movements. Such a role is not a clear one on the contemporary scene but a historical reference may help to illustrate some of its features. In the thirties, many professionals were attracted to the new CIO industrial unions, either as liberals seeing their potential for social reform or as Marxists who looked toward the working class as the vehicle for remaking society. Economists, social scientists, educators and others worked "on behalf of" these unions. This does not mean that they were necessarily paid employees or consultants; it means only that there was an identification and a devotion to issues that were of concern to labor and application of expert knowledge and skills to the solution of problems most crucial for labor. Some of this work was done under the aegis of autonomous or semiautonomous bodies; some through professional organizations and some from university bases.

The point of the historical example is not to try to make a forced analogy with the present but only to point up the fact that today, as in the past, there are some professionals concerned with basic social change who are not identifiable by their locus of work, (community or laboratory) by their specific function (activist or conceptual) or by a common theoretical frame of reference *within their discipline*. What they share is a certain kind of theorizing about contemporary society and, for some, a form of Marxist analysis of society may constitute the basis for their social involvement.

What are the implications for community psychology? "Social movement psychologists" may work in the same community programs as the social actionists (described below) but the basis for their participation may be quite different. They may work in settings far removed from the community, rendering diversified professional services in a voluntary capacity. They are likely to be concerned with many different kinds of social-political questions related to a number of different fields of psychology, rather than contributing primarily to the creation of a "new field" of community psychology. In terms of potentialities for theory development one thinks particularly of the possibilities of this group enriching the theory and practice of social movements, by subjecting to analysis and/or putting to the test certain "folk psychology" principles of how social and political organizations develop, function, and die.

In sum, in searching for what these psychologists have in common that enables us to "identify" them as a group, I would say that they share essentially a common *extra-psychological* frame of analysis for viewing contemporary social issues and a commitment to organized social movements as the major lever for social change.

II. "SOCIAL ACTION" PSYCHOLOGISTS

There seems to be a substantial group within community psychology that is interested in "social action to promote human betterment"—that is, in participating as professionals in programs directed at some specific social problem. As many have pointed out, there has been a proliferation of government-financed programs for human betterment in the last few years, dominated by the community mental health and poverty programs but encompassing such issues as juvenile delinquency, drug addiction, youth employment, and others. These programs have created certain new employment opportunities for psychologists and have helped to define community psychology as a new field.

In addition to government, other principal employers are philanthropic foundations and nonprofit research and service organizations. While they have always been large employers of psychological talent, there has been a shift in the nature of the programs funded,[2] creating the demand for different kinds of psychological skills as well as providing the opportunity for social-minded psychologists to engage in new professional responsibilities.

"Social action" psychologists often differ in the emphasis they place upon organizing the community. Some consider that the most significant aspect of contemporary social reform programs is their provision for "participation by the people" and they feel these programs will achieve real human gains only to the extent that they succeed in helping the disenfranchised, unorganized persons become actively engaged in common efforts to improve their life conditions. Other psychologists may be disinterested in organizing the recipients of services and feel they can perform a socially useful professional role simply through their own participation in these programs.

Even in programs which encourage people participation, however, the courses of action generally seem to be determined in most instances by the professional staff. *This is basically social action without commitment to political movements as forces for change.* In certain content areas, it may be social action without any clearly specified social goals while in others there may be varying degrees of professional consensus as to what the "desiderata" are.

The many content areas covered by these new programs are a source of great diversity, and so are the theoretical and scientific interests and the

[2]F. Riessman and M. Rein. The third force: an anti-poverty ideology. *The American Child,* November, 1965, **47**, 10-14.

values of the participating psychologists. It is hard to see how a common theory or body of knowledge can emerge from a group of practitioners who are not likely to even share a common definition of the psychological problem involved in a particular social program—say, for example, looting by Negro youths. To some the psychological problem may be that of correcting deviant behavior which interferes with individual progress, to others a matter of reducing intergroup hostility or controlling mass hysteria, or, conversely, a problem of raising the self-esteem of members of minority groups or of changing their child-rearing practices—and so on almost *ad infinitum*. While it undoubtedly would be rare to get any group of psychologists to "define the problem" similarly, it does seem that those who share an extra-psychological frame of reference toward social problems (as in the first group discussed) are more likely to exhibit a narrower conceptual range; their political "frame of reference" may operate, if ever so slightly, as a constraining and/or selective force on the way they identify and formulate issues.

The gain for theory building in the social action group, however, would be that more and more psychologists would be working with populations other than college sophomores and thus would come face to face with the deficiencies of many existing psychological constructs and be pressed to think creatively on their own.

On the level of practice and theory of practice, however, the picture is somewhat different. Working in somewhat similar settings with similar populations, these psychologists will be sharing certain common work interests and will be called upon to utilize certain practical skills not now in the general armanentarium of practitioners—action research, leadership development, adult education, new forms of consultation, to suggest a few. This would appear to justify the expectation that a new body of knowledge about technique or practice may be developed which will lay the basis for a certain generic approach to the training of a "community psychologist."

One might then consider this grouping of psychologists to be a kind of "conglomerate," made up of subgroups with subinterests and theories but sharing locations of work that have certain common humanistic goals and orientations and sharing certain common practical techniques.

As to whether a "common cement" of participation in action programs for human betterment will continue to hold together this conglomerate depends not so much on the subjective interests of the psychologists presently or future-ly involved, but on social, political and economic events. Will public funding continue for human betterment programs? Will they remain the same in character? Will the corporation replace the foundation as the "intervener" in the ghetto?[3] It is conceivable that changes in social action programs or experiences accumulated in them may promote the movement of some social action psychologists of today toward either the pole of "social movement psychologist" or of "social engineer." This would be the case if

[3]R. Cloward and F. Piven. Corporate imperialism for the poor. *Nation,* October 16, 1967.

the middle ground of applied psychology for human betterment through funded community action programs should disappear leaving psychologists either to affiliate with existing, more traditional public and institutional programs or to ally themselves (in voluntary, if not paid, capacities) with "grass-roots" action groups in the community.

III. "NEW CLINICAL" PSYCHOLOGISTS

A group that is both numerically and historically important to community psychology consists of clinical psychologists who are no longer willing to rely on individual face-to-face psychotherapy as the sole or primary means of remediating individual behavior. Their views have been well discussed in the literature and will not receive extended attention here.

For the future of community psychology, the important development would appear to be that more and more clinicians are departing from the medical model of mental illness, experimenting with new theoretical concepts and new techniques of environmental intervention. Because of these broadened interests and the changes in practice which take the clinician from the office or institution into new locations in the community, there is a growing basis for collaboration between him and the social action psychologist or the social engineer. Nonetheless, the clinical psychologist remains primarily oriented to a target individual and committed to evaluating intervention techniques on this basis.

Since this is the case, some of the questions considered central to the pursuit of community psychology—questions as to "how to achieve institutional change" or "how to involve people in social action" may or may not be relevant to the new clinical psychologists. Conversely a question meriting consideration is whether and how *their* knowledge and skills may be relevant to the other groupings involved in the community psychology enterprise.

IV. SOCIAL ENGINEER

Again this is a label of convenience intended to distinguish certain participants in community psychology from groups with other focal interests. Some attempt has been made to characterize "social engineers" in terms of the techniques of social change they employ. Generally, the criticism is made that their methods are heavily "manipulative" as compared to those which rely more on involvement of lay people in decision-making and planning.

This distinction by itself seems deficient, however, since social actionists and community organizers may also function in a manipulative way. Perhaps a better way to make a distinction is to suggest that what we mean by "social engineer" is someone directly focused on the system, organization, or institution. In other words, the system is his object and he is only indirectly concerned with the people whose behavior, experience or ideology is to be modified. The social actionist, on the other hand, is more related to the people who are to be served and/or activated and only indirectly to the system (Caveats again that any particular Mr. X may wear two hats, or any particular program may embody both approaches). The engineer's stock-in-trade is to diàgnose systems and systems effects, to help design and introduce changes in the system which are thought to lead to certain specified changes in people's behavior.

As I see it, the psychologist who participates in drawing up plans for a new kind of public housing is engaged in "social engineering;" so is the psychologist who sits in on meetings of a mayor's cabinet or who reorganizes the basic indoctrination program in the Army. As these examples are meant to suggest, the term "social engineer" is best used neutrally. There seems no reason why negative values should attach to it *per se* as is sometimes implied in discussions which cast social actionists in the role of "good guys" and "engineers" as the villains. With one as with the other, it would appear that the specific undertaking and its objective consequences should be evaluated, not the *ding-an-sich*. The trouble arises when claims are made for "social engineering" which are far too sweeping and imply that society will be remade by this approach. Used in this way, the same criticisms can be made against social science technocrats of today as were made against the "Technocracy" of the thirties—criticisms of the social, political and philosophical assumptions and policies of the scientific managers, not against their "legitimate" (that is, "technical") concerns. (I would just add that the exaggerated representations of some of the social actionists may equally well be considered unfounded and misleading.)

Applying the term "social engineer" broadly as here clouds over the extremely important consideration that there are many levels of system and system intervention. It has been more popular in the past to reserve the term "social engineer" to those working in the public sector at the higher levels of planning and policy-making. The number of "top-level" psychologists is likely to increase in the years ahead as professional organizations continue to press for greater participation by social scientists in government "in the national interest." Following the course taken by physical scientists, psychologists and other social scientists may be expected to take on added responsibilities in government posts, to shift more from the solely consultant role to that of key administrator, to disposal as well as proposal.

Psychologists functioning as social engineers are likely to be involved, too, in an increasing number of content areas as the public planning sphere is enlarged. They will be bringing different kinds of knowledge and expertise to their interventions, and no more than the other groups previously discussed, can they be expected to represent a common conceptual base. Moreover, as system intervention or social engineering approaches break into new fields we are likely to see new specializations developing, such as "architectural psychology" or "educational environment specialist." Finally, there is no reason to assume that the values, goals or objectives of psychologists attracted to this professional role are similar or harmonious or "humanistic" in the sense that this phrase is employed by some in community psychology. Recognition of this variance in values and ideology has already given rise to serious efforts to define a responsible role for the social engineer—one that will preserve his freedom to utilize his special knowledge and skills fully but that will ensure that his power to shape public policy is kept subject to the curbs and restraints of the lay citizenry.

What is shared in this group? Broadly speaking, it is a common interest in designing or shaping environments or systems to achieve certain behavioral or experimental consequences. And it is this group that might be expected to enrich psychology with data and theory in the ecological and systems analysis traditions.

Many might not agree with the interest groups that have been sketched out here or what has been said about them. But perhaps there is ground for agreement on some of these propositions:

1. Community psychology at the present time is a convenient umbrella term for psychologists who share a concern for a larger role for psychology on the social problems of the day but who have varying ideologies, values, psychological orientations and knowledge, skills and techniques;

2. Key constructs such as "acceptance of responsibility for problems of society," "social action" and "social change" have different content realms for individual psychologists depending on their interests and frame of reference;

3. It would be helpful in future discussions on the scope of community psychology to move from the level of acceptable but not very meaningful generality ("a new role for the psychologist is that of social change agent") to a more analytic level which specifies the different content realms and explores their implications.

While I have stressed the fact that the differences in background and the nature of present involvement of the various groupings in community psychology create varied potentialities for theory development, it does appear that on the level of practice, all the groupings share a common need—the need for more empirical knowledge about ecological and social system effects on individual behavior and experience. It may well be that the new roles performed by community psychologists will contribute to building a new data base which will make it possible for all psychologists—in the community or in the laboratory—to progress toward a more complete theory of human development and functioning.

What are the important variables one needs to identify, to understand and to work effectively in the community? It should be obvious that this question is all but unanswerable. There are an almost infinite number of kinds of data that one could wish to obtain about a community in order to achieve optimal effectiveness in community work. The outline given in the following article by Donald Klein taps many of the important variables. The view presented here is both a descriptive and dynamic view of the community and community processes. The variables discussed fall within the general categories of physical and topographical characteristics, the community's self-image, the nature of community groups and their interaction patterns, and the dynamic interplay of community forces. Klein's discussion of the various factors within these categories deserves close study.

the community and mental health: an attempt at a conceptual framework

Donald C. Klein

The clinical worker new to community work and his citizen collaborators in the community may question the need for a special conceptual view of community to guide them in their work. As life-long participants in multiple communities, they justifiably may lay claim to knowledge based on firsthand experience. To suggest that they do not have, on the basis of their experiences, sufficient understanding of the communities in which they work may seem strange to some. The suggestion is analogous to that of dynamic psychology when it questions the adequacy of the average person's common sense view of himself. This paper is based on the assumptions: (a) that it is important for professional mental health workers to maintain an objective and comprehensive view of community processes; and (b) that it is often difficult to do so, especially when the worker is confronted by community issues and events which are personally involving or which appear to threaten the very program to which he is committed.

The image of community which is developed in this paper is intended to serve as a rough territorial map which may help the mental health worker maintain some bearings as he functions within the complexities of the community. It is an attempt at a dynamic synthesis of a clinical point of view, with research and theory drawn from the social sciences, and empirical observations made within an ongoing community mental health program at the Human Relations Service of Wellesley, Inc.

It is believed that any comprehensive view of a community for mental health purposes should take into account (a) the physical and topographical characteristics of the setting, (b) the community's "self-image," that is, the view of the community held by its inhabitants, (c) the nature of community

Reprinted from the *Community Mental Health Journal*, 1965, **1**, 301-308, with the permission of Behavioral Publications, Inc. and the author.

groups and their characteristic interaction patterns, and (d) the dynamic interplay of dominant community forces. In the discussion of each area which follows, there is no attempt to be categorically comprehensive. Rather, the effort is made to indicate the scope of the phenomena and their implications for the development of mental health programs.

PHYSICAL CHARACTERISTICS
OF THE COMMUNITY

Where is the community located geographically and with respect to such things as: (a) natural resources, (b) trade and travel routes, and (c) other communities? It should be apparent to the casual observer that the natural resources available to any community dictate to a large extent the character of its economy. The suitable natural resources of some communities are organized around tourists and the tourist trade. Other communities find themselves engaged in mining and the extracting and processing of these natural resources. Other communities are manufacturing centers, and so on.

Trade and travel routes determine the extent to which residents of the community may be in contact with other areas and surrounding regions. Is this the kind of community which is accessible to the outer world? Is this a remote and isolated community into which strangers or "furriners" rarely come? Finally, is the community larger, smaller, or the same size as the surrounding communities? Is it a "satellite community," adjacent to a county seat, or a larger city or town in which are located most of the educational, trade, and cultural resources of its region? Perhaps it is one of the many burgeoning suburban towns growing up around our metropolitan areas from which wage earners emerge in the morning and to which they return at night, the so-called "bedroom" communities of modern America.

PHYSICAL SIZE

Size of a community can be expressed in population density and in trends of population growth or shrinkage, as well as in sheer physical dimensions. Most communities have grown since World War II, sometimes markedly so. Therefore, in most cases it is appropriate to consider what resources, what agencies, and what people in the community are paying attention to population trends? Is there any integrated plan with respect to this? What are some of the effects of this community's growth? What happens to the new people? Are there conflicts between newcomers and the old timers?

POPULATION DENSITY

The factor of population density is just beginning to be studied from the standpoint of mental health. Plant and animal biologists have some notion about the importance of this factor. When two kinds of distribution of the same number of items in the population exist, the conditions under which these trees and other plant and animal life live are very different. A striking and often used example, involves two groves of redwood trees, each consisting of one hundred trees. In one grove the trees are much closer together while in the other they are spread out over a considerable area. The sun penetrates one grove and not the other. Certain kinds of fauna and flora will flourish in one environment and not in the other. There have been some studies of urban communities which suggest that different kinds of behavior and emotional difficulties occur in the center of congested community areas than occurs in outer rings of a community. Outer rings are usually less densely inhabited, and inhabited by different kinds of individuals.

LOCATION AND RESOURCES

Another significant physical characteristic is the location in the community of the various services, agencies, and institutions: schools and hospitals, the main shopping areas, the main arteries within the town, and connecting roads that link one section of a community to another. The consideration of location is obviously important when thinking about the placement of a mental health center, since experience indicates that different clientele are attracted to a clinic depending upon its physical locus within the community. In some places, both the disadvantaged and elite groups in the population often reside in sections which are isolated from the main body of the community and which have few roads connecting them to the rest of the town. Such isolation may well affect the extent of use to which a mental health center or other community resource may be put by either group.

TOPOGRAPHY

Common sense recognizes the influence of topography upon community life. In literature it is common for authors to think of regional differences in terms of topographical features, i.e., the frequent reference to the "*rock-ribbed, reserved New Englander.*" Whether or not topography influences character formation, it does affect real estate values and population distributions. In many communities, for example, the more economically favored sections of the population are more apt to live in the geographically more elevated sections of town.

THE COMMUNITY'S VIEW OF ITSELF

Attention should be directed to the "phenomenology" of the community, that is, the ways in which residents view their community (Sanders, 1953).

Such perceptions constitute a kind of community self-image, usually based on history and traditions handed down from the past. How are such self-images organized? Each community seems to be able to say about itself, "We are such and such kind of folks." Some communities think of themselves as friendly places; others consist of people who "mind our own business;" a few communities have been studied where the residents accept a self-appraisal which essentially states "we are a bunch of no-goods;" another community may consist of "hustlers and go-getters;" and still another may be inhabited by "rugged individualists." It seems reasonable to expect that such differing community self-images would lead to quite varied responses to the introduction of mental health programs.

GUIDING VALUES

There are the values upheld in the community which guide and direct action: "We hold these truths to be self-evident" in *our* community. Some causes are readily mobilized around certain dominant values and still other causes will not flourish because they seem to be inconsistent or opposed to them.

Several often divergent and even conflicting values may coexist in a single community. Often separate values are upheld by different segments of the population but sometimes the same individuals may appear to subscribe to apparently conflicting value orientations. How does this affect the mental health field? As an example, one might think that the acceptable value of the need "to care for our own" would facilitate the organization of a local mental hygiene clinic to treat adults and children. On the other hand, such an enterprise might seem to conflict with a different value orientation espousing free enterprise because the mental health center becomes viewed as an expression of socialized medicine. Conflicting values in the same individual as well as in the same community are integrated in a variety of ways. But such integrations of dissonance are only beginning to be understood by students of personality, let alone observers of the modern community.

A value conflict frequently observed in such institutions as mental hospitals and in prisons is the conflict between the "soft," treatment-oriented, remedial values as opposed to the sterner, more "hard-headed," punitive and judgmental values. Both coexist and are strongly upheld in American society. Usually, mental health centers seem to have relatively little difficulty in entering into contact with the educational segments of the community, but have much more difficulty in establishing cooperative relationships with the law enforcement segments. It may be speculated that communities do not encourage a close cooperation between the "soft" values of the mental health center and the "hard" values upheld by the more punitive agents. Mental health enterprises in some communities may be allowed to flourish just because they do not unduly affect the conflicting values as often expressed and fulfilled by the law enforcement people, among others.

COMMUNITY STYLE

Each community seems to say in one way or another, "we have our own ways of doing things." It is useful to look at how decisions are made in a community and how new ideas may be proposed and implemented in the population. In one community, luncheon meetings seem to be favored; in another, letters to the editor have greater impact; and another may launch a new idea with great public fanfare in a central auditorium accompanied by considerable community-wide publicity.

In the organization of mental health associations and mental health centers, it would seem important to: (a) pay attention to the community's view of itself, (b) determine what kind of folks the inhabitants of this town feel they are, (c) ascertain which truths are upheld as self-evident when applied to human nature and community life, and (d) note the acceptable ways in which new ideas are proposed and decisions are made.

STRUCTURAL CHARACTERISTICS OF COMMUNITY GROUPING

The social-psychological structure of the community can be viewed from the standpoints of the socioeconomic characteristics of the population, and patterns of interaction between groups, agencies, and institutions. Looking first at socioeconomic characteristics, the observer would do well to note the nationality groups represented, the religious institutions present, the educational levels of the population, the occupations pursued, and the age distribution. Such factors would appear to influence the way in which the mental health resources as well as other community services are used. On the other hand, these factors also affect the nature of the problems to be found in the population. There is a growing body of evidence to suggest that mental illnesses are distributed differentially in the population according to socioeconomic characteristics. The studies by Hollingshead and Redlich (1958) indicate that, in New Haven at least, there is a far greater prevalence of diagnosed cases of schizophrenia among working class segments of the population than among middle and upper class groups. Even the nature of treatment provided by professionally trained people in the hospital setting differs according to the socioeconomic background of the patients.

It is useful for the observer of the community to attempt to map or diagram the patterns of interaction between groups, agencies, and institutions. What are some of the social-psychological features which can be noted from a structural point of view?

AUTHORITY

First, there are those segments of the community occupying positions of authority *vis-a-vis* other segments. Authority in this sense is being used to designate the formal responsibilities given to governmental and other bodies. Authority may or may not be accompanied by an equally high level of prestige. Such authority is often accompanied by power, but is by no means synonymous with it.

POWER

Power is the ability to influence decisions and actions of other people. Viewed in another sense, it is the extent of the individual's or group's ability to block or facilitate the gratification of the needs of other people. Power over all mankind would be secured almost immediately by the individual or group who learned how to control the supply of air which people breathe. Obviously, power viewed in this way can be seen to vary according to the area of need in question. For example, the county commissioners may have great influence and power over the mental health center where finances are involved but it may be counterbalanced by the commissioners' recognition of the professional skills which can be provided by the staff. Such a reciprocal or interdependent situation is perhaps the optimal one for the development of close working relationships and shared problem solving between the governmental body and the mental health center, a sharing based on recognition of mutual needs.

Power patterns in communities differ according to the degree to which they are stable and fixed, or unstable and fluctuating. Expanding population areas, for example, often seem to be typified by highly unstable power structures. They are often marked by sharp cleavages between the newcomers and the old timers. As a result, social planning for health, education, and social welfare enterprises may become inadvertently enmeshed in the already existing struggles for power on the part of different factions. A mental health center thus may become a political issue, although it would hardly appear that one political party would in actuality tend to be more mental health oriented than another. Such cleavages may run through all aspects of community life and may set up barriers to planning in the area of mental health until the reasonable issues regarding the mental health needs of the community are clearly separated from the less reasonable ones grounded in such factors as unstable power distribution.

The well-known studies by Hunter (1953), Freeman, et al. (1960,1962), and others indicate that recognized top power-figures or decision-makers in most communities are drawn from the following groups: those controlling natural resources, those controlling financial reserves, those in charge of means of production, as well as certain prestige-figures and certain professionals, with an occasional political leader thrown in for good measure. Hunter maintained that such top power-figures do not usually operate visibly in the community or through official channels. Later students of the subject have not confirmed his thesis, however.

A significant power group in the typical modern American community consists of those realtors who act as so-called "gatekeepers," occupying a role which may impinge upon the mental health of newcomers and others. To a greater or lesser extent, they determine into which communities people will move and into which neighborhoods they will settle. Often the realtors feel that economic security and success is bound up with their skill in assigning suitable newcomers to various sections of town. The criteria the realtor uses in his gatekeeper role and the consequences of the sorting process for mental health is not yet sufficiently understood.

PRESTIGE

Most community agencies seek to attract to their boards or other sponsoring bodies prestigious figures in the community. Prestige is usually based on social position, family background, and inherited wealth. It may also reside in individuals whose deep devotion and good sense is recognized when it comes to matters affecting the entire community. Hunter stresses that prestige-figures often may have a latent power position in their communities which they choose to use only on certain occasions.

COMMUNICATION

The communication network of a community represents an extremely important feature which often is dimly perceived and ill understood. Who talks to whom, about what and under what circumstances? Not only do people of similar socioeconomic characteristics sometimes reside close to one another, they also frequently interact with and communicate with one another more readily than with other groups in other sections.

Certain individuals or places in the community serve as communication centers. For example, in one New England community the largest supermarket was found to be the gossip center. Any item of information discussed in the supermarket would spread through the community. In other towns the barber shop, the beauty parlor, the local bar, and even the town dump may serve as gossip or communication centers.

In considering communication, it is customary to distinguish between formal and informal communication. The community observer would do well to note which open formal communication channels exist between various groups. Some groups have well-established intercommunications; between others there are no such channels. When formal communication channels do not exist, informal contacts between single individuals often are relied upon. Very often one group believes it has "communicated" with another group through an informal contact of this nature when in actuality no transmission of information has occurred on an intergroup basis. As a result, under some conditions, the first group may reject the second group and may fail to note possible points of alliance because it has misinterpreted inadequate communication to be rejection. Hunter's (1953) study of a southern city provides a case in point. He found that the top power-figures in the white community rarely knew and therefore could not communicate with their counterparts in the Negro community. Conversely the Negro power-figures were not in touch with the white leaders. Both top power-groups instead were in contact with "second echelon" power-figures in the other communities. Under such circumstances, it was very difficult indeed for these two subcommunities to come together to identify mutual needs and to solve mutual problems. It is clear that the board of a mental health agency cannot assume that effective communication with a group exists simply because a member of that group is "represented" on the board.

THE DYNAMIC INTERPLAY OF COMMUNITY FORCES

Because community structure and dynamics are closely interrelated, some issues of the dynamics of the community have been touched on in the foregoing discussions of power and communication. In order to consider this topic more systematically, it is useful to consider the community as an integrated field of forces. This assumption leads one to attempt to identify the instrumentalities whereby the various community values, interests, and groups become coordinated. Some communities have truly coordinative community councils or health bodies. In other communities, apparently coordinative groups in actuality represent restricted segments of the population. One may well raise the question of the extent to which the board of a mental health service should seek to serve the community in a coordinative way. To what extent can such a board attempt to assess and interpret community needs in the area of mental health? Is such a coordinative function possible when the agency must, at the same time, represent one of the value areas of the community and, in so doing, compete in the market place with other values and interests?

One of the most significant integrative dynamics of a community from a mental health standpoint concerns the processes whereby help is made available and sought by those in need. More simply stated, what kinds of problems are brought to which resources in the community? Some observers have suggested that in the lower socioeconomic groups as much as 80 per cent of the complaints brought to the general practitioners and health clinics have no organic basis but are instead an expression of social and emotional malfunction. Problems which arise from bereavement are obviously more apt to come to the clergyman. In recent years family agencies in many communities noted that they tended to serve lower socioeconomic groups and, in some cases, have attempted to alter this state of affairs. On the other hand, it appears that mental hygiene clinics are turned to most readily by middle class segments of the population. The community observer or planner may wish to ask himself and the community whether such patterns of helping should be altered or whether they should be reinforced and strengthened? The board and staff of a new mental health center may wish to consider what will happen to help-seeking and help-giving patterns as the center becomes established in a community. Should the mental health center take over responsibilities for certain psychiatric problems from the caretaking groups already dealing with them in one way or another? Or should the mental health center be in the position of strengthening these caretaking groups in their mental health operations?

The community is a dynamic system; each segment is related to each other segment. Moreover, the community is what Kurt Lewin (1951) called a "unified field." By this he meant that a change in one region would affect all other regions. Since the community is a dynamic system and a unified field, it follows that the entry of a mental health team will induce effects of one sort or another throughout the community. These reactions probably will be quite varied depending upon the ways in which the agency is perceived and experienced. One segment of the community may rush forward to collaborate with the mental health effort, and to make use of the resource. Another segment may attack the agency and perhaps even attempt to have it ejected as something alien or dangerous. Still another segment might simply seek to establish as much social psychological distance as possible between it and the agency. Whatever the pattern of response, the notion of the dynamic community would compel the assumption that these responses, in toto, represent an over-all pattern rather than haphazard reactions or reactions based primarily on idiosyncrasies of individual citizens or community leaders.

In the community there are groups which are highly receptive to certain influences from the outside, whereas other segments of the community are correspondingly hostile to or avoidant of outside influences. Which groups are receptive and which hostile depends on such factors as the nature of the community and of the outside influence itself. With respect to mental health issues, the pattern of response in various places throughout the country has appeared to be that of relatively greater receptivity on the part of the educational and certain religious systems, antagonism and attack on the part of exponents of law and order, and avoidance on the part of those people and groups most concerned with the maintenance of such cherished community values as neighborhood integrity, real estate land values, and the like.

As a dynamic system, a community exists in some kind of equilibrium or balance of its forces, which, while not static in nature, do act to maintain some form of homeostasis. In some communities, however, the regulatory mechanisms seem relatively poor and there are extremes of oscillation back and forth as, for example, in political power between radical and reactionary groups, or in the commonly observed alternation of government by reform movements and entrenched political bosses. In such communities, a mental health enterprise may enter as part of one phase in the oscillation and later may find itself under severe attack as the system moves back to the other extreme. Moreover, the entry of a mental health center may itself induce oscillation as opposing and restraining forces are mobilized. If not reckoned with, such oscillation might ultimately lead to unforeseen limitations on or even ejection of the center. It is wise for the board and staff of a mental health center to maintain continuing assessment of forces and factors opposing movement towards mental health values with the goal of understanding and, conceivably, altering and reducing rather than overriding them.

A social scientist may view the mental health movement with some skepticism. There are some who go so far as to postulate that the equilibrium of communities depends upon the existence of social pathology, delinquency, mental illness, and other deviant behaviors. This postulate suggests that the stable segment of the society in some way "needs" the unstable. Another way of putting this thesis is to ask, "How can we understand and practice virtue if we cannot observe and know about sin?" Those upholding this position assert that, even when causes of certain kinds of social pathology are well understood, communities seem remarkably unable to mobilize to deal effectively with them. They note, as further corroboration, the ready tendency of social groups to establish scapegoats and marginal members of one sort or another.

The writer's own observations indicate that in virtually every neighborhood area studied residents can and do identify individuals or families disliked by their neighbors. Those disliked are viewed as marginal or deviant in that they cause trouble, seem peculiar, are emotionally upset, or simply are "not like us." Neighborhoods appear to respond in a variety of ways to behaviors which are considered to be deviant, objectionable, or "sick." Under some conditions certain neighborhoods seem to be able to integrate marginal people and to deal effectively with certain problems. Under other circumstances some neighborhoods appear to reinforce and enhance the marginality through a hostile system of isolation and "quarantine." Such community processes are at present little understood. It seems clear, however, that neighborhood patterns and expectations may have considerable influence on the social learning of children, the quality of coping behavior, and the emotional well-being of individuals and families. The child who is having difficulties in relationships with parents, and is expressing these difficulties via destructive and aggressive behavior in the neighborhood, may find that neighborhood a force for health, or an additional force for emotional maladjustment, depending on how neighborhood forces are mobilized.

The foregoing cognitive map of community is necessarily limited. In addition to omissions arising from the author's inadequacies, there are inherent limitations common to most maps. The function of a map is to assist the user to accomplish certain specific purposes. Thus a map of transportation facilities may not include the elevations and other details needed for a topographical map. The objective of this paper has not been to provide specific guidance for the mental health worker in the community. Rather, it has been to stimulate his interest in the community and underscore patterned interactions having to do with certain fundamental functions for which communities exist. Clinically trained psychiatrists, psychologists, and social workers develop an ingrained feeling for the dynamics of personality as they are expressed in the behavior of their patients. It is hoped that, for some, these remarks will point the way towards the development of a similar "sense of community" as manifested by the behaviors of clients, consultees, board members, and the many other citizens with whom they work.

REFERENCES

Freeman, L. C. et al. *Local community leadership*. Syracuse: University College, 1960.

Freeman, L. C. et al. *Metropolitan decision making*. Syracuse: University College, 1962.

Hollingshead, A. and Redlich, F. *Social class and mental illness: A community study*. New York: John Wiley & Sons, 1958.

Hunter, F. *Community power structure: A study of decision makers*. Chapel Hill: University of North Carolina Press, 1953.

Lewin, K. *Field theory in social science*. New York: Harper & Brothers, 1951.

Sanders, I. *Making good communities better*. Lexington: University of Kentucky Press, 1953.

Sanders, I. *The community: An introduction to a social system*. New York: Ronald Press, 1958.

The following American Psychological Association position paper by M. Brewster Smith and Nicholas Hobbs stresses the importance of involving the community if the community mental health center is to fulfill its promise. The community mental health center legislation has made possible many significant program developments in recent years. It is also true that in actual practice the implementation of the legislation has frequently fallen short of its potential, often because the guidelines offered in this paper have not been effectively incorporated. A major point of the article is that compre-hensive community mental health centers should exist to satisfy the needs of the community first and foremost. What the community needs is not always what the professional wishes to give. Smith and Hobbs discuss the range of services involved in a comprehensive center. Five "essential services" and the five "additional services" were outlined in the original legislation. The article emphasizes contacting people who are hard to reach, devising preventive activities and work with children, and working with problem groups that are often avoided by professionals. The authors also emphasize the need for training, research, and evaluation of programs.

Some feel that the community mental health center is too limited in scope. Ultimately, the most viable alternative may be the community service center wherein a comprehensive collection of health and welfare services are brought together to deliver coordinated services to the community.

the community and the community mental health center[1]

M. Brewster Smith and Nicholas Hobbs

Throughout the country, states and communities are readying themselves to try the "bold new approach" called for by President John F. Kennedy to help the mentally ill and, hopefully, to reduce the frequency of mental disorders. The core of the plan is this: to move the care and treatment of the mentally ill back into the community so as to avoid the needless disruption of normal patterns of living, and the estrangement from these patterns, that often come from distant and prolonged hospitalization; to make the full range of help that the community has to offer readily available to the person in trouble; to increase the likelihood that trouble can be spotted and help provided early when it can do the most good; and to strengthen the resources of the community for the prevention of mental disorder.

The community-based approach to mental illness and health attracted national attention as a result of the findings of the Joint Commission on Mental Illness and Health that was established by Congress under the Mental Health Study Act of 1955. After 5 years of careful study of the nation's problems of mental illness, the Commission recommended that an end be put to the construction of large mental hospitals, and that a flexible array of services be provided for the mentally ill in settings that disrupt as little as possible the patient's social relations in his community. The idea of the comprehensive community mental health center was a logical sequel.

In 1962, Congress appropriated funds to assist states in studying their

[1]This statement was adopted on March 12, 1966, by the Council of Representatives as an official position paper of the American Psychological Association.

needs and resources as a basis for developing comprehensive plans for mental health programs. Subsequently, in 1963, it authorized a substantial Federal contribution toward the cost of constructing community mental health centers proposed within the framework of state mental health plans. It appropriated $35,000,000 for use during fiscal year 1965. The authorization for 1966 is $50,000,000 and for 1967 $65,000,000. Recently, in 1965, it passed legislation to pay part of the cost of staffing the centers for an initial period of 5 years. In the meantime, 50 states and 3 territories have been drafting programs to meet the challenge of this imaginative sequence of Federal legislation.

In all the states and territories, psychologists have joined with other professionals, and with nonprofessional people concerned with mental health, to work out plans that hold promise of mitigating the serious national problems in the area of human well-being and effectiveness. In their participation in this planning, psychologists have contributed to the medley of ideas and proposals for translating the concept of comprehensive community mental health centers into specific programs. Some of the proposals seem likely to repeat past mistakes. Others are fresh, creative, stimulating innovations that exemplify the "bold new approach" that is needed.

Since the meaning of a "comprehensive community mental health center" is far from self-evident, the responsible citizen needs some guidelines or principles to help him assess the adequacy of the planning that may be underway in his own community, and in which he may perhaps participate. The guidelines and discussion that are offered here are addressed to community leaders who face the problem of deciding how their communities should respond to the opportunities that are opened by the new Federal and state programs. In drafting what follows, many sources have been drawn upon: the monographs and final report of the Joint Commission, testimony presented to Congress during the consideration of relevant legislation, official brochures of the National Institute of Mental Health, publications of the American Psychiatric Association, and recommendations from members of the American Psychological Association who have been involved in planning at local, state, and national levels.

The community mental health center, 1966 model, cannot be looked to for a unique or final solution to mental health problems: Varied patterns will need to be tried, plans revised in the light of evaluated experience, fossilized rigidity avoided. Even as plans are being drawn for the first comprehensive centers under the present Federal legislation, still other bold approaches to the fostering of human effectiveness are being promulgated under the egis of education and of economic opportunity programs. A single blueprint is bound to be inadequate and out of date at the moment it is sketched. The general approach underlying these guidelines may, it is hoped, have somewhat more enduring relevance.

Throughout, the comprehensive community mental health center is considered from the point of view of members of a community who are seeking good programs and are ultimately responsible for the kind of programs they get. The mental health professions are not to be regarded as guardians of mental health, but as agents of the community—among others—in developing and conserving its human resources and in restoring to more effective functioning people whose performance has been impaired. Professional people are valuable allies in the community's quest for the health and wellbeing of its members, but the responsibility for setting goals and major policies cannot be wisely delegated.

COMMUNITY INVOLVEMENT AND COMMUNITY CONTROL

For the comprehensive community mental health center to become an effective agency of the community, community control of center policy is essential.

The comprehensive community mental health center represents a fundamental shift in strategy in handling mental disorders. Historically, and still too much today, the preferred solution has been to separate the mentally ill person from society, to put him out of sight and mind, until, if he is lucky, he is restored to normal functioning. According to the old way, the community abandoned its responsibility for the "mental patient" to the distant mental hospital. According to the new way, the community accepts responsibility to come to the aid of the citizen who is in trouble. In the proposed new pattern, the person would remain in his own community, often not even leaving his home, close to family, to friends, and to the array of professional people he needs to help him. Nor would the center wait for serious psychological problems to develop and be referred. Its program of prevention, detection, and early intervention would involve it in many aspects of community life and in many institutions not normally considered as mental health agencies: the schools, churches, playgrounds, welfare agencies, the police, industry, the courts, and community councils.

This spread of professional commitment reflects in part a new conception of what constitutes mental illness. The new concept questions the appropriateness of the term "illness" in this context, in spite of recognition that much was gained from a humanitarian viewpoint in adopting the term. Mental disorders are in significant ways different from physical illnesses. Certainly mental disorder is not the private misery of an individual; it often grows out of and usually contributes to the breakdown of normal sources of social support and understanding, especially the family. It is not just an individual who has faltered; the social systems in which he is embedded through family, school, or job, through religious affiliation or through friendship, have failed to sustain him as an effective participant.

From this view of mental disorder as rooted in the social systems in which the troubled person participates, it follows that the objective of the center staff should be to help the various social systems of which the community is composed to function in ways that develop and sustain the effectiveness of the individuals who take part in them, and to help these community systems regroup their forces to support the person who runs into trouble. The community is not just a "catchment area" from which patients are drawn; the task of a community mental health center goes far beyond that of purveying professional services to disordered people on a local basis.

The more closely the proposed centers become integrated with the life and institutions of their communities, the less the community can afford to turn over to mental health professionals its responsibility for guiding the center's policies. Professional standards need to be established for the centers by Federal and state authorities, but goals and basic policies are a matter for local control. A broadly based responsible board of informed leaders should help to ensure that the center serves in deed, not just in name, as a focus of the community's varied efforts on behalf of the greater effectiveness and fulfillment of all its residents.

RANGE OF SERVICES

The community mental health center is "comprehensive" in the sense that it offers, probably not under one roof, a wide range of services, including both direct care of troubled people and consultative, educational, and preventive services to the community.

According to the administrative regulations issued by the Public Health Service, a center must offer five "essential" services to qualify for Federal funds under the Community Mental Health Centers Act of 1963: *(a) inpatient care* for people who need intensive care or treatment around the clock; *(b) outpatient care* for adults, children, and families; *(c) partial hospitalization*, at least day care and treatment for patients able to return home evenings and weekends, perhaps also night care for patients able to work but needing limited support or lacking suitable home arrangements; *(d) emergency care* on a 24-hour basis by one of the three services just listed; and *(e) consultation and education* to community agencies and professional personnel. The regulations also specify five additional services which, together with the five "essential" ones, "complete" the comprehensive community mental health program: *(f) diagnostic service; (g) rehabilitative service* including both social and vocational rehabilitation; *(h) pre-care and after-care,* including screening of patients prior to hospital admission and home visiting or halfway houses after hospitalization; *(i) training* for all types of mental health personnel; and *(j) research and evaluation* concerning the effectiveness of programs and the problems of mental illness and its treatment.

That the five essential services revolve around the medically traditional inpatient-outpatient core may emphasize the more traditional component of the comprehensive center idea somewhat at the expense of full justice to the new conceptions of what is crucial in community mental health. Partial hospitalization and emergency care represent highly desirable, indeed essential, extensions of the traditional clinical services in the direction of greater flexibility and less disruption in patterns of living. Yet the newer approach to community mental health through the social systems in which people are embedded (family, school, neighborhood, factory, etc.) has further implications. For the disturbed person, the goal of community mental health programs should be to help him and the social systems of which he is a member to function together as harmoniously and productively as possible. Such a goal is more practical, and more readily specified, than the elusive concept of "cure," which misses the point that for much mental disorder the trouble lies not within the skin of the individual but in the interpersonal systems through which he is related to others. The emphasis in the regulations upon consultation and public education goes beyond the extension of direct patient services to open wide vistas for imaginative experimentation.

The vanguard of the community approach to mental health seeks ways in which aspects of people's social environment can be changed in order to improve mental health significantly through impact on large groups. Just as a modern police or fire department tries to prevent the problems it must cure, so a good mental health center would look for ways of reducing the strains and troubles out of which much disorder arises. The center might conduct surveys and studies to locate the sources of these strains; it might conduct training programs for managers, for teachers, for ministers to help them deal with the problems that come to light. By providing consultation on mental health to the governing agencies of the community, to schools, courts, churches, to business and industry, the staff of the center can bring their special knowledge to bear in improving the quality of community and family life for all citizens. Consultation can also be provided to the state mental hospitals to which the community sends patients, to assist these relics of the older dispensation in finding a constructive place in the new approach to mental health. Preferably, revitalized state hospitals will become integral parts of the comprehensive service to nearby communities.

In performing this important and difficult consultative role, the mental health professionals of the center staff do not make the presumptuous and foolish claim that they "know best" how the institutions of a community should operate. Rather, they contribute a special perspective and special competencies that can help the agencies and institutions of community life—

the agencies and institutions through which people normally sustain and realize themselves—find ways in which to perform their functions more adequately. In this endeavor, the center staff needs to work in close cooperation with other key agencies that share a concern with community betterment but from different vantage points: councils of social agencies, poverty program councils, labor groups, business organizations, and the like. To promote coordination, representatives of such groups should normally be included in the board responsible for the center's policies.

Communities may find that they want and need to provide for a variety of services not specifically listed among the "additional services" in the regulations issued by the Public Health Service: for example, a special service for the aged, or a camping program, or, unfortunately, residences for people who do not respond to the best we can do for them. The regulations are permissive with respect to additional services, and communities will have to give close and realistic attention to their own needs and priorities. For many rural areas, on the other hand, and for communities in which existing mental health services are so grossly inadequate that the components of a comprehensive program must be assembled from scratch, the present regulations in regard to essential services may prove unduly restrictive. Communities without traditions of strong mental health services may need to start with something short of the full prescribed package. So long as their plan provides for both direct and indirect services, goes beyond the traditional inpatient-outpatient facility, and involves commitment to movement in the direction of greater comprehensiveness, the intent of the legislation might be regarded as fulfilled.

Many of the services that are relevant to mental health will naturally be developed under auspices other than the comprehensive center. That is desirable. Even the most comprehensive center will have a program that is more narrowly circumscribed than the community's full effort to promote human effectiveness. What is important is that the staff of the center be in good communication with related community efforts, and plan the center's own undertakings so as to strengthen the totality of the community's investment in the human effectiveness of its members.

FACILITIES

Facilities should be planned to fit a program and not vice versa.

The comprehensive community mental health center should not be thought of as a place, building, or collection of buildings—an easy misconception—but as a people-serving organization. New physical facilities will necessarily be required, but the mistake of constructing large, congregate institutions should not be repeated. The danger here is that new treatment facilities established in medical centers may only shift the old mental hospital from country to town, its architecture changed from stone and brick to glass and steel. New conceptions are needed even more than new facilities.

Small units of diverse design reflecting specific functions and located near users or near other services (such as a school or community center) might be indicated, and can often be constructed at a lesser cost than a centralized unit linked to a hospital. For example, most emotionally disturbed children who require residential treatment can be effectively served in small residential units in a neighborhood setting removed from the hospital center. Indeed, there is the possibility that the hospital with its tense and antiseptic atmosphere may confirm the child's worst fears about himself and set his deviant behavior.

Each community should work out the pattern of services and related facilities that reflects its own problems, resources, and solutions. The needs and resources of rural areas will differ radically from those of urban ones. Every state in the nation has its huge mental hospitals, grim monuments to what was once the latest word in treatment of the mentally ill, and a major force in shaping treatment programs ever since. It should not be necessary to build new monuments.

CONTINUITY OF CONCERN

Effective community action for mental health requires continuity of concern for the troubled individual in his involvements with society, regardless of awkward jurisdictional boundaries of agencies, institutions, and professions.

A major barrier to effective mental health programing is the historical precedent of separating mental health services from other people-serving agencies—schools, courts, welfare agencies, recreational programs, etc. This is partly a product of the way of thinking that follows from defining the problem as one of illness and thus establishing the place of treatment and the professional qualifications required to "treat" it. There are thus immense gaps in responsibility for giving help to people in trouble. Agencies tend to work in ignorance of each other's programs, or at cross purposes. For example, hospital programs for emotionally disturbed children often are operated with little contact with the child's school; a destitute alcoholic who would be hospitalized by one community agency is jailed by another.

Current recommendations that a person in trouble be admitted to the total mental health system and not to one component of it only fall short of coming to grips with the problem. The laudable aim of these recommendations is to facilitate movement of a person from one component to another—

from hospital to outpatient clinic, for example, with minimum red tape and maximum communication among the professional people involved. Such freedom of movement and of communication within the mental health system is much to be desired. But freedom of movement and of communication between systems is quite as important as it is within a system.

No one system can comprise the range of mental health concerns to which we are committed in America, extending from serious neurological disorders to include the whole fabric of human experience from which serious —and not so serious—disorders of living may spring. Mental health is everyone's business, and no profession or family of professions has sufficient competence to deal with it whole. Nor can a mental health center, however comprehensive, encompass it. The center staff can and should engage in joint programing with the various other systems with whom "patients" and people on the verge of trouble are significantly involved—school, welfare, industry, justice, and the rest. For such joint programing to reflect the continuity of concern for the individual that is needed, information must flow freely among all agencies and "systems." The staff of the center can play a crucial role in monitoring this flow to see to it that the walls that typically restrict communication between social agencies are broken down.

REACHING THOSE WHO MOST NEED HELP

Programs must be designed to reach the people who are hardly touched by our best current efforts, for it is actually those who present the major problems of mental health in America.

The programs of comprehensive community mental health centers must be deliberately designed to reach all of the people who need them. Yet the forces generated by professional orthodoxies and by the balance of public initiative or apathy in different segments of the community—forces that have shaped current "model" community mental health programs—will tend unless strenuously counteracted to restrict services to a favored few in the community. The poor, the dispossessed, the uneducated, the "poor treatment risk," will get less service—and less appropriate service—than their representation in the community warrants, and much, much less service than their disproportionate contribution to the bedrock problem of serious mental illness would demand.

The more advanced mental health services have tended to be a middle-class luxury; chronic mental hospital custody a lower-class horror. The relationship between the mental health helper and the helped has been governed by an affinity of the clean for the clean, the educated for the educated, the affluent for the affluent. Most of our therapeutic talent, often trained at public expense, has been invested not in solving our hardcore mental health problem—the psychotic of marginal competence and social status—but in treating the relatively well-to-do educated neurotic, usually in an urban center. Research has shown that if a person is poor, he is given some form of brief, mechanical, or chemical treatment; if his social, economic, and educational position is more favored, he is given long-term conversational psychotherapy. This disturbing state of affairs exists whether the patient is treated privately or in a community facility, or by a psychiatrist, psychologist, or other professional person. If the community representatives who take responsibility for policy in the new community mental health centers are indignant at this inequity, their indignation would seem to be justified on the reasonable assumption that mental health services provided at public expense ought to reach the people who most need help. Although regulations stipulate that people will not be barred from service because of inability to pay, the greatest threat to the integrity and usefulness of the proposed comprehensive centers is that they will nonetheless neglect the poor and disadvantaged, and that they will simply provide at public expense services that are now privately available to people of means.

Yet indignation and good will backed with power to set policy will not in themselves suffice to bring about a just apportionment of mental health services. Inventiveness and research will also be indispensable. Even when special efforts are made to bring psychotherapy to the disturbed poor, it appears that they tend not to understand it, to want it, or to benefit from it. They tend not to conceive of their difficulties in psychological terms or to realize that talk can be a "treatment" that can help. Vigorous experimentation is needed to discover ways of reaching the people whose mental health problems are most serious. Present indications suggest that methods hold most promise which emphasize actions rather than words, deal directly with the problems of living rather than with fantasies, and meet emergencies when they arise without interposing a waiting list. Much more attention should also be given to the development of nonprofessional roles for selected "indigenous" persons, who in numerous ways could help to bridge the gulf between the world of the mental health professional and that of the poor and uneducated where help is particularly needed.

INNOVATION

Since current patterns of mental health service are intrinsically and logistically inadequate to the task, responsible programing for the comprehensive community mental health center must emphasize and reward innovation.

What can the mental health specialist do to help people who are in trouble? A recent survey of 11 most advanced mental health centers, chosen to suggest what centers-in-planning might become, reveals that the treatment of choice remains individual psychotherapy, the 50-minute hour on a one-to-one basis. Yet 3 minutes with a sharp pencil will show that this cannot conceivably provide a realistic basis for a national mental health program. There simply are not enough therapists—nor will there ever be—to go around, nor are there enough hours, nor is the method suited to the people who constitute the bulk of the problem—the uneducated, the inarticulate. Given the bias of existing facilities toward serving a middle-class clientele, stubborn adherence to individual psychotherapy when a community can find and afford the staff to do it would still be understandable if there were clear-cut evidence of the superior effectiveness of the method with those who find it attractive or acceptable. But such evidence does not exist. The habits and traditions of the mental health professions are not a good enough reason for the prominence of one-to-one psychotherapy, whether by psychiatrists, psychologists, or social workers, in current practice and programing.

Innovations are clearly required. One possibility with which there has been considerable experience is group therapy; here the therapist multiplies his talents by a factor of six or eight. Another is crisis consultation: a few hours spent in active intervention when a person reaches the end of his own resources and the normal sources of support run out. A particularly imaginative instance of crisis consultation in which psychologists have pioneered is the suicide-prevention facility. Another very promising innovation is the use under professional direction of people without professional training to provide needed interpersonal contact and communication. Still other innovations, more radical in departure from the individual clinical approach, will be required if the major institutional settings of youth and adult life—school and job—are to be modified in ways that promote the constructive handling of life stresses on the part of large numbers of people.

Innovation will flourish when we accept the character of our national mental health problem and when lay and professional people recognize and reward creative attempts to solve it. Responsible encouragement of innovation, of course, implies commitment to and investment in evaluation and research to appraise the merit of new practices.

CHILDREN

In contrast with current practice, major emphasis in the new comprehensive centers should go to services for children.

Mental health programs tend to neglect children, and the first plans submitted by states were conspicuous in their failure to provide a range of services to children. The 11 present community programs described as models were largely adult oriented. A recent (1965) conference to review progress in planning touched occasionally and lightly on problems of children. The Joint Commission on Mental Illness and Health bypassed the issue; currently a new Joint Commission on Mental Health of Children is about to embark upon its studies under Congressional auspices.

Most psychiatric and psychological training programs concentrate on adults. Individual psychotherapy through talk, the favored method in most mental health programs, is best suited to adults. What to do with an enraged child on a playground is not normally included in curricula for training mental health specialists. It would seem that our plans and programs are shaped more by our methods and predilections than by the problems to be solved.

Yet an analysis of the age profile of most communities—in conjunction with this relative neglect—would call for a radically different allocation of money, facilities, and mental health professionals. We do not know that early intervention with childhood problems can reduce later mental disorder, but it is a reasonable hypothesis, and we do know that the problems of children are receiving scant attention. Sound strategy would concentrate our innovative efforts upon the young, in programs for children and youth, for parents, and for teachers and others who work directly with children.

The less than encouraging experience of the child guidance clinic movement a generation and more ago should be a stimulus to new effort, not an occasion for turning away from services to children. The old clinics were small ventures, middle-class oriented, suffering from most of the deficiencies of therapeutic approach and outreach that have been touched upon above. A fresh approach to the problems of children is urgently needed.

We feel that fully half of our mental health resources—money, facilities, people—should be invested in programs for children and youth, for parents of young children, and for teachers and others who work directly with children. This would be the preferable course even if the remaining 50% were to permit only a holding action with respect to problems of adults. But our resources are such that if we care enough we can move forward on both fronts simultaneously.

The proposal to place the major investment of our mental health resources in programs for children will be resisted, however much sense it may make, for it will require a thoroughgoing reorientation of the mental health establishment. New facilities, new skills, new kinds of professional people, new patterns for the development of manpower will be required. And new and more effective ways must be found to reach and help children where they are—in families and schools—and to assist these critically important social systems in fostering the good development of children and in coming to the child's support when the developmental course goes astray. This is one reason why community leaders and other nonprofessionals concerned with the welfare and development of people should be centrally involved in establishing the goals of community mental health centers. They can and should demand that the character of the new centers be determined not by the present habits and skills of professional people but by the nature of the problem to be solved and the full range of resources available for its solution.

PLANNING FOR PROBLEM GROUPS THAT NOBODY WANTS

As a focus for community planning for mental health, the comprehensive center should assure that provision is made to deal with the mental health component in the problems of various difficult groups that are likely to "fall between the stools" of current programs.

Just as good community programing for mental health requires continuity of concern for the troubled individual, across the many agencies and services that are involved with him, so good programing also requires that no problem groups be excluded from attention just because their problems do not fit neatly into prevalent categories of professional interest, or because they are hard to treat.

There are a number of such groups of people, among whom problems of human ineffectiveness are obvious, yet whose difficulties cannot accurately or helpfully be described as mainly psychological: for example, addicts, alcoholics, the aging, delinquents, the mentally retarded. It would be presumptuous folly for mental health professionals to claim responsibility for solving the difficult social and biological problems that are implicated in these types of ineffectiveness. But it would also be irresponsible on the part of persons who are planning community mental health programs not to give explicit attention to the adequacy of services being provided to these difficult groups and to the adequacy of the attack that the community is making on those aspects of their problems that are accessible to community action.

Recently, and belatedly, national attention has been focused on the mentally retarded. This substantial handicapped group is likely to be provided for outside the framework of the mental health program as such, but a good community mental health plan should assure that adequate provision is in fact made for them, and the comprehensive center should accept responsibility for serving the mental health needs of the retarded and their families.

Some of the other problem groups just mentioned—e.g., the addicts and alcoholics—tend to get left out partly because treatment by psychiatric or psychological methods has been relatively unproductive. Naturally, the comprehensive center cannot be expected to achieve magical solutions where other agencies have failed. But if it takes the approach advocated here—that of focusing on the social systems in which problem behavior is embedded—it has an opportunity to contribute toward a rational attack on these problems.

The skills that are required may be more those of the social scientist and community change agent than those of the clinician or therapist.

In planning its role with respect to such difficult groups, the staff of the center might bear two considerations in mind: In the network of community agencies, is humanly decent care being provided under one or another set of auspices? And does the system-focused approach of the center have a distinctive contribution to make toward collaborative community action on the underlying problems?

MANPOWER

The present and future shortage of trained mental health professionals requires experimentation with new approaches to mental health services and with new divisions of labor in providing these services.

The national effort to improve the quality of life for every individual—to alleviate poverty, to improve educational opportunities, to combat mental disorders—will tax our resources of professional manpower to the limit. In spite of expanded training efforts, mental health programs will face growing shortages of social workers, nurses, psychiatrists, psychologists, and other specialists. The new legislation to provide Federal assistance for the staffing of community mental health centers will not increase the supply of manpower but perhaps may result in some minor redistribution of personnel. If adequate pay and opportunities for part-time participation are provided, it is possible that some psychiatrists and psychologists now in private practice may join the public effort, adding to the services available to people without reference to their economic resources.

The manpower shortage must be faced realistically and with readiness for invention, for creative solutions. Officially recommended staffing patterns for community mental health centers (which projected nationally would require far more professionals than are being trained) should not be taken as setting rigid limitations. Pediatricians, general medical practitioners, social workers other than psychiatric ones, psychological and other technicians at nondoctoral levels should be drawn into the work of the center. Specific tasks sometimes assigned to highly trained professionals (such as administrative duties, follow-up contacts, or tutoring for a disturbed child) may be assigned to carefully selected adults with little or no technical training. Effective communication across barriers of education, social class, and race can be aided by the creation of new roles for specially talented members of deprived groups. New and important roles must be found for teachers, recreation workers, lawyers, clergymen. Consultation, in-service training, staff conferences, and supervision are all devices that can be used to extend resources without sacrificing the quality of service.

Mental health centers should find ways of using responsible, paid volunteers, with limited or extended periods of service. There is a great reservoir of human talent among educated Americans who want to contribute their time and efforts to a significant enterprise. The Peace Corps, the Vista program, Project Head-Start have demonstrated to a previously skeptical public that high-level, dependable service can be rendered by this new-style volunteer. The contributions of unpaid volunteers—students, housewives, the retired—can be put to effective use as well.

PROFESSIONAL RESPONSIBILITY

Responsibility in the comprehensive community mental health center should depend upon competence in the jobs to be done.

The issue of who is to be responsible for mental health programs is complex, and not to be solved in the context of professional rivalries. The broad conception of mental health to which we have committed ourselves in America requires that responsibility for mental health programs be broadly shared. With good will, intelligence, and a willingness to minimize presumed prerogatives, professional people and lay board members can find ways of distributing responsibility that will substantially increase the effectiveness of a center's program. The tradition, of course, is that the director of a mental health center must be a psychiatrist. This is often the best solution, but other solutions may often be equally sensible or more so. A social worker, a psychologist, a pediatrician, a nurse, a public health administrator might be a more competent director for a particular center.

The issue of "clinical responsibility" is more complex but the principle is the same: Competence rather than professional identification should be the governing concern. The administration of drugs is clearly a competence-linked responsibility of a physician. Diagnostic testing is normally a competence-linked responsibility of a psychologist; however, there may be situations in which a psychiatrist or a social worker may have the competence to get the job done well. Responsibility for psychotherapy may be assumed by a social worker, psychiatrist, psychologist, or other trained person. The director of training or of research could reasonably come from one of a number of disciplines. The responsible community member, to whom these guidelines are addressed, should assure himself that there is a functional relationship in each instance between individual competence and the job to be done.

This issue has been given explicit and responsible attention by the Congress of the United States in its debates and hearings on the bill that authorizes funds for staffing community mental health centers. The intent of Congress is clear. As the Senate Committee on Labor and Public Welfare states in its report on the bill (Report No. 366, to accompany H.R. 2985, submitted June 24, 1965):

There is no intent in any way in this bill to discriminate against any mental health professional group from carrying out its full potential within the realm of its recognized competence. Even further it is hoped that new and innovative tasks and roles will evolve from the broadly based concept of the community mental health services. Specifically, overall leadership of a community mental health center program may be carried out by any one of the major mental health professions. Many professions have vital roles to play in the prevention, treatment and rehabilitation of patients with mental illnesses.

Similar legislative intent was established in the debate on the measure in the House of Representatives.

Community members responsible for mental health centers should not countenance absentee directorships by which the fiction of responsiblity is sustained while actual responsibility and initiative are dissipated. This is a device for the serving of professions, not of people.

TRAINING

The comprehensive community mental health center should•provide a formal training program.

The need for centers to innovate in the development or reallocation of professional and subprofessional roles, which has been stressed above in line with Congressional intent, requires in every center an active and imaginative training program in which staff members can gain competence in their new roles. The larger centers will also have the self-interested obligation to participate in the training of other professionals. Well-supervised professional trainees not only contribute to the services of a center; their presence and the center's training responsibilities to them promote a desirable atmosphere of self-examination and openness to new ideas.

There should be a director of training who would be responsible for: (a) in-service training of the staff of the center, in the minimum case; and, in the larger centers, (b) center-sponsored training programs for a range of professional groups and including internships, field placements, postdoctoral fellowships, and partial or complete residency programs; and (c) university-sponsored training programs that require the facilities of the center to give their students practical experience. Between 5% and 10% of the center's budget should be explicitly allocated to training.

PROGRAM EVALUATION AND RESEARCH

The comprehensive community mental health center should devote an explicit portion of its budget to program evaluation. All centers should incul-

cate in their staff attention to and respect for research findings; the larger centers have an obligation to set a high priority on basic research and to give formal recognition to research as a legitimate part of the duties of staff members.

In the 11 "model" community programs that have been cited previously, both program evaluation and basic research are rarities; staff members are commonly overburdened by their service obligations. That their mental health services continue to emphasize one-to-one psychotherapy with middle-class adults may partly result from the small attention that their programs give to the evaluative study of program effectiveness. The programs of social agencies are seldom evaluated systematically and tend to continue in operation simply because they exist and no one has data to demonstrate whether they are useful or not. In this respect the "model" programs seem to be no better.

The whole burden of the preceding recommendations, with their emphasis on innovation and experimentation, cries out for substantial investment in program evaluation. Only through explicit appraisal of program effects can worthy approaches be retained and refined, ineffective ones dropped. Evaluative monitoring of program achievements may vary, of course, from the relatively informal to the systematic and quantitative, depending on the importance of the issues, the availability of resources, and the willingness of those responsible to take the risks of substituting informed judgment for evidence.

One approach to program evaluation that has been much neglected is hard-headed cost analysis. Alternative programs should be compared not only in terms of their effects, but of what they cost. Since almost any approach to service is likely to produce some good effects, mental health professionals may be too prone to use methods that they find most satisfying rather than those that yield the greatest return per dollar.

All community mental health centers need to plan for program evaluation; the larger ones should also engage in basic research on the nature and causes of mental disorder and on the processes of diagnosis, treatment, and prevention. The center that is fully integrated with its community setting will have unique opportunities to study aspects of these problems that elude investigation in traditional clinic and hospital settings. That a major investment be made in basic research on mental health problems was the recommendation to which the Joint Commission on Mental Illness and Health gave topmost priority.

The demands of service and of research are bound to be competitive. Because research skills, too, are scarce, it is not realistic to expect every community mental health center to have a staff equipped to undertake basic research. At the very least, however, the leadership in each center should inculcate in its training program an attitude of attentiveness to research findings and of readiness to use them to innovate and change the center's practices.

The larger centers, especially those that can establish affiliation with universities, have an obligation to contribute to fundamental knowledge in the area of their program operations. Such centers will normally have a director of research, and a substantial budget allocation in support of research, to be supplemented by grants from foundations and governmental agencies. By encouraging their staff members to engage in basic studies (and they must be sedulously protected from encroaching service obligations if they are to do so), these centers can make an appropriate return to the common fund of scientific and professional knowledge upon which they draw; they also serve their own more immediate interests in attracting and retaining top quality staff and in maintaining an atmosphere in which creativeness can thrive. As a rough yardstick, every center should devote between 5% and 10% of its budget to program evaluation and research.

VARIETY, FLEXIBILITY, AND REALISM

Since the plan for a comprehensive community mental health center must allocate scarce resources according to carefully considered priorities tailored to the unique situation of the particular community, wide variation among plans is to be expected and is desirable. Since decisions are fallible and community needs and opportunities change, provision should be made for flexibility and change in programs, including periodic review of policies and operations.

In spite of the stress in these guidelines on ideal requirements as touchstones against which particular plans can be appraised, no single comprehensive center can be all things to all men. Planning must be done in a realistic context of limited resources and imperfect human talent as well as of carefully evaluated community needs, and many hard decisions will have to be made in setting priorities. In rural areas, especially, major alterations in the current blueprint would seem to be called for if needed services are to be provided. As a result, the comprehensive community mental health centers that emerge should be as unique as the communities to whose needs and opportunities they are responsive. This is all to the good, for as it has been repeatedly emphasized, there is no well-tested and prefabricated model to be put into automatic operation. Variety among centers is required for suitability to local situations; it is desirable also for the richer experience that it should yield for the guidance of future programing.

The need for innovation has been stressed; the other side of the same coin is the need for adaptability to the lessons of experience and to changing requirements of the community. Flexibility and adaptiveness as a characteristic of social agencies does not "just happen;" it must be planned for. The natural course of events is for organizations to maintain themselves with as little change as possible, and there is no one more conservative than the proponent of an established, once-radical departure. Plans for the new centers should therefore provide for the periodic self-review of policies and operations, with participation by staff at all levels, and by outside consultants if possible. To the extent that active program evaluation is built intrinsically into the functioning of the center, the review process should be facilitated, and intelligent flexibility of policy promoted. Self-review by the center staff should feed into general review by the responsible board of community leaders, in which the board satisfies itself concerning the adequacy with which the policies that it has set have been carried out.

This final recommendation returns once more to the theme, introduced at the outset, that has been implicit in the entire discussion: the responsibility of the community for the quality and adequacy of the mental health services that it gets. The opportunities are now open for communities to employ the mechanism of the comprehensive mental health center to take major strides toward more intelligent, humane, and effective provision for their people. If communities rise to this opportunity, the implications for the national problem of mental health and for the quality of American life are immense.

The following people read an early draft of this statement and made suggestions for its improvement. Their assistance is gratefully acknowledged. They in no way share responsibility, of course, for errors of fact or judgment that may be in the paper.

George W. Albee
Roger Bibace
Arthur J. Bindman
Hedda Bolgar
Joseph E. Brewer
Mortimer Brown
John D. Cambareri
Robert C. Challman
Emory L. Cowen
Joseph J. DeLucia
Gordon F. Derner
Morton Deutsch
Paul R. Dingman
Herbert Dörken
Henry Dupont

J. Wilbert Edgerton
John C. Glidewell
Leonard D. Goodstein
Lee Gurel
Robert A. Harper
Ira Iscoe
Nelson C. Jackson
James G. Kelly
Oliver J. B. Kerner
Barbara A. Kirk
Lewis B. Klebanoff
Sheldon J. Korchin
Maurice Kott
Harry Levinson
John J. McMillan

Harry V. McNeill
Sherman E. Nelson
J. R. Newbrough
Nancy Orlinsky
Thomas F. A. Plaut
David B. Ray
Sheldon R. Roen
Joseph Samler
Bernard Saper
Guy Scott
Saleem A. Shah

Edwin S. Shneidman
Franklin C. Shontz
George A. Silver
Hans Strupp
Donald E. Super
Harold C. Taylor
Forrest B. Tyler
Mrs. Bernard Werthan
Stanley F. Yolles
Alvin Zander

Ecology is the study of the relationship between the organism and its environment. A behavioral ecological model for community psychology and community mental health is a viable alternative to a "mental illness" model. In the following article James Kelly discusses human ecology and its potential application in the mental health field. From an ecological viewpoint, Kelly has derived four basic principles: the community as client; reducing the use of community services; strengthening community resources; and planning for change. Ecology, a concept developed by biological science, has great value for the social sciences.

ecological constraints on
mental health services[1]

James G. Kelly

The concept of ecology is particularly relevant for defining a community mental health program. While the Federal legislation for the construction of community health centers implicitly approaches a conceptual statement, the legal language of the legislation does not make explicit reference to public health principles or an ecological thesis (Community Mental Health Centers Act, 1964). In this paper I will review community mental health programs as a problem for human ecology.

An ecological analysis of mental health services refers to at least three different types of problems. One type of problem is essentially an analysis of social or organizational systems such as a study of the relationship between mental health services and other community services. The assumption for this type of problem is that any change in the operation of one service unit will affect the operation of all other service units. An increase in admissions to one local mental health facility, for example, can be attributed to a decrease in service opportunities at another facility or may indicate changes in stress tolerance for the social structure of the local population. This type of problem is often defined as operations research.

A second type of ecological problem is the study of the relationship between the physical environment and individual behavior. Studies of population density, response of local population groups to public housing, or

[1]Paper presented in symposium, "Psychology and Community Mental Health: Prospects and Preparation," at American Psychological Association, Chicago, September 1965.

effects of urban renewal upon styles of living are examples for evaluating the effects of nonpersonal structures upon behavior (Calhoun, 1963; Fried, 1963; Wilner, Walkley, Pinkerton, and Tayback, 1962). The assumption for this type of problem is that urban design has observable constraining or unfolding effects upon social behavior (Lynch, 1958, 1960).

A third type of problem is the study of the relationship of the individual to his immediate social environment (French, 1963). Here emphasis is upon interrelations between individuals in specific behavior settings (Raush, Dittman, and Taylor, 1959; Raush, Farbman, and Llewellyn, 1960; Sells, 1963a, 1963b). The most apt example of this type of work is Barker's taxonomic studies of a midwest town (Barker, 1960, 1963, 1965) as well as the work of naturalists and animal ecologists in their investigations of the social behavior of animals (Etkin, 1964; Klopfer, 1962; Lorenz, 1952). The most well-documented and replicated finding of this wide range of work is that group size has significant effects upon individual behavior in such diverse units as high schools and bee colonies (Barker and Gump, 1964; Forehand and Gilmer, 1964; Thomas and Fink, 1963). The small social group has fewer status differentials, fewer expressions of maladaptive behavior, and a higher work output per unit than larger social groups. For this last type of problem the assumption is that social structure and individual behavior are reciprocal. It is this premise that is most provocative for considering community mental health programs.

Each of these three types of problems defines a specific social environment, examines the discrete psychological activities within that environment, and then studies the behavior of individuals who are members of the particular social environment. The ecological thesis is that there are predictable patterns of individual behavior which are characteristic of any one social situation and that the expressive behavior of individuals changes in a newly defined social setting.

The Federal legislation with the opportunity to construct approximately 500 mental health centers over the next 3 fiscal years will definitely affect the visibility and, it is hoped, the effectiveness of mental health services in most metropolitan areas. Unless there is a clear conception of programing that is independent of brick and mortar these centers may perpetuate treatment methods which are increasingly outmoded, rather than initiating a new conception of psychological service. While I recognize that the National Institute of Mental Health is actively supporting changes in treatment concepts, we who can benefit from the legislative program are not always ready for the challenge of innovation unless the philosophy for the social change is readily apparent (LaPiere, 1965; Vickers, 1964).

As an initial attempt to express a point of view, I will offer four principles for community mental health programing that are consistent with an ecological thesis.

PRINCIPLE ONE: THE COMMUNITY AS THE CLIENT

The first principle is that assessment methods are focused on the total population rather than on those persons who presently receive a mental health service. Special attention is given to changes in the quantity and form of maladaptive behavior in the population. Under this principle the staff of the community mental health program in cooperation with other community resources is concerned with predicting the effects of the physical and social structure of the community upon persons who have different styles of living. The community mental health staff also is concerned with anticipating the effects of services upon the adaptive behavior of the population. It is an assumption of an ecological analysis that the expression of adaptive behavior will vary from place to place. Hence services should also be designed to be multiple and varied. In order to implement this principle new kinds of basic data will be needed, such as analyses of population movement and knowledge of how persons in the local community manage crises (Klein and Lindemann, 1961). The primary research task is to accurately assess the type of behavior which will be adaptive in one situation and maladaptive in another.

The model for such a program is not clinical psychiatry, psychiatric social work, or even clinical psychology. Instead, it is community development. Mental health services become one part of a total array of services dealing with the emergent behavior of a local population. The generation of new services is closely linked with a continuous evaluation of behavior perceived by representative segments of the local population as problem behavior. In addition to the linkage of mental health services with other community services there are other alterations in the assessment process. The psychologist active in community mental health work is equally concerned with the analysis of behavior settings as he is with the individual motivations of a client, and he spends as much time in the community as he spends when he is insulated from the community in his private office. In sum, the program is sufficiently accessible to the population so that adequate analysis can precede intervention (Caplan, 1964).

PRINCIPLE TWO: REDUCING THE USE OF COMMUNITY SERVICES

One of the advantages of such an approach is that persons who have demonstrated a high risk for service can be identified in their natural setting. The second principle that I am proposing is that mental health services are designed to reduce a high risk for community service. In some communities high-risk groups consist of persons who have demonstrated that they are chronic recipients of multiple community services. In other localities or for other groups of population a high-risk status may consist of persons who have had multiple contacts but with only one type of service. In both instances failure to respond to therapeutic efforts may represent multiple factors, including the provision of professional help which is divergent from the client's culture. A client's apparent maladaptive behavior also may indicate attempts to attain an adaptive solution to an anticipated new role. Deficiencies in mental health services to persons in lower-class cultures can be attributed to inaccessible professionals, which has reduced the creation of workable interventions (Phillips, 1963; Reissman, Cohen, and Pearl, 1964). Another basis for proposing as a fundamental principle of community programing services to high-risk groups is that mental health services should focus on negatively valued behaviors that are visible but are unserviced. Commitment to the community's unsolved problems helps acquire knowledge that is necessary for effective prevention. The administration of community health programs has indicated that prevention services that reduce the incidence of maladaptive behavior require changes in the social structure of the local population. Before recommendations for change can be considered, knowledge of the current ineffective social structure is essential.

PRINCIPLE THREE: STRENGTHENING COMMUNITY RESOURCES

In addition to a preference for the continuous analysis of community behavior and a commitment to services for the high-risk populations, a third principle for community mental health programing is the creation of professional and research services to local community resources. By initiating the informal coordination of current services, the community mental health program helps to create specific *new* community services as needed. The range of such new services is open. Consultation programs and educational services have been identified in the Federal legislation, but these are not exhaustive. Collaboration activities, the creation of staff development institutes, and provision of multiple research services are other examples. To the extent that mental health programing is participating as a community resource, the mental health program takes the leadership in creating a valid basis for problem solving. Implementing this principle has direct effects on professional training. In addition to competence in psychotherapeutic techniques, this new professional also acquires competence in other methods for producing change (Albee, 1964). Knowledge of consultation concepts, collaboration methods, community organization skills, as well as basic methods for community development becomes essential (Gelfand and Kelly, 1960; Kelly, 1965). As the mental health professions acquire these skills they also become more familiar with the role of the layman and the indigenous leader as effective change agents (Kelly, 1964b). Active participation in community programing not only has the advantage of developing effective services, but it increases the chances of the mental health professions becoming more closely aware of the consequences of any particular intervention upon the client's behavior. In this way programing helps to clarify the relative effectiveness with which services are responding to the expression of community problems.

PRINCIPLE FOUR: PLANNING FOR CHANGE

As the community mental health program participates in a continuous assessment of adaptive behavior of the local population, and as services are provided to high-risk groups as well as selected community resources, the program achieves a fourth important function: planning for change (Kelly, 1964a). I do not mean scheming for change, or proclaiming utopias, but I refer to mobilizing anticipatory problem solving not only for clients but for professionals as well (Perloff, 1963; Seeley, 1962). This principle also refers to a responsible caution for the outcome of programs, and considers the effects of valid as well as invalid outcomes upon the organization of services or the structure of the community. I would hypothesize that as the planning function accelerates in a community the local area will become more efficient and productive but less comfortable. While the planning function can facilitate economic development and more effective use of resources—the planning process itself changes the social structure and can lead to temporary disruption of the regulation of normative behavior.

The planning function becomes particularly salient in large metropolitan areas where mental health services are increasingly a part of government operations along with other health and welfare services. As funds for mental health services become a major budget item, closer attention will be given to the clarity of program objectives as well as the criteria for program evaluation. Establishing this type of planning function should help to manage an increasing problem for public mental health services, namely distinguishing political objectives from professional objectives *prior* to program development. For the ecologist who is involved in the analysis of community structure and the development of services, the planning orientation is basic. The elements of the planning cycle include data sources which provide continuous input of the interdependent and reciprocal effects of three elements: the plan, community services, and the population at risk.

THE ECOLOGY OF THE INDIVIDUAL: ASSERTIONS

The above comments have been presented as one alternative conception of community mental health work based upon the ecological thesis that adaptive programs change (Dubos, 1959, 1962). The concept of ecology is also particularly valid for the assessment of individual behavior in social situations and provides a redefinition of clinical practice. The client is viewed as an individual in a specific social situation with the consequence that expressive behavior is assessed in terms of the structure and function of the social setting in contrast to an analysis of intrapsychic motivations. In the same way explanations of behavior change are not restricted to the interaction between an expert and a client but are viewed as taking place in multiple settings. A change agent becomes a person who alters behavior independent of formally designated helping roles. The social effectiveness of indigenous leaders under this model becomes as relevant a research topic as the efficacy of treatment institutions or treatment techniques.

One of the primary features of an ecological conception of behavior is the redefinition of pathology. Behavior is not viewed as sick or well but is defined as transactional—an outcome of reciprocal interactions between specific social situations and the individual. Adaptive behavior then can be expressed by any individual in a restricted number of social settings or in a variety of environments, and can vary from time to time as well as from place to place. The research task is to clarify the precise relationships between individual behavior and social structure that differentially affect various forms of adaptive behavior. The work of Orth (1963) in his studies of the Harvard Business School, Mechanic (1962) in his analysis of a graduate department in the behavioral sciences, Becker's analysis of the socialization of medical school students (Becker, Blanche, Hunger, and Strauss, 1961), and Barker and Gump's (1964) pioneering analysis of a midwestern high school illustrate the potential for studying adaptation to social structures.

The present writer is presently conducting a study of teenagers' social adaptation to high schools. The study is concerned with the response of socially and geographically mobile youths to the life of a high school environment. The purpose of this research is to clarify the socialization process of high school youths that is relevant for understanding the variability of adaptation in different high schools, changes in adaptation over time and across situations, as well as the effects of various patterns of mobility history upon adaptation. To date pilot work and scattered impressions from the literature suggest that the social structure of the high school is a primary setting for the learning of subsequent adaptations (Kantor, 1965). This study is another example of research that I consider relevant for understanding individual behavior in large social units and the type of work that is basic for an ecological conception of community mental health programs. This type of study, and the point of view that has generated this research, I hope may contribute to a psychological understanding of the social environment and help to grasp a clearer sense of man's versatility.

REFERENCES

Albee, G. W. Psychotherapy: Panacea or dead-end? Presidential address presented at Ohio Psychological Association, Columbus, Ohio, April 1964.

Barker, R. G. Ecology and motivation. M. R. Jones, ed., *Nebraska symposium on motivation: 1960.* Lincoln: University of Nebraska Press, 1960. Pp. 1-49.

Barker, R. G. On the nature of the environment. *Journal of Social Issues,* 1963, **19**, 17-83.

Barker, R. G. Explorations in ecological psychology. *American Psychologist,* 1965, **20**, 1-14.

Barker, R. G., and Gump, P.V. *Big school, small school.* Stanford: Stanford University Press, 1964.

Becker, H. S., Blanche, G., Hunger, E., and Strauss, A. *Boys in white: Student culture in medical school.* Chicago: University of Chicago Press, 1961.

Calhoun, J. B. Population density and social pathology. L. J. Duhl, ed., *The urban condition: People and policy in the metropolis.* New York: Basic Books, 1963. Pp. 33-44.

Caplan, G. *Principles of preventive psychiatry.* New York: Basic Books, 1964.

Community Mental Health Centers Act of 1963. (Pub. L. 88-164, Tit. II, Regs. 5951-5956) *Federal Register,* 1964, May 6.

Dubos, R. *Mirage of health.* Garden City, N. Y.: Harper, 1959.

Dubos, R. *The torch of life.* New York: Simon & Shuster, 1962.

Etkin, W., ed. *Social behavior and organization among vertebrates.* Chicago: University of Chicago Press, 1964.

Forehand, G. A., and Gilmer, B. Von H. Environmental variation in studies of organizational behavior. *Psychological Bulletin,* 1964, **62,** 361-382.

French, J. R. P. The social environment and mental health. *Journal of Social Issues,* 1963, **19**, 39-56.

Fried, M. Grieving for a lost home. L. J. Duhl, ed., *The urban condition: People and policy in the metropolis.* New York: Basic Books, 1963. Pp. 151-172.

Gelfand, S., and Kelly, J. G. The psychologist in community mental health: Scientist and professional. *American Psychologist,* 1960, **15**, 223-226.

Kantor, M. B. *Mobility and mental health.* Springfield, Ill.: Charles C. Thomas, 1965.

Kelly, J. G. The community mental health center and the study of social change. Paper read in Community mental health: Individual adjustment or social planning? Symposium presented at IXth Inter-American Congress of Psychology, Miami, December 1964. (a)

Kelly, J. G. The mental health agent in the urban community. L. J. Duhl, ed., *Urban America and the planning of mental health services.* (Symposium No. 10) New York: Group for the Advancement of Psychiatry, 1964. Pp. 474-494. (b)

Kelly, J. G. Graduate training in community mental health. Position paper presented at Conference on Professional Preparation of Clinical Psychologists, Chicago, August 27-September 1, 1965.

Klein, D. C., and Lindemann, E. Preventive intervention in family crisis situations. G. Caplan, ed., *Prevention of mental disorders in children.* New York: Basic Books, 1961. Pp. 283-306.

Klopfer, P. H. *Behavioral aspects of ecology.* Englewood Cliffs, N. J.: Prentice-Hall, 1962.

LaPiere, R. T. *Social change.* New York: McGraw-Hill, 1965.

Lorenz, K. A. *King Solomon's ring.* New York: Crowell, 1952.

Lynch, K. Environmental adaptability. *Journal of the American Institute of Planners,* 1958, **24**, 16-24.

Lynch, K. *The image of a city.* Cambridge, Mass.: M.I.T. Press and Harvard University Press, 1960.

Mechanic, D. *Students under stress: A study in the social psychology of adaptation.* Glencoe, Ill.: Free Press, 1962.

Orth, C. D. *Social structure and learning climate: The first year at the Harvard Business School.* Boston: Harvard University, Graduate School of Business Administration, 1963.

Perloff, H. S. Social planning in the metropolis. L. J. Duhl, ed., *The urban condition: People and policy in the metropolis.* New York: Basic Books, 1963. Pp. 331-347.

Phillips, D. L. Rejection: A possible consequence of seeking help for mental disorders. *American Sociological Review,* 1963, **28**, 963-972.

Raush, H. L., Dittmann, A. T., and Taylor, T. J. Person, setting, and change in social interaction. *Human Relations,* 1959, **12**, 361-378.

Raush, H. L., Farbman, I., and Llewellyn, L. G. Person, setting, and change in social interaction. *Human Relations,* 1960, **13**, 305-332.

Riessman, F., Cohen, J., and Pearl A. *Mental health of the poor.* New York: Free Press of Glencoe, 1964.

Seeley, J. R. What is planning? Definition and strategy? *Journal of the American Institute of Planners,* 1962, **28**, 91-97.

Sells, S. B. Dimensions of stimulus situations which account for behavior variance. S. B. Sells, ed., *Stimulus determinants of behavior.* New York: Ronald Press, 1963. (a)

Sells, S. B. An interactionist looks at the environment. *American Psychologist,* 1963, **18**, 696-702. (b)

Thomas, E. J., and Fink, C. F. Effects of group size. *Psychological Bulletin,* 1963, **60**, 371-384.

Vickers, G. The psychology of policy making and social change. *British Journal of Psychiatry,* 1964, **110**, 465-477.

Wilner, D. M., Walkley, R. P., Pinkerton, T. C., and Tayback, M. *The housing environment and family life.* Baltimore: Johns Hopkins Press, 1962.

suggested additional readings

Cowen, E. L., Gardner, E. A., and Zax, M., eds. *Emergent approaches to mental health problems.* New York: Appleton-Century-Crofts, 1967.

Golann, S. E. *Coordinate index reference guide to community mental health.* New York: Behavioral Publications, 1969.

Iscoe, I. and Spielberger, C. D., eds. *Community psychology: Perspectives in training and research.* New York: Appleton-Century-Crofts, 1970.

Klein, D. C. *Community dynamics and mental health.* New York: Wiley, 1968.

Shore, M. F. and Mannino, F. V. *Mental health and the community: Problems, programs and strategies.* New York: Behavioral Publications, 1969.

two   primary prevention and crisis intervention

The belief that social and emotional disorders can be prevented, or at least reduced in severity, is, of course, an optimistic one. Nevertheless, it makes a good deal of sense to have prevention as a goal. It is quite likely that in the long run prevention will be more economical than reparation of damages, just as maintenance is usually less expensive and more desirable than repair. Most of the basic support for prevention in mental health comes from the fields of preventive medicine and public health. There are many instances that can be recalled where relatively simple techniques, such as mosquito control, have led to an increase in the health of a population. There are also many instances where the prevention of the disease required much more tedious and involved development. One example would be the perfection of a vaccine for poliomyelitis.

It would seem reasonable that the burden of proof be upon the detractors of prevention. That is, those who question the feasibility of prevention should have to show that individual treatment is effective and economical and that prevention is not possible or not effective and not economical. This may be the reality for some conditions. At the same time the proponent of prevention is not excused from attempting to evaluate preventive interventions in order to demonstrate their efficacy.

If prevention can be demonstrated to be effective, it will be desirable to mount intensive and extensive economic and social action programs. Sometimes it happens that large-scale attacks are mounted in advance of reasonable proof that they will be effective (see the Rossi article in Section six for a further discussion of program evaluation). It is easy to be critical when a program precedes supporting evidence. On the other hand, when the traditional techniques of meeting social and emotional problems have proven ineffective, there is a definite pragmatic appeal in trying something new and seeing if it works. The critical element here is to see if the program does indeed have an effect on the problem. The article in this section is a review of primary prevention.

Gerald Caplan must be acknowledged as one of the "fathers" of community mental health. His work, along with the work of Lindemann, has had a profound influence directly and indirectly on nearly everybody in the community mental health and community psychology fields. Here, with Henry Grunebaum, Caplan reviews the literature on primary prevention, a concept that is at the very root of community mental health.

The authors begin by defining the three types of prevention. Primary prevention *is directed at reducing the incidence (i.e., the occurrence of new cases) of social and emotional problems in a population. The goal of* secondary prevention *is to shorten the duration of disorders thereby reducing the prevalence (the number of cases "on the books" at any one time) of disorder in a population. The goal of* tertiary prevention *is to reduce the "community rate of residual defect" which also serves to reduce the prevalence of disorder. The authors discuss long-term and short-term factors in prevention. Long-term factors include physical resources, psychosocial resources, sociocultural resources, and the provision of these resources. The short-term factors are crisis factors and the authors review crisis theory and discuss the applications of crisis theory in prevention, such as the reduction of the severity of crises and provision of services to increase the community's ability to cope with crises. Among the techniques used are education of caregivers, mental health consultation, education of the public, crisis intervention, and anticipatory guidance. This article is, then, a review of much of the important subject matter of preventive psychiatry and community mental health. Caplan's model shows its public health origins, and is, of course, only one model for prevention.*

perspectives on primary prevention: a review

Gerald Caplan and Henry Grunebaum

In recent years psychiatrists have come to realize that psychological maldevelopment, maladaptation, and illness are so prevalent that treatment of established cases can never be expected to deal adequately with more than a fraction of the cases which occur. Therefore, one must consider how to reduce the incidence of mental illness, as well as to promote mental health. Primary prevention is that preventive effort which is concerned with studying the population-wide patterns of forces influencing the lives of people in order to learn how to reduce the risk of mental disorder.

Although we currently have little definite knowledge of the specific factors which are etiologic in specific mental diseases, there exists a body of plausible assumptions about various factors which may be significant in primary prevention. Some of these assumptions are based on experiments on human beings and animals, others are inferred from theory. Some are based upon experiences in psychotherapy, psychoanalysis, and clinical research. Others are derived from epidemiological studies which demonstrate the existence of different sets of conditions in communities which have high rates of mental disorder, as contrasted with those which have low rates.

TYPES OF PREVENTION

Preventive psychiatry can be considered under three main headings.

Primary Prevention aims at reducing the incidence of new cases of mental disorder and disability in a population. Efforts are focused both on modifying the environment and strengthening individual capacities to cope

Reprinted from the *Archives of General Psychiatry*, 1967, **17**, 331-346, with the permission of the American Medical Association and the authors.

with situations. We will discuss primary prevention in this paper, and it can best be understood if secondary and tertiary prevention are also briefly described.

Secondary Prevention aims at reducing the duration of cases of mental disorder which will inevitably occur in spite of the programs of primary prevention. By shortening the duration of existing cases, the prevalence of mental disorder in the community is reduced. This may be accomplished by organizing case-finding, diagnostic, and remedial services so that mental disorders are detected early and are dealt with efficiently and effectively.

Tertiary Prevention aims at reducing the community rate of residual defect which is often a sequel to acute mental illness. It seeks to ensure that people who have recovered from mental disorder will be hampered as little as possible by their past difficulties in returning to full participation in the occupational and social life of the community. Alienation of the patient from work, family, and social groups during and after mental illness may be diminished by programs to rehabilitate ex-patients, so that symptom reduction will be complemented by the recovery of old occupational and social skills or the acquisition of new ones.

All three preventive effects focus on groups within the total population and seek to reduce the community rates of mental disorder and its effects. This is the new approach advocated in 1963 by the late President Kennedy. It contrasts with an approach which provides therapists and institutions with responsibilities restricted to their individual patients. There are now increasing efforts to take into account those individuals who define themselves as patients and seek assistance, those who do not avail themselves of help yet who suffer from mental illness, and those who are currently healthy.

In order to effect prevention there will, of necessity, have to be planned programs so that the deployment of specialized resources will be related to appropriate aims; and evaluation of effectiveness will have to be built into the programs from the outset. Mental health programs will have to be coordinated with other programs in the community which influence the psychological life conditions of its citizens. Clearly community planning, organization, and coordination are fundamental elements in effecting preventive psychiatry. Thus the key factors which influence mental health in the community must be delineated in the areas of economics, politics, public health, religion, welfare, and education, to name a few. It will be obvious that the lines between the roles of psychiatrist, social planner, and social activist will often not be clear. Each individual will have to decide for himself which of these tasks he will undertake at any given time, just as he must decide to what extent to focus his efforts on individuals or groups, research or education. Insofar as possible, primary prevention is the most desirable and potentially most effective approach to a solution of the problem of mental disorder in our communities. At the present, however, primary prevention is clearly more a hope than a reality.

PRIMARY PREVENTION

In order to deal systematically with primary prevention, the following conceptual framework will be used to order the data. According to this model, the rate of mental disorder in a community is related to the interaction of both long-term and short-term factors which impinge on adaptive capacities of its members. However, the individual person is not merely the passive recipient of what the environment provides, but actively organizes his environment to obtain what he may need. Any individual's ability to cope with his environment will, of course, vary over the long and short term. Similarly, the human environment varies widely in its richness, organization, and comprehensibility. We may call those environmental factors which impinge on the individual *resources*, if it is clear that we are not merely interested in the quantity of a resource but also in its organization, timing, duration, quality, and other relevant variables. (The word "resource" is not entirely satisfactory, and "supplies" and "opportunities" are possible alternatives.)

Over the long term, the likelihood of psychological dysfunction is increased if specified basic resources are not adequately provided for the population; these resources may be classified as physical, psychological, and sociocultural. A program of primary prevention will seek to evaluate these resources and ensure their optimal provision in the population.

The *short-term* focus of this preventive model is on the pattern of adaptation to developmental and situational life crises. It appears likely that the direction of a person's psychological development throughout life, whether toward mental health or disorder, is most sensitive to influence at times of crisis. These crises represent transition points, at each of which the person may move nearer or further away from adaptive patterns of functioning. Primary preventive efforts are often directed toward modifying the field of forces at times of crisis in the belief that efforts may be more effectively and more efficiently applied at these times.

NATURE OF LONG-TERM RESOURCES

Physical resources include food, shelter, adequate living space,[1] sensory stimulation,[2] and opportunities for exercise, sleeping,[3] dreaming,[4] etc. These are necessary for growth and development, and for the maintenance of the bodily health upon which mental health is dependent. Protection is necessary from bodily damage, such as that by radiation, microorganisms, trauma, or chemical poisons, both before and after birth.

Psychosocial resources include the stimulation of a person's intellectual and emotional development through personal interaction with significant

The superscript numbers refer to the References found at the end of this article—Ed.

others. These include members of his family, peers, and other persons in school, church, and work. In face-to-face interchanges the person satisfies his needs for love and affection, limitation and control, and participation in joint activity which provides opportunities for identification and identity formation. Inadequate provision of psychosocial resources may be conducive to mental disorder for example, if there is a disorder in the relationships with parents, or if satisfactory relationships are interrupted through illness, death, or departure.

Sociocultural resources include those influences on personality development and functioning which are exerted by the social structure of community and culture. The expectations by others of a person's behavior have a profound influence on psychological development and the growth of self-esteem. Man's place in the structure of his society is determined by others to a large extent, and they prescribe his path in life to a considerable degree. If a person happens to be born into an advantaged group in a stable society, his social roles and their expected changes over a lifetime will tend to provide him with adequate opportunities for healthy personality development. If, on the other hand, he belongs to a disadvantaged minority, suffers from economic deprivation,[5] or is a member of an unstable society, as Leighton[6] has shown, he may find his progress blocked and he may be deprived of opportunity and challenge. This may have an adverse effect on his mental health. Calhoun[1] has demonstrated the deleterious effects of overcrowding on the laboratory animal, and it may well be the case that for psychological health there is an optimal human population in any given area, just as there is an optimal population for a given level of food supplies.

IMPROVING THE PROVISION OF LONG-TERM RESOURCES

Primary prevention involves studying the provision of resources in a population and attempting to improve the situation when necessary—usually by modifying community-wide practices through changing laws, regulations, administrative patterns, or widespread values and attitudes. The following examples are illustrative.

PHYSICAL OR NONHUMAN RESOURCES

Examples of host factors which may be influenced to prevent the development of mental disorder include efforts to prevent prematurity, which adversely influences intellectual development; to provide appropriate nutrition for children with genetic defects, such as phenylketonuria;[7] and the provision of iodinated salt in areas where iodine supplies may be inadequate, as to prevent the endemic cretinism which causes mental retardation.[8] Another example is the prevention of psychosis due to the pellagra caused by vitamin B deficiency. This has been much reduced in the southern part of the United States by social policies and community education programs which have fostered changes in the food habits and food supplies of the population.[9] The environment, on the other hand, may provide easy access to poisons: For example, lead poisoning in slum children from eating lead paint off decaying woodwork is not uncommon.[10] This could be prevented by laws requiring landlords to replace old lead-containing paint with modern lead-free varieties.

The effect of inadequate environmental stimulation and its consequent effect on cognitive development is at present under intensive investigation. Already, however, the work of Hess[11] and Deutsch[12] is sufficient to indicate the importance of the early perceptual experiences of the child for later intellectual development. It has been found that the cognitive environment of severely deprived groups impairs later learning.[13, 14] Efforts at cognitive enrichment for pre-school children through education, as in Operation Headstart (Office of Economic Opportunity, Washington, D.C.), are being undertaken, and evaluations of such programs are urgently needed.

In a different area, it is found that the sensory deprivations or distortions experienced by patients undergoing cataract operations[15] or cardiac surgery[16] can cause a transient psychosis which may be prevented by appropriate intervention. These examples would appear to imply strongly that certain aspects of the physical environment have direct psychological consequences of significance to mental health.

PSYCHOSOCIAL RESOURCES

Under this heading we will comment upon those factors which impinge on an individual in his face-to-face interchanges with others. These include the stimulation of an individual's intellectual and emotional development through personal interaction with significant people in his family, peer group, and people in authority.

A central issue here is the maintenance of a healthy family environment. For instance, legislators and administrators who plan manpower distribution should be influenced to ensure that fathers be given work opportunities in the localities where their families live. Employment regulations concerning pregnant women and mothers of young children should allow them time off to care for their children. In some countries, graduated family allowances encourage mothers of young children to stay at home with them. Divorce laws and legal practices relating to custody of children are an important field for the consultative services of the psychiatrist. In Denmark, for instance, a mental health specialist is consulted whenever a couple with children seeks a divorce, and his advice influences court decisions on custody and visiting.

Illness, hospitalization, or death of the mother are common problems often leading to fragmentation of the family; the children are separated and sent to unstable placements with relatives or to foster homes and residential institutions. For instance, Rice[17] found in a study of the children of women who were hospitalized for psychosis, that no professional assistance in arranging care for the children was sought or offered in these cases, and that the children experienced many placements at the very time when they needed extra emotional support.

The works of Spitz,[18] Bowlby,[19] and Provence and Lipton[20] have demonstrated the importance of adequate mothering and the deleterious effects of impersonal institutions on child development. Yet it is not institutions qua institutions which are harmful. Skeels[21] has recently reported a remarkable 20-year follow-up of two matched groups of orphans, one of which was raised in an impersonal institution and the other in a home for the mentally retarded, where the children received much attention and stimulation prior to adoption. The second group of children was functioning in the community as adults while the first group remained, with one exception, institutionalized. The human and financial costs of these two types of institutions differ strikingly; this study points out again that institutions need not have adverse effects, but can, under certain conditions, irreversibly damage development. The care of children by Aid to Dependent Children[22] and those in public institutions are striking instances where psychiatric knowledge[23,24] is sufficiently expert to provide adequate guidelines for planning, yet where public policy lags tragically behind what is known.[25] A preventive program would seek to ensure provision by the community of both an adequate homemaker service, so that families could be kept together in their own homes as much as possible, and the provision of adequate institutions when necessary.

The effect of loss of the mother when a child is hospitalized has been recently reviewed by Mason.[26] This remains a classical example of the failure to provide for essential psychosocial needs, and it could be avoided by regulations promoting daily visiting of hospitalized children by their parents, modification of hospital structure and functioning to allow mothers to stay with and help nurse their children (which might alleviate in small part the shortage of personnel), changes in the professional practice of pediatrics as advocated by Prugh,[24] and efforts to treat sick children at home rather than in hospital as much as possible.

The maintenance of family ties is not only important in childhood but throughout life, particularly in old age. Significant developments in present-day urban life are the relative increase in the number of the aged due to improvements in general health care, and the difficulty of maintaining regular contact between the older and younger generations. This is partly caused by policies and the attitudes of both generations. Understanding psychological factors might influence city planners to provide more large apartments, especially in housing projects, so that grandparents need not be pushed out of the family home. Planners, on the other hand, could be counseled to build special housing for the aged in relatively small units spread throughout the community, so that old people can live near and maintain contact with their children and grandchildren.

One of the programs of the antipoverty effort, "Foster Grandparents" (Older Persons Program, Office of Economic Opportunity, Washington, D.C.), has been to provide foster grandparents for poor children. In this instance, children and old people are brought together who are not related by blood but by geographical proximity. These programs have seemed beneficial to both sets of participants and need not be limited to the poor. It may be possible to combat the attitudes of rejection of the aged by programs of public education to help younger people understand the problems and potentials of their parents and grandparents in much the same way that we try to increase their understanding of children.

SOCIOCULTURAL RESOURCES

The most obvious example of ensuring the provision of sociocultural resources in efforts at primary prevention is that of influencing the educational system. The role of psychiatrists in offering consultation to educators to help them improve the psychological atmosphere of the school is well known. It is also true that psychiatrists are increasingly becoming involved in the social and educational environment of colleges and universities,[27] and a recent report by the Group for the Advancement of Psychiatry entitled "Sex and the College Student,"[28] illustrates an attempt to inform college administrators about psychological issues of direct relevance to them.

Barger[29] has studied the epidemiology of failure to graduate in a university community. He delineated groups of students at special risk, discovered times of increased incidence of breakdown, and then instituted social action, including anticipatory orientation sessions for freshmen, consultation to caregivers such as chaplains, and specially supportive dormitory arrangements for individuals identified as being at risk. The effectiveness of this program is being studied now.

Another example is Upward Bound (Community Action Program, Office of Economic Opportunity, Washington, D.C.), a preventive program which has recently been initiated in a metropolitan slum. In this area the scholastic levels of many young people who leave high school were no longer sufficient to the demands of the labor market because of rapid technological advances leading to diminished needs for unskilled labor. The result was rising unemployment among young people with inadequate education, which had obvious effects on their psychological health that led to frustration, depression, and tendencies to rebel against the social order which they felt was rejecting them. The neighborhood had an increased incidence of delinquency, alcoholism, drug addiction, illegitimate pregnancies, abortion, and venereal disease—all signs of social disorganization. Attempts to deal with these problems by traditional casework and remedial psychiatric practices had about as much effect as trying to bail out a flooded room with a small bucket while the water continued to pour in from a burst pipe. Now, a new preventive service has been instituted which attempts to handle the problems at their sources. A systematic program of improving the educational offerings of the school system in that neighborhood has been instituted. Extra teachers of high caliber were hired, and more modern educational techniques were instituted. At the same time, efforts at raising the levels of aspiration of the students and their families were begun by involving the entire community in an adult educational campaign in an attempt to increase the motivation of the students to stay at school and to study as hard as students in middle-class school districts, with the hope and the confidence that the technologically advanced labor market will be open to them. Here again, a plausible program has been initiated, but an evaluation of the results has not been reported.

The sociocultural needs of the aged population may be met by modifying retirement laws and regulations so that older people who retain their capacities are not forced to retire suddenly and prematurely and may be offered part-time or light-work opportunities as their powers diminish. Old age assistance and retirement pensions could take up the slack in income as earning capacity is reduced by age if regulations did not penalize a person for working. In certain cases, at present, the lowered earning capacity of older people means that their income may be less if they work than if they were entirely unemployed and drawing full welfare assistance. Studies, such as that in progress at Harvard Medical School's Laboratory of Community Psychiatry under McEwan and Sheldon are urgently needed so that retirement can be planned in terms of individual needs and capacities, and so that those who are vulnerable to postretirement difficulties may be identified and assisted.

Social isolation is a potent factor in promoting mental disorders in the aged.[30] A preventive program would foster the provision of social and recreational facilities, administered in a way to stimulate the activity and independence of the aged rather than permitting them to become the passive recipients of care. In preparation for retirement, health education programs aimed at the middle-aged population can use anticipatory guidance, so that people can face in advance the implications of old age and see this period as one in which they will be expected and encouraged to remain interested in the social, political, welfare, and recreational life of their community, and productively active in formal work, service, or in sheltered occupations.

In all examples of these kinds, it is necessary to identify the physical, psychosocial, or sociocultural factors at work in the community, and to modify social policy. Education of professional or lay groups and efforts at influencing legislators and administrators to modify laws, regulations, and policies may be necessary. These efforts are often successful, and psychiatrists and psychologists have been influential in changing policies in such institutions as industry[31,32] and the Army.[33] Thus, the Army has found that treating neuropsychiatric casualties as close to the front lines as possible has led to a much higher salvage rate than was the case when they were treated far from their unit.

It is worth emphasizing that this is not government by psychiatrists. Legislators and administrators will perforce take into consideration many economic, social, and political issues before making their decisions. Primary prevention, however, involves the psychiatrist as a participant in social planning and social action, so that those who govern may take into account the mental health needs of their populations. It is to be hoped that if these are infringed upon, it is done with some knowledge and consideration of the consequences. For example, the psychiatrist may point out that an urban relocation program is likely to have an adverse effect on the aged inhabitants of a condemned area. Fried,[34] in particular, has demonstrated the results of an ill-conceived urban renewal program on the inhabitants of a lower-class but highly organized community. Nevertheless, the economy of the city may demand that the slum be torn down and replaced by modern apartment houses. The legislators, who have been informed of the psychological sequelae of renewal, may then feel obligated to provide extra social work and home nursing service to the old people, to give them special help in handling their relocation difficulties. According to communications from the Visiting Nurses Association, this did in fact occur in the city under discussion. Legislators may also be inclined to solicit the advice of psychiatrists in planning other measures to cushion the blow, such as making provision for ethnic and extended family groups to be rehoused near each other and near the places where their old social and recreational agencies have been relocated.

SHORT-TERM OR CRISIS FACTORS

Up to this point we have discussed the preventive psychiatric implications of impairments or inadequacies of the host-environment interaction; this interaction, long term in duration, affects the steady process of psychological development. Sometimes, however, individuals face immediate problems from which they cannot escape, and which are beyond their capacities to solve. This results in states of temporary disequilibrium in the relatively smooth trajectory of development. These emotionally significant turning points, or crises,[35] are short periods usually marked by psychological upsets.

Crisis theory has been derived from a series of research projects carried out over the past 15 years. Some typical examples are the crisis of bereavement,[36,37] the reactions of parents to the birth of a normal or of a premature child,[38,39] and the crisis of surgery.[40] There are recent studies of the crises experienced by Peace Corps volunteers exposed to unexpected cultural problems in their overseas assignments,[41] and by engaged and newly married couples in dealing with the ordinary upsets of early married life.[42] Clinical work suggests that deterioration of mental health often occurs following such crises; and it appears that during the crisis significant psychological changes must occur. On the other hand, healthy coping has also been described, such as in the work of Silber et al, [43,44] with competent adolescents. Findings to date point to the potential value of studying the psychological processes which take place during crises in order to find leverage points for improving the outcome. Parad's[45] book of readings covers many aspects of clinical and investigative work in this field.

The terminology in the field is unsettled; thus, the word "crisis" was originally used by Lindemann and Caplan to refer to personal reaction after such traumatic events as sudden bereavement or the birth of a premature child. Erikson, on the other hand, uses the same word to refer to a series of normal developmental steps such as those of puberty or menopause. Crisis may thus be employed to refer to both normal and unusual transitions which necessitate specific tasks of interpersonal and intrapsychic readjustment. Recently Rapoport,[46] who has studied couples through engagement, honeymoon, and early marriage, has called attention to the social aspects of this transition by calling it a "critical role transition."[46] On the other hand, Parkes (unpublished), using an approach influenced by Kurt Lewin, suggests using the term "change in life space." He criticizes the word "crisis" as referring to the emotional results of the transition which may in fact be absent, as in a delayed grief reaction. In the interests of simplicity we will continue to employ the term "crisis," recognizing that certain examples are marked by society for recognition through ritual and may be called "critical role transitions." Others are due to alteration in the life space, while yet others are due to biological maturation. All of these junction points involve change in role as well as interpsychic and intrapsychic balance; the differentiation is one of emphasis.

Crisis may be due to either internal or external changes necessitating adaptation. The internal changes may be developmental or due to illness or trauma, while the external changes involve (a) the loss of a significant person or source of need satisfaction, (b) the threat of loss, or (c) a challenge which threatens to overtax adaptive capacities. This list strikingly resembles the causes of neurosis delineated by Freud,[47] who in 1912 mentioned (1) frustration due to loss of an object, (2) inability to adapt to a challenge such as marriage, (3) inhibition in development, and (4) biologic maturation.

During crisis the individual's usual pattern of functioning becomes disorganized. He feels anxious, and thought processes are often confused and ineffective. Particularly evident is a preoccupation with the problem which precipitated the upset, and memories of similar problems from the past. Feelings of frustration and helplessness are common. Crises usually last for a period of up to four to six weeks. By the end of that time the anxiety usually diminishes, and the person returns to a steady psychological and physiological state as he works out a solution. It is of interest that recent investigations demonstrate specific biochemical concomitants of specific phases of emotional crisis.[48] The problem may be dealt with in an adaptive way by realistic modification of the environment and by intrapsychic readjustments. On the other hand, the solution may be (1) postponed, as in delayed grief; (2) maladaptive; or (3) development of psychiatric symptoms. It is believed that the methods of crisis resolution used by the individual—whether healthy or maladaptive—will become henceforward a part of his coping repertoire and may be used in dealing with future problems. Thus the individual may emerge from the crisis with increased adaptive capacities and confidence in his ability to tolerate stress and to cope. On the other hand, he may emerge with lower adaptive capacities and a greater vulnerability to mental disorder. Therefore, we can say that crises represent mental health turning points. The individual will be helped or hindered in finding a healthy outcome by his family and friends. Work has recently suggested that conjoint family interviews at times of crisis offer insight into the degree to which the family is helping the person toward an adaptive or maladaptive solution.[49] He may also be helped by community caregivers, such as doctors, lawyers, teachers, clergymen, and social workers. This is of importance, because a person in crisis both feels a greater need for help than when he is in his usual psychological state, and *is usually more easily influenced* during this period than at other times.[49] He is in unstable equilibrium. A crisis, therefore, represents a leverage point; this means that assistance may produce a greater effect if focused on people at times of crisis than during periods of stable equilibrium, and an opportunity is thus available to maximize the potential of our scarce mental health specialists.

APPLICATIONS OF CRISIS THEORY

Preventive psychiatric efforts, based on studies of crises, have been attempted and are focused on two broad goals.

REDUCING SEVERITY OF CRISES

It is not possible to prevent crises altogether. Temporarily insurmountable problems are an inevitable aspect of life; and there will always be unexpected and stressful situations to be faced, such as illness, death, accidents, and operations. Normal development implies coping with change. Even if it were possible to avoid all stress and challenge, we would not wish to do so; *The Happy Prince* by Oscar Wilde illustrates the grief that befalls one who attempts to avoid all the sadness consequent to life. The successful mastery of challenge provides the opportunity for personality growth and enrichment, as Zetzel[50] pointed out recently in a paper on the problems that individuals who have never developed the capacity for dealing with grief and depression must face.

It does appear, however, that if stress can be kept within tolerable bounds, the crisis will be less intense and there will be a better chance of healthy adaptive responses. It may be useful to study the living conditions of the community in order to identify those circumstances which precipitate crisis in significant numbers of the population, and to modify these circumstances, if possible, so that their impact is reduced.

For example, it was found in a midwestern community[51] that many young married couples with several children were seeking assistance from social agencies, ministers, and physicians because of disturbance in their children or dissatisfaction with their marriage. Clinical and epidemiological investigation turned up the pertinent fact that a significant number of these couples had married because of premarital pregnancy. When the pregnancy was first discovered, they had consulted their ministers, priests, or physicians, and these caregivers had encouraged them to marry. When the later consequences of these marriages were discussed with the persons who had been consulted at the time of crisis, they realized that a deeper review of the problem of premarital pregnancy and due consideration of alternative solutions might have been more useful in the long run. The effects of this changed approach to a crisis situation are now under study. It may be added that one of the counselors, a priest, had come to the same conclusion as the psychiatrist independently on the basis of his own experience.

SERVICES TO FOSTER HEALTHY CRISIS-COPING

It has already been stated that the outcome of a crisis is influenced by the quality of help which the individual receives from family, friends, and community caregivers in trying to work out a new adaptation. The psychiatrist is part of this potentially helpful influence network. Since he cannot personally help large numbers of people in crisis, his major impact can only come from indirect action, which may take the following paths.

Ensuring that Communities Provide Professional Help During Crisis. In order for professionals to help an individual in crisis, it is necessary for them to understand the nature of crisis reactions and to have the necessary therapeutic skill. In addition, administration policy must be such that they are immediately available to offer help during relatively short periods of crisis disequilibrium when critical choices of coping pattern are being made. The increased desire for help during crisis will impel the person to ask for assistance; but, unless he can gain access to the agency and the helper during the crisis period itself—a period no longer than a few weeks in duration—he will have to cope unaided.

This situation presents no problem in many types of crises, because the predicament itself is so clearly a life emergency that immediate contact with a community agency or caregiving professional is mandatory: for example, a surgical emergency, a road accident, or a death in the family. In many other instances, however, the predicament, apart from the psychological crisis, is not an obvious emergency: examples are the crises of adolescence, early marriage, change of jobs, entrance into nursery school, or retirement. In these cases the individual or his family must reach out for help from a health, welfare, education, or religious agency. Unfortunately, many of these agencies are not prepared to handle new cases quickly. They have long waiting lists, and their clientele are usually chronic cases involving treatment long in duration but not necessarily immediately available. Such agencies usually conceive an "emergency case" as one of obvious and dramatic severity, and only such cases are likely to be given priority on waiting lists. Crisis upsets are often not dramatic despite their importance, and therefore would not be given priority. Agency policy should attempt to shorten and abolish waiting lists, and staff should be available for immediate help. Centers for the prevention of suicide, available 24 hours a day, are an example in this direction,[52] although, their effectiveness over time must be studied. Reeducation of staff may be necessary to accomplish these changes.

A survey of commonly occurring crises may disclose that some fall outside the sphere of current agency operations. If this is the case, it may be necessary to attempt to influence the community planning and governing bodies either to assign new jurisdictions to old agencies, or to establish new agencies to cover areas of unmet need. A common example of a lacuna in agency practice is the absence of adequate homemaker services in many communities. Their provision would ensure that families facing the temporary absence of mothers may be kept together in their homes, thus ameliorating the stress of this crisis.[53] In many communities no agencies are available to assist widows or parents who are divorced. The Cruse clubs[54] in England and Parents Without Partners[55] in this country have grown up in recent years as a response to these problems. The development of such community initiatives should clearly be encouraged. On the other hand, in many rural areas traditional family and child welfare agencies are completely absent; their provision must be a major goal of those involved in the primary prevention of mental disorder.[56]

Preventive Intervention with Individuals in Crisis. Klein and Lindemann,[57] Waldfogel and Gardner,[58] and Rapoport[46] have discussed techniques of preventive intervention by mental health specialists during the period of disorganization of a crisis in an individual and his family. Parad[59] has recently surveyed the efforts of a number of projects concerned with various styles of time-limited crisis intervention to individuals and families. Unpublished studies at the Laboratory of Community Psychiatry of Harvard Medical School confirm this approach and suggest the importance of the following methodological points.

Timing. The most economic utilization of professional efforts is achieved by repeated visits at short intervals during the four to six week period of the crisis rather than by interviews at weekly intervals for many months.

Family Orientation. Intervention should support the integrity of the family in its own home if possible and prevent its fragmentation in order to conserve its capacity to support the family member who is most directly affected by the crisis. Thus, if a parent is absent or deceased, a replacement from within the family or by a homemaker should be obtained. Families can be helped to share the painful affect consequent to the crisis and comfort and support each other, as well as assist each other in household tasks. To these ends, interviews in the home with couples and whole families may be useful.

Avoiding Dependency. Individuals in crisis are more dependent; however, long-term dependency does not appear to be fostered by active intervention during crises. In fact, the more help given during the crisis, the more independent are the clients when the crisis has been resolved. Undue dependency is also avoided by dealing with current realities rather than exploring the antecedents of the problem.

Fostering Mastery. The focus of crisis-oriented intervention is to enable the individual to master the problem by confronting it, despite the unpleasant affect it arouses, and the frustration of an unknown outcome. The individual requires all the information possible to deal effectively with the problem and to understand its predictable phases; so a useful model is the one of education. Task-oriented activity is thus to be encouraged and hope maintained. An individual frequently releases tension associated with crisis by such nongoal-directed activities as redecorating a house, moving, or scapegoating a child; this wasteful activity has to be discouraged.

Outside Supports. During the crisis period, the individual not only needs additional family support but the outside support of extended family, friends, clergy, and other agencies is most important. These are often not utilized for fear that asking for help is a sign of weakness. Clients can appropriately be reassured that this is not the case. It seems likely that nonprofessionals can often be most useful in offering support during a crisis, particularly if they themselves have experienced a similar one in the past.

Goals. The goal of crisis intervention is to enable the individual to cope effectively with the current situation regardless of what past maladaptive experiences he may have had. The effort is thus to achieve an improvement in present functioning, rather a "cure." Since the focus of the work is on the final common path of going through the steps necessary to resolve the crisis rather than exploring its antecedents, it may not require specialized psychological knowledge or sophistication; nonprofessionals can thus be trained and supported in carrying it out.

Education of Caregivers. The caregiving professionals—doctors, nurses, clergymen, teachers, lawyers, etc.—are the major resource to whom people in crisis turn. To ensure that these caregivers attend to the mental health implications of the crisis and act skillfully, they must be appropriately educated in the necessary skills. They must learn enough about specific crises to know what psychological tasks are involved in ameliorating each, as well as what is within the range of healthy and unhealthy patterns of coping in order to identify and aid those individuals who are proceeding on a maladaptive course. For example, recent research[60] has shown that normal children experience a considerable degree of difficulty in going to elementary school, and it takes a surprisingly long time for them to adapt. Among others, Bower[61] has been interested in how we may aid children to better manage the transitions inherent in schooling.

Careful studies have shown that the premature birth of a child is a crisis for a family and that physicians and nurses can be made aware that the pattern of the mother's initial adjustment to the situation may have a significant effect on her subsequent relationship to and care of her child.[62,63] Mothers who are coping poorly can be identified; for example, the mother who seems overly cheerful and unconcerned about the situation, who shows little curiosity about her baby's progress and about the meaning of prematurity, who visits him infrequently in the premature baby nursery, and who does not seek help from family members, friends, or professionals in dealing with the problems involved, indicates that on the whole she tends to evade or deny. A mother such as this can often be helped to recognize some of her realistic problems, and can be supported in admitting to consciousness and mastering her natural feelings of anxiety, guilt, and sadness. She can be encouraged to visit her baby regularly and learn how to understand and predict his progress by observing his behavior and getting relevant information about prematurity from the nurses. She can also be assisted to enlist the support of clergymen, public health nurses, and physicians as indicated, to help her with the problems which emerge.

Knowledge of the predictable emotional crises in the community can be communicated to the appropriate community caregivers by taking part in their preprofessional education or by participating in on-the-job training, as in postgraduate seminars for teachers, clergymen, or general practitioners.

However, knowledge often lies fallow, as Mason has pointed out in a recent article. He noted the disparity between what is known about the adverse effects on children of separation from their parents during hospitalization, and the lag in pediatric practice and attitudes that still prevails.[26] This article illustrates how difficult it is to influence other professionals and organizations and should lead to humility about our effectiveness. It also points up the need for studies which may enable us to be more successful in this task.

Mental Health Consultation.   However well educated the community caregivers are with regard to crises, it is inevitable that they will encounter unexpected difficulties as they deal with emotional problems. In order to consolidate a program of preventive work by caregivers, it is important to provide them with opportunities for consulting a mental health specialist. Various methods of consultation have been developed for use by mental health specialists in recent years.[64] For instance, in one city a mental health consultant goes for about two hours every week into each of the 20 health stations from which the nurses of the Public Health Department and the Visiting Nurse Association operate. Nurses who find themselves unable to understand particularly difficult cases or psychologically complicated problems in their patients are free to seek consultation in order to clarify the complexities. This enables them and their supervisors to work out improved ways of helping their patients.[35] Similar consultation programs exist in many communities, in schools, and in other community agencies.

Much work is necessary to devise and evaluate the appropriate techniques for consultation with different professions in their unique work situations. Although evaluation of the efficacy of consultation is just beginning, a study of consultation with nurses has recently been completed by Howe and Caplan (unpublished). It suggests that if issues emotionally relevant to the nurse are foci of the consultation, it is useful in the long run. However, space does not permit adequate coverage of this rapidly growing field; it deserves a review in its own right.

Education of Informal Caregivers.   Individuals in crisis often turn for help not to professional caregivers, but to people who live or work near them, whom they have learned to know and respect. Such informal caregivers include neighbors, druggists, bartenders, hairdressers, industrial foremen, etc. They are chosen by people as confidants because of special personality gifts—capacity for empathy and understanding and interest in their fellow men.

These informal caregivers exert a significant influence on the mental health of the population, and pose a major challenge for preventive psychiatry. How can we make contact with them, and how can we educate them so that they give wise counsel to those in crisis who seek them out? They have had no formal training, and we have had no hand in selecting them. Currently, pioneering efforts are being made to train and utilize indigenous workers in many places and in many programs. The work of Christmas,[65] Rieff[67] and Reissman,[66] and our own experiences[68] are examples.

Another way of reaching informal caregivers may be through mass media such as articles, radio, or TV. An example is an article entitled "Crisis in the Family,"[69] addressed to and hopefully read by those to whom people in crisis turn for help. It offers a series of guidelines or basic principles which may be useful in the helping process. Another example is illustrated by "Trouble in the family," (Audio-Visual Center, National Educational Television Film Service) a television program which was recently honored by the American Psychiatric Association Strecker Award. A series of family therapy interviews conducted by Dr. Norman Paul was presented, with a commentary on the efforts of the family to improve their relationship with a problem child.

Personal Preparation for Healthy Crisis Coping Through Education. The effort here is to modify the content and methods of the education of children and youth so that skills are acquired for dealing adequately with unexpected and temporarily insoluble problems. An example is the attempt developed in Iowa by Ojemann[70] to improve the problem-solving capacities of children. The nature of American education, he observes, leads to what he calls "surface thinking," in which behavior in any situation is rather simply and automatically determined as a reaction to the overt manifestations of the problem. In place of this he advocates a "causal approach," in which the person learns to uncover the causes of the observed manifestations and then systematically works out a plan of action to deal with the most crucial of these causes. Ojemann has rewritten school textbooks and has trained teachers in methods of teaching causal thinking as an integral part of a normal school curriculum. The results were evaluated by comparing children taught along these lines with children from traditional classes; they clearly demonstrate that children taught the causal approach are better able to solve novel intellectual problems. They develop an increased capacity to persevere in the face of ambiguity, as well as an increased tolerance of frustration;[71] these are precisely the attributes which foster an improved capacity to deal adaptively with crisis. Biber[72] and others at the Banks Street School have been similarly interested in modifying the school experience to promote healthier adjustment and more successful problem-solving by preschool and elementary school children.

Another approach is that of Kurt Hahn[73] and the Outward Bound movement in Britain, a program which was one of the forerunners of the Peace Corps. This program attempts character building experiential education for adolescents and young adults. The students are exposed to situations of natural hazard, such as climbing mountains or ocean sailing— or, in the Peace Corps, physical deprivation and cultural conflict. The stress is graduated to be just beyond the usual capacity of the student. He experiences an induced crisis, but is then provided with adult support and guidance in working his way to a healthy adaptation. This, it seems likely, will lead to a strengthening and maturing of his personality, with increased independence and awareness of his own capacities and improved skills in making use of the help of others.

These apparently relatively successful attempts point to the possibility of modifying our educational system on a wide population basis to improve the potential of students to master life crises. It is a field in which collaboration of psychiatrists with educators may yield important results in the future.

Anticipatory Guidance. Here the effort is to prepare an individual for an impending crisis. An example is discussed in a recent study by Janis, of Yale,[74] which shows that among patients awaiting operation in a surgical ward, it is possible to predict which ones will have the least difficult postoperative psychological adjustment. Patients who are moderately worried about the operation and ask a lot of questions about the pain and discomfort ahead adapt more easily afterwards than those who seem unusually cheerful and express unconcern about the impending stress. The study suggests that if a person facing a crisis knows ahead of time what he must cope with and begins to master it, he will be better prepared psychologically to handle the stress when the situation is upon him. Janis recommends, on the basis of careful studies of postoperative patients, that patients awaiting operation should be given a sort of "emotional inoculation," wherein they are told in some detail what is likely to happen. Similarly, work in the Anesthesiology Department of the Massachusetts General Hospital[75] demonstrates that it is possible to reduce the postoperative narcotic requirements by approximately half through preoperative guidance discussions. In addition, it is striking that the 46 patients receiving encouragement and education were ready for discharge an average of 2.7 days before the 51 matched control cases.

Attempts in public health have been made for some years to prepare pregnant women for childbirth and for dealing with expectable problems in the growth and development of their children. Anticipatory guidance techniques are also used in the Peace Corps to prepare volunteers to face the challenges of overseas service. Some of this preparation has been done by psychiatrists in a special mental health sequence in Peace Corps training programs, and a pamphlet, *Adjusting Overseas*,[35] is given to every trainee. It describes the many stresses, such as loneliness, strange living conditions, different value systems, boredom, and lack of obvious signs of accomplishment, which volunteers must expect in their assignments, and tells them that they will probably become depressed, anxious, angry, and confused when exposed to these conditions. The psychiatrist then meets with the trainees in a small group to discuss in advance some of the negative feelings they are likely to have as they go through these difficulties; they may then be better prepared to accept their feelings, to master them and to seek the emotional support of their associates and of the Peace Corps staff.

No discussion of primary prevention would be complete without reference to the problems of conceptualization and evaluation, particularly when the focus is on a population. These are the areas where the greatest problems exist and the least work has been done. The conceptual model used in this paper is to divide the environmental influences on human development into long- and short-term factors, and to subdivide the nature of the factors into physical, psychosocial, and sociocultural. Bloom (unpublished), on the other hand, has suggested that one may consider primary prevention programs as focusing on the total community; on individuals who are passing a certain milestone in their lives; and on high-risk groups. Bolman and Westman[76] have suggested that preventive programs dealing with young children can be divided into society-centered, family-centered, and child-centered efforts. It is clear that these different conceptualizations are not contradictory, but complementary. The schema used in the present paper focuses attention on the vicissitudes of human growth and development and the forces which foster or impede it, while the other two focus attention on specific goals and methods of programs of primary prevention. Indeed, in the absence of great knowledge as to the etiology of mental illness and psychological maldevelopment, any conceptual framework will be a temporary expedient adopted for pragmatic purposes. As this is the case for all sciences, whether exact and highly developed or primitive and inexact, we should not be too troubled.

The efficacy of preventive efforts has been assessed in too few of the programs discussed in this review. While many ideas about primary prevention seem plausible, are based on clinical judgment, or are transpositions of findings from one area of research to another, we will only gain greater certitude if we make evaluative studies. Yet the problems of evaluation are many, as in evaluating the effects of psychotherapy, but on a much larger scale. This discussion will be brief and focus on the salient issues of goals, controls, and assessment techniques; and the reader is referred to reviews of the field, such as those by Hyman,[77] Freeman,[78] Etzioni,[79] and Mac-Mahon.[80]

The problem of specifying the goals of an intervention program is a particularly knotty one. For example, Brim,[81] in his discussion of parent education, notes that the aims of such education depend not only on the particular psychological theory which one espouses, but also on the values which one holds. It is impossible to educate without advocating, and so too, efforts at prevention involve issues of value. Thus, to express one's grief at a loss may be useful for one's mental health, but it is antithetical to the value of stoicism. Furthermore, the goals of preventive efforts are rarely single and simple; they are usually multiple and complex. As Brim points out, education may influence the parent in the direction of being both more knowledge-able about his influence on his child, and less anxious at the same time. These objectives may in fact conflict; but even if they do not, the results of programs designed to effect them require quite different evaluative techniques. The problems of determining goals thus involves matters of both value orientation and of clarifying the various aims of any given program.

Problems of specifying and obtaining adequate controls are also difficult. Most programs of prevention involve the individual's consent and participation, and it is well known that these are aspects of personality which may influence outcome. If one obtains a person's agreement to participate in a program which will be helpful to him, can one then refuse to let him participate? A choice has to be made whether the control group is to be offered no intervention at all or some placebo program, since there are likely to be effects on individuals from just giving them some attention entirely apart from the specific aims of any given program of prevention. Furthermore, in many programs which last over time, there is the problem of dropouts. Such individuals clearly do not terminate randomly, and dropping out is likely to be associated with other characteristics of personality which may influence outcome. It is clear that to specify the appropriate controls for use in evaluating attempts at intervention and what program, if any, to offer is difficult, particularly when the focus is on a population.

Bloom (unpublished), who comments that the field is a "nightmare," describes four types of research which often are considered as evaluative: (1) program description; (2) evaluation based on judgments made by recipients; (3) evaluation based on judgments made by professionals; and (4) evaluations based on analysis of objective data without recourse to intervening interpretive judgments. Only the last three can truly be considered evaluative, yet each has its own built-in problems of reliability, validity, and bias. The last type of evaluation, based on objective data, may seem to be the most plausible, yet it too has its problems. For instance, hospitalization rates depend heavily on admission policies; thus, a high rate of admission can lead by a change of administrative policy to many more psychotics living with their families, without affecting the prevalence of psychosis. In this example, it can be seen that seemingly objective data, i.e., admission rates, may be dependent on unseen and unstudied subjective factors of both patients and families, and of professionals. It appears that different methods of evaluation will be most appropriate for different programs—for some, subjective reports by recipients of increased happiness or decreased familial discord will be appropriate; for others, professional assessment of symptom change or increase in IQ; and for still others, lowered rates of suicide. In all cases, it is necessary that evaluation be attempted and focused as far as possible on the specific objectives of the program, so that we may learn which aspect of a given program influences which aspects of its recipients.

In conclusion, in view of the vast amounts of money being spent on programs which are primarily psychological, social, and rehabilitative in nature, it is useful to consider costs. Sherwood (unpublished data) points out that it is cost per unit of output alone that should be considered. A program which costs little per person and serves large numbers may be highly wasteful if little is accomplished, when compared with a program which spends the same amount of money on far fewer recipients but accomplishes more, not only with each recipient, but in total.

SUMMARY

It is clear from this review of the literature on primary prevention that much has been learned from clinical experience and research; yet, unfortunately, it must be admitted that what is known is often not used. To cite but one example, the short-term effects of hospitalization on infants and small children are well known and thoroughly documented. And yet, it remains true that all too few hospitals take into account the emotional needs of their child patients, and large impersonal institutions exist for the care of the wards of the state. Why this should be so is an important question for psychiatrists to answer. It may well be that we are better prepared and willing to deal with the needs of individual patients than to enter the broad field of implementing social change; yet it is clear that much of the knowledge on primary prevention suggests that we must change institutions, not only individuals. Eisenberg[25] asks, in his presidential address to the American Orthopsychiatric Association, "If not now, when?" Pellagra and cretinism are prevented, not by treating individuals, but by altering the nutritional patterns of groups; so, too, "hospitalism" and the adverse effects of institutionalization can only be prevented by altering organizations. In conclusion, it may be said that while the specific etiological factors which lead to specific mental illnesses are not known and much remains to be learned, a great deal is known about the prevention of psychological maldevelopment, maladaptation, and misery; and much remains undone.

REFERENCES

1. Calhoun, J.B. Population density and social pathology. L.J. Duhl, ed., *The urban condition*. New York: Basic Books, 1963. Pp.33-43.
2. Kubzansky, P.E. The effects of reduced environmental stimulation on human behavior: A review. A.D. Biderman and H. Zimmer, eds., *The manipulation of human behavior*. New York: Wiley, 1961. Pp.51-95.
3. Kleitman, N. *Sleep and wakefulness*, Second Edition. Chicago: University of Chicago Press, 1965.
4. Hartman, E.L. The D-state. *New England Journal of Medicine*, July 8, 1965, **273**(2), 87-92.

5. Srole, L., et al. *Mental health in the metropolis.* New York: McGraw-Hill, 1961. Vol. 1.
6. Leighton, D., et al. *The character of danger.* New York: Basic Books, 1963.
7. Moncrieff, A.A. Treatment of phenyl ketonuria: Report to the Medical Research Council of the Conference on Phenyl Ketonuria. *British Medical Journal*, 1963, **1**, 1691-1697.
8. Means, J.H., DeGroot, L.J., and Stanbury, J.B. *The thyroid and its diseases*, Third Edition. New York: McGraw-Hill, 1963.
9. Wohl, M.D., and Goodhart, R.S., eds. *Modern nutrition and disease.* Philadelphia: Lea & Febiger, 1960.
10. University of Cincinnati. Symposium on lead. *Archives of Environmental Health*, 1964, **8**, 202-354.
11. Hess, R.D., and Shipman, V.C. Early experience and the socialization of cognitive modes in children. *Child Research*, 1965, **36**(4), 869-886.
12. Deutsch, M. The role of social class in language development and cognition. *American Journal of Orthopsychiatry*, 1964, **35**, 78-87.
13. John, V.P. The intellectual development of slum children: Some preliminary findings. *American Journal of Orthopsychiatry*, (Oct) 1963, **33**(5), 813-822.
14. Keller, S. The social world of the urban slum child: Some early findings. *American Journal of Orthopsychiatry*, (Oct) 1963, **33**(5), 823-831.
15. Weisman, A., and Hackett, T.P. Psychosis after eye surgery: Establishment of a specific doctor-patient relation in the prevention and treatment of "Black Patch Delirium." *New England Journal of Medicine*, 1958, **258**, 1284.
16. Kornfeld, D.S., Zimberg, S., and Malm, J.K. Psychiatric complications of open-heart surgery. *New England Journal of Medicine*, 1965, **273**, 287-292.
17. Rice, E.P., and Krakow, S.G. Hospitalization of a parent for mental illness: A crisis for children. Read before the 42nd annual meeting of the American Orthopsychiatric Association, New York, March 17-20, 1965.
18. Spitz, R.A. Hospitalism: An inquiry into the genesis of psychiatric conditions in early childhood. O. Fenichel et al., eds., *Psychoanalytic study of the child.* New York: International Universities Press, 1945. Vol. 1, pp. 53-74.
19. Bowlby, E.J.M. *Maternal care and mental health.* World Health Organization Bulletins, Monograph No. 2. Geneva: World Health Organization, 1951. Vol. 3, pp. 355-533.
20. Provence, S., and Lipton, R.C. *Infants in institutions.* New York: International Universities Press, 1962.
21. Skeels, H.M. *Adult status of children with contrasting early life experiences: A follow-up study.* Society for Research in Child Development Monograph, 1966, **31**, No. 105.
22. Wiltse, K.T. Orthopsychiatric programs for socially deprived groups. *American Journal of Orthopsychiatry*, (Oct) 1963, **33**(5), 806-813.
23. Eisenberg, L. The sins of the fathers: Urban decay and social pathology. *American Journal of Orthopsychiatry*, (Jan) 1962, **32**(1), 5-17.
24. Prugh, D., et al. A study of emotional reactions of children and families to hospitalization and illness. *American Journal of Orthopsychiatry*, 1953, **23**, 70-106.
25. Eisenberg, L. If not now, when? *American Journal of Orthopsychiatry*, (Oct) 1962, **32**(5), 781-791.
26. Mason, E.A. The hospitalized child—his emotional needs. *New England Journal of Medicine*, (Feb) 1965, **272**(8), 406-414.

27. Committee on the College Student. *The college experience: A focus for psychiatric research* (GAP Report no. 52). New York: Group for the Advancement of Psychiatry, 1962.

28. Committee on the College Student. *Sex and the college student* (GAP Report No. 60). New York: Group for the Advancement of Psychiatry, 1965.

29. Barger, B. The University of Florida Mental Health Program. *Higher Education and Mental Health*. Gainesville, Fla.: University of Florida, 1964.

30. Williams, R.H., Tibbetts, C., and Donahue, W., eds. *The process of aging*. New York: Atherton, 1963.

31. French, J.R.P., Jr. The industrial environment and mental health. Read before the First International Congress of Social Psychiatry, August 1964.

32. Tureen, L., and Wortman, M. A program sponsored by a labor union for treatment and prevention of psychiatric conditions. *American Journal of Orthopsychiatry*, (April) 1965, **35**(3), 594-597.

33. Glass, A.J. Observations upon the epidemiology of mental illness in troops during warfare. Walter Reed Army Institute of Research, *Symposium on preventive and social psychiatry*. Washington: U.S. Government Printing Office, 1958. Pp. 185-198.

34. Fried, M. Effects of social change on mental health. *American Journal of Orthopsychiatry*, 1964. **34**(3), 3-28.

35. Caplan, G. *Principles of preventive psychiatry*. New York: Basic Books, 1964.

36. Lindemann, E. Symptomatology and management of acute grief, *American Journal of Psychiatry*, 1944, **101**, 141-148.

37. Engel, G.L. Is grief a disease? *Psychosomatic Medicine*, 1961, **23**(1), 18-22.

38. Caplan, G. Patterns of parental response to the crisis of premature birth. *Psychiatry*, (Nov) 1960, **23**(4), 365-374.

39. Caplan, G., Mason, E.A., and Kaplan, D.M. Four studies of crisis in parents of prematures. *Community Mental Health Journal*, (Summer) 1965, **1**(2), 149-161.

40. Tichener, J.L., and Levine, M. *Surgery as a human experience*. New York: Oxford University Press, 1960.

41. English, J.T., and Colman, J.G. Biological adjustment patterns of Peace Corps volunteers. *Psychiatric Opinion*, 1966, **3**, 29.

42. Rapoport, R. Transition from engagement to marriage. *Acta Sociologica*, 1964, **8**, 1-2.

43. Silber, E., et al. Adaptive behavior in competent adolescents coping with the anticipation of college. *Archives of General Psychiatry*, 1961, **5**, 354-365.

44. Silber, E., et al. Competent adolescents coping with college decisions. *Archives of General Psychiatry*, 1961, **5**, 517-527.

45. Parad, H.J. *Crisis intervention: Selected readings*. New York: Family Service Association of America, 1965.

46. Rapoport, L. Working with families in crisis: An exploration in preventive intervention. *Social Work*, 1962, **7**, 48.

47. Freud, S. Types of onset of neurosis. J. Strachey, ed. and trans., *The standard edition of the complete psychological works of Sigmund Freud*. London: Hogarth Press, 1958. Vol. 12, pp. 231-238.

48. Hamburg, D.A. Plasma and urinary corticosteroid levels in naturally occuring psychologic stresses. Association for Research in Nervous and Mental Disease. *Ultrastructure and metabolism of the nervous system*. Baltimore: Williams and

Wilkins, 1962. Vol. 40, pp. 406-413.

49. Caplan, G. *An approach to community mental health.* New York: Grune & Stratton, 1961.

50. Zetzel, E.R. Depression and the incapacity to bear it. M. Schur, ed., *Drives, affects, behavior.* New York: International Universities Press, 1965. Vol. 2.

51. Kiessler, F. Is this psychiatry? S.E. Goldston, ed., *Concepts of community psychiatry: A framework for training,* Public Health Service Publication No. 1319. Washington: Department of Health, Education and Welfare, 1965. Pp. 147-157.

52. Faberow, N. L., and Shneidman, E. S. *The cry for help.* New York: McGraw-Hill, 1961.

53. Aldrich, C.K. Homemaker service: Adjunct in mental hygiene and socio-psychiatric rehabilitation. *Progress in Psychotherapy,* 1959, **4,** 159-162.

54. Torric, M., ed. *The Cruse Club Chronicle: Monthly Newsletter of the Counselling Service for Widows and their Families.* Richmond, Surrey, England: E.H. Baker & Co.

55. Egleson, J., and Egleson, J.F. *Parents without partners.* New York: Dutton, 1961.

56. Robinson, R., Demarche, D.F., and Wagle, M.K. *Community resources in mental health,* No. 5, Joint Commission on Mental Illness and Health Monograph Series. New York: Basic Books, 1960.

57. Klein, D.C., and Lindemann, E. Preventive intervention in individual and family crisis situations. G. Caplan, ed., *Prevention of mental disorders in children.* New York: Basic Books, 1961.

58. Waldfogel, S., and Gardner, G.E. Intervention in crises as a method of primary prevention. G. Caplan, ed., *Prevention of mental disorders in children.* New York: Basic Books, 1961.

59. Parad, H.J. The use of time-limited crisis intervention in community mental health programming. *Social Service Review,* 1966, **40,** 275-282.

60. Moore, T. Difficulties of the ordinary child in adjusting to school. *Journal of Child Psychology and Psychiatry,* 1966, **7,** 17-38.

61. Bower, E.M. The modification, mediation and utilization of stress during the school years. *American Journal of Orthopsychiatry,* (July) 1964, **34**(4), 667-674.

62. Bibring, G.L., et al. A study of the psychological processes in pregnancy and of the earliest mother-child relationship: I. Some propositions and comments. R.S. Eissler et al., eds., *Psychoanalytic study of the child.* New York: International Universities Press, 1961. Vol. 16, pp. 9-24.

63. Bibring, G.L., et al. A study of the psychological processes in pregnancy and of the earliest mother-child relationship: II. Methodological considerations. R.S. Eissler et al., eds., *Psychoanalyatic study of the child.* New York: International Universities Press, 1961. Vol. 16, pp. 25-92.

64. Caplan, G. *Theory and practice of mental health consultation.* New York: Basic Books, 1970.

65. Christmas, J.J. Sociopsychiatric treatment of the disadvantaged psychotic. Read before the American Orthopsychiatric Association Meeting, San Francisco, April 13-16, 1966.

66. Pearl, A., and Riessman, F. *New careers for the poor.* New York: Free Press, 1965.

67. Rieff, R., and Riessman, F. The indigenous non-professional: A strategy of change in community action and community mental health programs, National Institute of Labor Education Report No. 3. Washington, (Nov) 1964.
68. Palmbaum, P.J. Apprenticeship revisited. *Archives of General Psychiatry*, 1965, **13**, 304-309.
69. Cadden, V. Crisis in the family. G. Caplan, ed., *Principles of preventive psychiatry*. New York: Basic Books, 1964.
70. Ojemann, R.H. Investigations on the effects of teaching an understanding and appreciation of behavior dynamics. G. Caplan, ed., *Prevention of mental disorders in children*. New York: Basic Books, 1961. Pp. 378-397.
71. Morgan, M.I., and Ojemann, R.H. The effect of a learning program designed to assist youth in an understanding of behavior and its development. *Child Development*, (Sept) 1942, **13**(3), 181-194.
72. Biber, B., et al. *The psychological impact of school experience*. New York: Bank Street College of Education, 1962.
73. Hahn, K. Origins of the Outward Bound Trust. D. James, ed., *Outward Bound*. London: Routledge & Kegan Paul, 1957.
74. Janis, I.L. *Psychological stress*. New York: Wiley, 1958.
75. Egbert, L.D., et al. Reduction of postoperative pain by encouragement and instruction of patients. *New England Journal of Medicine*, (April) 1964, **270**, 825-827.
76. Bolman, W.M., and Westman, J.C. Prevention of mental disorder: An overview of current programs. *American Journal of Psychiatry*, 1967, **128**, 1058-1068.
77. Hyman, E., et al. *Application of methods of evaluation*. Berkeley, Calif.: University of California Press, 1965.
78. Freeman, H.E., and Sherwood, C.C. Research in large-scale intervention programs. *Journal of Social Issues*, 1965, **21**, 11-28.
79. Etzioni, A. Two approaches to organization analysis: A critique and a suggestion. *Administrative Science Quarterly*, (Sept) 1960, **5**, 257-278.
80. MacMahon, B., Pugh, T.F., and Hutchison, G.B. Principles in the evaluation of community mental health programs. *American Journal of Public Health*, 1961, **7**, 963-979.
81. Brim, O.G., Jr. *Education for childrearing*. New York: Russell Sage Foundation, 1959.

suggested additional readings

Caplan, G., ed. *Prevention of mental disorders in children*. New York: Basic Books, 1961.

Caplan, G. *Principles of preventive psychiatry*. New York: Basic Books, 1964.

Lambert, Nadine M. *The protection and promotion of mental health in schools*. Mental Health Monograph Number 5, U.S. Department of Health, Education, and Welfare, 1965.

Parad, H.J. *Crisis intervention: Selected readings*. New York: Family Service Association of America, 1965.

three   mental health consultation

The provision of consultation and education to community caregivers and agencies is one of the five "essential" services called for under the Community Mental Health Centers Act of 1963. Consultation probably has received more attention than any other technique of primary prevention. One reason may be that, as Lorene Stringer notes, no one objects to being called a consultant. As the reader will see from the articles in this section, mental health consultation is a sophisticated technique. It is not simply a matter of an expert telling someone what to do about a problem. Consequently a large number of people currently act as "consultants" without actualizing the full potential of the consultation process.

Mental health consultation is a very good example of the application of the "participant-conceptualizer" role for the community specialist. The consultant must both participate and conceptualize in order to bring about changes which will promote mental health. Mental health consultation refers to the technique and process by which a *consultant* attempts to help a *consultee* or consultees with the problem of a *client* or client-system. The problem may reside in the client. It may also be a problem the consultee has in dealing with a client or client-system. Or, as is the case in social system consultation, the problem may exist within the consultee-system or client-system. In the consultation relationship, the consultee retains the responsibility and initiative for action. The consultant uses his understanding and knowledge of human behavior as well as social systems to help the consultee arrive at adaptive approaches to the resolution of the problematic situation. Whenever possible, the consultant would like to create a change in the consultee or the social system that has broader implications and more lasting impact than does the solution of a single presenting problem. This last point is a prominent feature of mental health consultation. The question is: Can the consultant work with the consultee in such a way that, in addition to solving the problem at hand, the consultee becomes more competent to solve problems of a similar nature in the future?

Elsewhere, Spielberger and Iscoe (1970) view the participant-conceptualizer role as a specific rather than a general role for the community psychologist and differentiate between the mental health consultant and the participant-conceptualizer. They view the mental health consultant as bringing mental health expertise to the consultation situation. The participant-conceptualizer makes his contribution through his ability to participate, conceptualize, clarify, and expedite. In our experience one community psychologist in particular exemplifies a participant-conceptualizer. He was repeatedly sought out as a valued committee member, advisor, and consultant, not just because of his expertise in mental health, personality dynamics, and human relations, nor because of his administrative position in a community mental health center. It was quite clear that his value largely sprang from his ability to conceptualize and clarify objectives, tasks, functions, and issues. Thus he was able to influence substantially the development of community programs, as a good consultant does. While the two functions can be distinguished, the participant-conceptualizer role remains a superordinant one for the community psychologist.

The mental health aspects of case consultation are clearly recognizable. The mental health implications of program or social system consultation are sometimes more subtle. It can be argued, however, as Nagler and Cooper do in Section four, that contributions to the articulation of programs and changes in social systems have greater potential for enhancing community mental health than does any case-centered technique.

A variety of aspects of mental health consultation are discussed in the four articles of this section. The articles in Section four are a continuation of the subject of consultative intervention and deal with planned social system and organizational change.

REFERENCE

Spielberger, C.D. and Iscoe, I. The current status of training in community psychology. I. Iscoe and C.D. Spielberger, eds., *Community psychology: Perspectives in training and research.* New York: Appleton-Century-Crofts, 1970.

In the first article in this section, Lorene Stringer discusses some of the fundamental considerations in consultation. She highlights some of the important aspects of what it means to be a consultant—what people expect of the consultant, what are some of the pitfalls and what are the consultant's tasks. It will be seen from the article that it is not easy to be a good consultant and that professional expertise is not the only prerequisite. To be a consultant requires training and skills beyond those usually derived from professional education. The article is a valuable introduction to some of the more important and subtler considerations of consultation.

Miss Stringer's comments are based on her experience as a mental health consultant in schools. Traditionally the schools have been a prime target of mental health consultation.

consultation: some expectations, principles, and skills

Lorene A. Stringer

Ten years ago the St. Louis County Health Department began a program now known as the School Mental Health Services. Under contract arrangements with a number of county school districts, psychiatric social workers from the Mental Health Division are assigned to specified schools where they work, on regular schedules, in ways comparable to those of district-employed school social workers. What happened to us in the early years of the program is what can be expected to happen to most school social workers—mushrooming demands that could not be met on any case-by-case basis within the existing limits of staff time. Some of us, therefore, ventured into consultant relationships with principals and superintendents, believing that we could thus increase our effectiveness, at no extra cost or effort at all, but simply by a change of focus. What we have learned, in general, follows.

No one, apparently, will object to being called a consultant. The term has prestige value, the quietly unassailable dignity of a hallmark. *Being* a consultant, however, is something else again and not often carried off with "quietly unassailable dignity." It is likely to be either a thankless or a most arduous undertaking; the former if we do it poorly, the latter if we do it well.

The discrepancy between title and task need not concern us. Titles, after all, are intended to yield gratification, to compensate in some measure for the headaches commonly occurring in the performance of the duties that go with them. But there is a major peculiarity in the consultant's situation that adds enormously to the number of headaches he suffers. Whereas most professional titles (e.g., *physician, sanitarian, social worker, nurse, health educator*) are bestowed only on people specifically trained to perform the duties

Reprinted from *Social Work*, Vol. 6. No. 3 (July 1961), 85-90, with the permission of the National Association of Social Workers and the author.

associated with them, the title of *consultant* is regularly bestowed on people trained only for some other kind of work (*e.g.,* medicine, sanitation, social work, and so on).

We can have some fine consultants in spite of this, people who have been able to train themselves, on the job, to effective performance. Not everyone has talent for self-training, but we usually overlook that fact, particularly when our attention is concentrated on the larger and sorrier fact that our staffs are never big enough to meet the community need for direct services, of all the kinds that fall within the realm of settings in which social work is practiced. To be so concerned about this is appropriate, but is it equally appropriate to resort to expediency to allay our concern? And is it truly expedient if, whenever we find ourselves short of service staff, we pull a few more out of direct service, dub them "consultants," increase the number of their assignments while decreasing their time for each, and then just trust to luck?

We need consultants. It is highly improbable that we shall ever have staff resources to provide all the direct service needed; it is open to argument whether we should if we could. But we need trained consultants, because the job they have to do requires a good deal more than just that they be highly skilled in their own discipline, whatever that may be. Consider, even briefly, some of the problems they encounter as they work.

ROLE EXPECTATIONS

The consultant may or may not conceive of himself as an oracle, but many people who ask for consultation harbor a hope (unrecognized until it explodes) that he will speak-as-an-oracle-and-tell-them-exactly-what-they-want-to-hear—not just one or the other of these but always the two together. A tenth or a hundredth part of the time he may be able to do this in good conscience. The rest of the time he must choose between (1) not speaking as an oracle, which will disconcert and disappoint his listeners and raise real question about his competence, and (2) speaking as an oracle but telling them what they do not want to hear, which will upset and anger them and stimulate ideas about how they can prove him wrong. (If there appears to be another obvious choice, let us note merely that to score only once in two tries is bad enough, but not to score at all is worse.)

Let us assume, however, that all parties are reasonable and view the consultant merely as an expert in the field of his own specialization. He is still expected to be able to package his expertness neatly and have it always deliverable on demand, ready for immediate use. Here is another cluster of difficulties. In the first place, the packaging is itself an art, the end result of which must be neither too little nor too big, neither too light nor too heavy, neither too full nor too nearly empty. Moreover, the deliverable-on-demand condition is taxing. Most of us tend to mislay certain pieces of knowledge that are not often called for—to forget about this technique or that resource that proved useful once but has not been needed since. Even if one can remain unembarrassed while fumbling around the dusty shelves of one's mind, it is always frustrating to have only a dim recollection that we have something suitable somewhere, if we could just remember what and where. Third, the people who are to use this packaged expertness are not themselves experts in the consultant's specialization. They will be less than expert in it, and possibly expert in some other field. What the consultant says in his language, then, they will hear in their language, and when—not getting his message—they counter with arguments and objections, the confusion is all too often further compounded: now they speak in their language, and he hears in his.

But assume that the puzzle of semantics has been solved and communication has become full and free. There remains still a triad of odd expectations that are sometimes acted out but almost never voiced, for obvious reasons: (1) that the consultant will somehow effect the necessary changes to make everything shipshape, although he has no executive authority at all, (2) that whenever the outcome is good he will have the decency to keep out of sight, so that the credit can go to those onstage, and (3) that whenever the outcome is bad he will have the equal decency to remain out front and center, to take full blame, while the others ease quietly out of sight. All this seems patently unreasonable and unfair, but it is tightly adherent to (maybe really inherent *in*) the consultant function, so that it has to be dealt with somehow.

We are not yet being forced to set up programs for training consultants to deal with problems like these. We can doubtless go on for a long time in our present makeshift way, if only because it does not seem to be costing very much. However, this is mere seeming, and the true cost is a tremendous amount of work going undone that could be done if we had more good consultants. We are not likely to have them until we train them; and we are not going to be able to train them until we know, rather more clearly and specifically than we do now, what particular attributes and skills differentiate a good consultant from a poor one. It is to this point that we need to address ourselves first, and it may be as good a beginning as any simply to consider how a good consultant might deal with the problems just mentioned.

THE TASK

A good consultant will not conceive of himself as an oracle. If he is truly expert in his own field, he is—by virtue of that fact—well aware that he is not omniscient. In the process of becoming expert he will have experienced failures and reversals often enough to leave him more impressed with the unpredictable and the uncontrollable than with his own ability to predict and control. All the same, when his best counsel happens to accord with what the counsel-seekers want to hear, and they therefore regard his utterance as oracular, it is tempting to offer no disclaimer but just for a little while to bask in their high esteem. It is tempting—and dangerous—for it invites them to listen more reverently the next time, when his advice may not be so much to their liking and their disappointment will therefore be sharper. He will be better off to do here, gratuitously and against whatever resistance they offer, what he has to do when his counsel is unpopular: grant that he is not infallible, admit that he cannot guarantee, and remind them and himself that his recommendation is simply his chosen way of committing himself to the as yet unknown.

In stressing the as yet unknown, however, the good consultant will not overlook or slight the matter of his own commitment. Rejecting the oracular role does not mean injecting so many ifs, ands, and buts into the discussion as to throw one's listeners into confusion and dismay, and it does not mean burdening them with all the unpredictables one can think of. This would be tantamount to rejecting the consultant role as well, because to counsel means to lend one's knowledge *and its strength*. The good consultant, therefore, will have to be able to select, out of whatever knowledge he possesses, only so much as will make the issue as clear as possible to his listeners; and whatever he proposes he will propose explicitly and firmly, committing himself unreservedly to both his recommendation and its risks, but leaving his listeners perfectly free to accept or reject it as they choose. Until the consultant so commits himself, the counsel-seekers remain shackled, not only with their own misgivings, but with their consultant's doubts and uncertainties, too.

What happens, then, when one cannot formulate a recommendation that warrants such commitment? Simply, the consultant needs to know how to say "I don't know" in a way that will inspire more rather than less confidence in him. It takes no more than forthright honesty to give this statement a good, clean impact, but if the consultant stops with that, the consultation process is likely to stop there, too. There must be follow-through, for these three unembroidered, unabashed words can open doors to fuller communication and more productive collaboration. But this counts for nothing unless the consultant moves in to stimulate new interest or encourage experimentation or suggest another point of view.

In sum, if the consultant himself has no great need to be an oracle, he can learn how to avoid the pitfalls associated with this.

It is by no means so easy a matter to learn how to make his expertness fully serviceable through consultation. The tools of his trade and his own hard-won skills are almost irrelevant now, because he is not to do the job himself, whatever the job may be; he is only to help someone else do a job—someone who, lacking the consultant's skills, will not be able to use the consultant's tools. The consultant expert now has to transmute himself somehow into an expert consultant, and the problem is how.

In the first place he must take the time and invest the effort necessary to become familiar with the field to which he is consulting—with its prevalent practices, its historical great and its current local authorities, its major problems whether chronic or acute, its more important schools of thought, its terminology and jargon. He may acquire such familiarity in any of several ways, but he will not acquire it effortlessly nor in an hour or two, and until he has acquired it, he will not be able to comprehend adequately the job to be done.

In the second place he must be able to appraise with reasonable accuracy the person who is to do the job, so that the tool can be matched as well as possible to the user. If the consultant either underestimates or overestimates the user, the tool will be ill-chosen—inefficient in the one case, risky or dangerous in the other. For that matter, the right tool may not be ready to hand; often enough the consultant has to be able to adapt an old tool or invent a new one before he has something right for the particular person and the specific job.

Finally, and by far the trickiest task of the three, the consultant must discover how to teach the person to use the tool so as to do the job successfully. This sounds simple, and yet it is precisely here that we are most likely to be tripped up by a suddenly erupting need to display our own expertness: we toss off a few highly technical terms and an abstruse reference or so, as a passing and surely innocent self-indulgence, and recognize too late, if at all, that these have thrown the other person off stride. We may even be tempted into mystifying rather than teaching, into saying in effect, "I have a hunch that I can't quite explain, but I think *seven* is our answer," when we could say, "Here are two, and here two more, and over there are three, making seven in all." It is not only the churlish consultant who falls into this kind of error; it awaits us all until we have learned to find it more rewarding to be a good consultant than to show off our expertness.

WHAT KIND OF PERSON?

By now, as we come to that triad of odd expectations that always attend the consultant, it is obviously time to ask what kind of person it takes to make a good one. The answer seems almost to leap full-formed out of the expectations: it takes a person mature enough to fill a parental role, supporting, encouraging, guiding, protecting whenever that is needed, entrusting whenever that is safe. What other kind of person could without bitterness take the blame when things go wrong, and yield the credit when credit is forthcoming?

The trouble with this answer is that the counsel-seekers are not children.

They may be teachable and tractable, but they may be opinionated and head-strong, and they are never answerable to the consultant. Not only may they fail to be grateful for having been coached to a creditable performance, but they are often the first to attack and accuse when the coaching has not led to success. To behave parentally toward some of them is like trying to pet a porcupine.

But this is the trouble with the answer—which is not to say that the answer is altogether wrong. On the contrary, it points quite clearly to the basic and indispensable element without which no consultant can be good: the capacity to devote his energies happily and productively to building strength and furthering growth in someone else.

Again this sounds simple and is not so. It necessarily implies that the consultant has already attended adequately to his own needs and that, as new needs arise in him, he is quick to become conscious of them and able to handle them so that they do not interfere with his consultative functioning. It means, further, that he is discriminating in the investment of his energies, neither demanding that his consultees be able to make full use, right now, of as much as he can offer, nor masochistically pouring out effort for consultees too rigid or panicked to use him at all. And it means, still further, that whatever he does is ordered, as best he can order it, to the purpose of building strength and promoting growth, not of overprotecting or overindulging or doing for.

Given this capacity to enjoy work in behalf of someone else, it becomes possible for a consultant to deal with our triad of odd expectations. Since he does not have clamoring needs of his own to distract him, he can take cognizance of certain facts that we all too often ignore: that the counsel-seekers, like grown-up children, have attained their majority, won their independence, and proved their competence in their own field; that, though they are not answerable to the consultant, they are answerable to others, somewhere, and are well aware of it; and that they have far more at stake, personally, in any issue on which they ask help than the consultant has. In the light of these facts, their expectations no longer look so unreasonable and unfair, and we may even begin to suspect that they looked that way earlier chiefly because the consultant's expectations were out of line; he was either too needy himself to be willing to work in behalf of someone else, or he did not know how to work except with executive authority, or both.

SPECIAL SKILLS

The truth is that a good consultant *can* effect change without benefit of executive authority. By sensitive listening and lucid speaking, by concerning himself to understand the consultee's problems and his potentialities, by thinking with him but from a different orientation and out of a different backlog of experience, he can move with his consultee from one new vantage point to another until the consultee begins to gain new perspective, conceive new ideas, and glimpse how they may be suited to his need. The consultant's essential function is not to do, but to enable another to do, and the most brilliant ideas the consultant may have are useless until the consultee reconceives them and makes them his own. From that point on, of course, the consultee is entitled to credit when credit is forthcoming, and the good consultant not only concedes it but points it up, knowing that the real increment of strength for the consultee, the real stimulant to his further growth, lies not so much in the credit as in the knowledge that he earned it.

Two of our three "odd" expectations are thus easily met if the consultant is willing and able to work primarily in behalf of the consultee. The third expectation, however, calls for a higher refinement of this capacity—its distillation, as it were, through further learning and greater discipline. The basic fair-mindedness that operates productively to fulfill the first two expectations now operates productively only as it *changes*, rather than fulfills, the third. The consultant cannot build the consultee's strength or promote his growth by taking all blame when things go wrong; for him to be a scapegoat helps no one in the long run. He must, of course, be ready to take his share of blame if he has share in it, but he must also know how to help the consultee tolerate as much as is his due.

This had best be done—perhaps can only be done—in advance of the outcome. A clear allocation of responsibility before the fact is always wiser than attempts to divide the blame afterward. But the consultant must be alert to perceive when the consultee is following him with more docility than conviction. Unless such following is promptly checked, a fiasco is almost inevitable, because anything that the consultee (or anyone else) does reluctantly or apprehensively is likely to be ill-done. It is usually less costly to stop and try to bring the unvoiced reservations into the open than to risk their lingering backstage to spoil the show.

One further issue that sometimes arises in this connection merits note. Though the good consultant works in behalf of the consultee, the fact remains that these two people belong to two different disciplines, each imposing its own peculiar obligations and restrictions; and situations do occur in which the two differing sets of demands are irreconcilable. To the consultee who places great confidence in his consultant, these situations are extremely threatening. For example: a juvenile court judge found himself caught between the law, which required him to sentence a young third offender to reform school, and the recommendation of his trusted psychiatric consultant, which was in unconditional opposition to such action. What the consultant had to do in this case was to support the judge in acting *against* his (the consultant's) recommendation—to clarify for him that neither of them could ethically dodge the obligations of their different professions, but that conflict between these obligations need not impair the consultative relationship at all —on the contrary, the conflict could illumine the issues that most urgently demanded their continuing collaborative effort. This point is made because we tend to assume too easily that collaboration requires that the parties to it either think and work alike or move through a succession of compromises toward thinking and working alike. Compromise doubtless has its uses, but we need to be quite sure that it is kept subordinate to the maintenance of professional integrity, without which the consultation process becomes mere politicking.

CHALLENGE AHEAD

The aim of this discussion is to support a plea for the training of consultants, specifically those consultants who are expected to substitute somehow for unavailable service staff. It is no fun to be an untrained consultant, it is frustrating and exasperating to try to get help from a poor consultant, and it is cold comfort in either case to know that in the higher echelons a great deal of effort is going into study of the consultation process. We need research, certainly; we need good theory and thoughtful over-all planning; but meanwhile we need training, too, at the grass-roots level. And while it is true that we do not yet know how to train for this function, it is equally true that it would break no precedent in the field of social work if we were to learn by doing. We shall never learn enough without doing, and now is not too soon to begin.

In the following article, Gerald Caplan presents a definition of mental health consultation. As was pointed out in Section two, Caplan has been one of the leaders in the community health movement. No doubt everyone who is concerned with mental health consultation has been directly influenced by his views on the subject. According to Caplan, consultation is concerned with the kind of interaction that takes place between a consultant and a consultee. He discusses four varieties of mental health consultation: Client-Centered Case Consultation, Program-Centered Administrative Consultation, Consultee-Centered Case Consultation, and Consultee-Centered Administrative Consultation. In his discussion he pays particular attention to consultee-centered case consultation and presents material illustrating theme interference, *a consultation concept associated with Caplan's views and undoubtedly derived from his psychoanalytic background.*

types of mental health consultation[1]

Gerald Caplan

In this paper the term "consultation" is used in a quite restricted sense to denote the process of interaction between two professional persons—the consultant, who is a specialist, and the consultee, who invokes his help in regard to a current work problem with which the latter is having some difficulty, and which he has decided is within the former's area of specialized competence. The work problem involves the management or treatment of one or more clients of the consultee, or the planning or implementation of a program to cater to such clients.

An essential aspect of consultation, as defined here, is that the professional responsibility for the client remains with the consultee. The consultant may offer helpful clarifications, diagnostic interpretations, or advice on treatment, but the consultee will be free to accept or reject all or part of this help. Action for the benefit of the client that emerges from the consultation is the responsibility of the consultee.

Another essential aspect of this type of consultation is that the

[1]The views expressed in this paper have been developed by the author in collaboration with several colleagues in the Boston area. The earliest work was done at the Wellesley Human Relations Service, with Erich Lindemann, Donald Klein and Elizabeth Lindemann. For eight years, consultation techniques have been explored within the framework of the community mental health activities of the Commonwealth of Massachusetts Division of Mental Hygiene in conjunction with its Directors, Warren T. Vaughan, Bellenden Rand Hutcheson, and their colleagues. During the past four years, the main focus of the work has centered on an evaluative study at Harvard School of Public Health, financed by Grant No. M-3442 from the National Institute of Mental Health. The staff members of this project have made major contributions to the development of the conceptual framework. Significant help has been obtained from Charlotte E. Owens, Louisa P. Howe, David M. Kaplan, Thomas F. A. Plaut, Leonard J. Hassol, Thomas McDonald, and Lenin A. Baler.

consultant engages in the activity, not only in order to help the consultee with his current professional problem in relation to a specific client or program, but also in order to add to his knowledge and to lessen areas of misunderstanding, so that he may be able in the future to deal more effectively on his own with this category of problem.

The above definition applies not only to a single consultant dealing with one consultee, but equally to one consultant and a group of consultees, or a group of consultants and a single consultee or group of consultees.

In defining consultation in this narrow way there is no implication that this is the "correct" usage of the term and that other authorities are "wrong" in their different use of it; on the contrary there is the intention to recognize that confusion exists because so many workers legitimately use the term in so many different ways, and the desire to single out one among the various activities for special study and evaluation. A specialist formally or informally designated "a consultant" may engage in many types of professional activity that resemble each other to some extent in regard to goals, methods and techniques. These include inspection, administrative manipulation, coordination, supervision, teaching, casework, psychotherapy, counseling, negotiation, liaison, collaboration, mediation and so on. I believe that we will attain a higher level of professional functioning when the specialist is able to differentiate these various activities and employ each of them consistently in relation to his assignment, his professional goals and his understanding of the demands of each situation. In a previous publication I have made a preliminary attempt to differentiate consultation from supervision, education, psychotherapy and collaboration.[2] In a forthcoming publication I intend to deal with this topic in greater detail.[3]

What has been said so far refers to consultation as a generic form of specialist professional activity. By the term "mental health consultation," we designate the use of this method as part of a community program for the promotion of mental health and for the prevention, treatment and rehabilitation of mental disorders. The reports of the Joint Commission on Mental Illness and Health emphasize the fact that much, if not most, of the work with actual or potential patients in such programs is currently being carried out by professional workers who have no specialized training in psychiatry, psychology or psychiatric social work—namely nurses, teachers, family doctors, pediatricians, clergymen, probation officers, policemen, welfare workers and the like. Recruitment and training possibilities in the mental health professions are such that this state of affairs is likely to con-

[2]G. Caplan. Concepts of Mental Health and Consultation—Their Application in Public Health Social Work. Children's Bureau Publication 373. U. S. Department of Health, Education, and Welfare. Washington, D. C., 1959.
[3]G. Caplan. Theory and Practice of Mental Health Consultation. Basic Books. New York, N. Y., 1970.

tinue indefinitely. Consequently, it seems important that a significant proportion of the time and energies of mental health specialists should be focused upon improving the operations of these other caregiving professionals in relation to mental health and mental disorder. Mental health consultation is one of the methods that have been developed to achieve this goal. It provides an opportunity for a relatively small number of consultants to exert a widespread effect in a community through the intermediation of a large group of consultees. In order to be effective along these lines, the amount of time devoted by a consultant to helping a consultee deal with the mental health problems of a current case must be relatively short, and there must be the maximum educational carry-over to the consultee's work with other cases. It is also worth emphasizing that, in a comprehensive program of community psychiatry, mental health consultation should be used in appropriate balance with other community methods, such as education about mental health issues in the preprofessional and in-service training of caregiving agents, and planning and coordination of caregiving agencies.

TYPES OF MENTAL HEALTH CONSULTATION

It is of value to differentiate four fundamental types of mental health consultation, each of which is associated with characteristic technical demands upon the consultant. A consultation may focus upon (A) the consultee's problems in handling a specific client, as contrasted with (B) his administrative problems in initiating and maintaining a program, and a consultant may have the immediate goal of improving the client or the program, as contrasted with improving the insights, skills and professional objectivity of the consultees. The four types have become known as (A1) Client-Centered Case Consultation, (B1) Program-Centered Administrative Consultation, (A2) Consultee-Centered Case Consultation, and (B2) Consultee-Centered Administrative Consultation. In the following brief description of these types of mental health consultation, Type A2 will be discussed in greater detail, because of its special technical interest.

TYPE A1.   CLIENT-CENTERED CASE CONSULTATION
In this type of consultation the problems encountered by the consultee in dealing with a professional case are the major focus of interest; the immediate goal is to help the consultee find the most effective treatment for his client. Increasing the knowledge of the consultee so that he may be better able to deal unaided with this client or class of clients in the future is a subsidiary goal. Since the primary goal is to improve the client, the consultant's fundamental responsibility is to make a specialized assessment of the client's condition and to recommend an effective disposition or method of treatment

to be undertaken by the consultee. This means that the consultant's attention is centered mainly upon the client, whom he probably will examine with whatever methods of investigation his specialized judgment indicates are necessary to arrive at an adequate appraisal of the nature of his difficulty. On the other hand, the consultant will pay attention to what the consultee says, to ascertain what type of help the latter is requesting—sometimes the consultee may ask for "consultation" when he really wishes to refer a patient for treatment by the specialist, and he will be angry when the patient is sent back with a diagnosis and a prescription for nonspecialist management. Sometimes all he is requesting is help with screening so that he can decide to which specialized agency he should refer the patient. In that event he is not interested in receiving a complicated diagnostic formulation, and the consultant might well spare himself the expenditure of time and effort in working this out. Here, as elsewhere in community psychiatry, energy expended on diagnostic investigation should be no greater than that necessary to answer the questions that will meaningfully affect disposition or treatment.

The consultant will also pay attention to what the consultee says, to learn how to communicate with him. The more the consultant knows about the consultee's language, conceptual framework and ways of working, the better will he be able to formulate his diagnosis in understandable words and to suggest treatment that the consultee can carry out effectively in his professional setting. Too many consultants write reports in which they communicate only with themselves and with their specialist reference group! This would not affect the welfare of the client, if the specialist were carrying out the treatment, but in consultation the treatment is carried out by the consultee, and only messages that improve his operations will help the client. Needless to say, the consultant must make a correct diagnosis and must suggest effective treatment in order to improve the client's condition. The content as well as the manner of the communication is important for success.

TYPE B1   PROGRAM-CENTERED ADMINISTRATIVE CONSULTATION

In this type of consultation the consultant is called in by a consultee, or more often by a group of consultees, to help with current problems in the administration of programs for the prevention, treatment or rehabilitation of mental disorders. The problems may relate to any aspect of the program, including the planning and administration of services and policies governing the recruitment, training and effective utilization of personnel. In response to the needs expressed by the consultees, the primary focus of the consultant is upon making a specialized assessment of the current program or policy predicament, and then recommending a plan of action to resolve the difficulty. As in Type A1, education of the consultees to be better able to deal on their own with such a difficulty is a subordinate goal.

In contrast with client-centered case consultation, the consultant may make much use of the efforts of his consultees in collecting the data about the workings of the institution upon which he will base his analysis of the problem. He will, however, take into account that the consultees will inevitably distort and bias their reports. He will collect some of the essential data himself, using his own specialized methods. And he will cross check the other data, since in this type of consultation the assessment of the problem is his responsibility alone and is not to be shared with the consultees, however actively he may enlist their cooperation in assembling the facts. His reason for the latter is that he will probably need as many agents as possible in collecting the large amount of complicated data necessary to understand the problems of an institution. An important aspect of these problems may involve the interrelationships of the staff, which he can observe in action as he works with them. Also, through his own interactions in this process, he can learn about the language, values and traditions of the institution, so that his recommendations for remedial action will be expressed in understandable words and will be feasible within the current and future reality of the institution.

Administrative consultants will usually be requested to present their analysis of the institutional problems, and their recommendations for solution, in a written report. This will often deal with short-term solutions that are possible with the current staff and in line with the current administrative framework. It will also contain long-term suggestions of an ideal type, which may act as distant goals toward which the institution may strive in the future. The long-term recommendations will be based largely upon the general knowledge and the experience of the consultant in a variety of other programs, as well as upon his professional value system. They will of course also be directed toward the local situation, but in formulating them the consultant will be minimally influenced by the ideas of the consultees.

On the other hand, if the short-term recommendations are to be acceptable and implemented, they must fit closely within the expectations and the capacities of the consultee group. Experienced administrative consultants find that the best way of ensuring the latter is to communicate their developing judgments in their formative stages to the consultee group, and then progressively to modify these recommendations in the light of the reactions of the consultees. The responsibility for the recommendations is not shared with the consultees, and the disagreement of one or more of them with certain of the recommendations will not necessarily persuade the consultant to change them; but the discussions will enable him to see how closely his plan fits the culture of the group, and the working-through process will prepare the consultees to live with his eventual report. When the consultees read the consultant's report, they should find little in it that he has not already discussed with them, and upon which they have not been able to express an opinion as to feasibility.

An interesting variant of this type of consultation deals, not with programs for the promotion of mental health and the prevention and control of mental disorders, but with the mental health aspects of other programs. In this consultation the mental health specialist is asked for help in regard to those problems of administration that may influence the mental health or the interpersonal effectiveness of personnel or of recipients of the program. His specialized knowledge of personality dynamics and interpersonal relationships in social systems is exploited to help administrators behave more effectively and, at the same time, with a greater regard for the human needs of their colleagues, subordinates and clients. Operational efficiency in an institution such as a hospital or a factory can be achieved in different ways. Some of these may frustrate fundamental needs of the participants and may lead to an increased risk of mental disorder. The mental health specialist may be able to help the administrators maintain or raise the productivity of their institution, while also improving the mental health potential of the workers.

TYPE A2.   CONSULTEE-CENTERED CASE CONSULTATION

The primary focus of the consultant in this type of consultation is upon the consultee, rather than upon the particular client with whom the consultee is currently having difficulties. True, the problems of this client were the direct stimulus for the consultation request, and they will form the main content area of the consultation discussions. Also, a successful consultation will usually lead to an improvement in the consultee's handling of the current case, with consequent benefit for the client. But in contrast to client-centered case consultation, in which the consultant's main interest is in diagnosing the difficulties of the client, his primary endeavor in the present instance is to assess the nature of the consultee's work difficulty and to help him handle this. Most or all of the consultant's time will be spent talking to the consultee about the client, and little or no time will be spent in specialist examination of the client. The consultant realizes that, because the consultee is having difficulties with the client, his perceptions and understanding of the case are probably distorted, and that a correct diagnosis of the client by the consultant is unlikely if his data are restricted to this information but, since his goal is to improve the consultee's functioning and not to make a diagnosis of the client, this is not important. In fact, in this type of consultation it is the very distortions and omissions in the consultee's report on the client that provide the consultant with his basic material. He does not need to learn the "objective" reality of the client to be able to identify these distortions and omissions. Instead, he appraises them by identifying internal inconsistencies in the consultee's story, and from verbal and nonverbal cues in both the consultee's behavior and that of others in the consultee institution. When the consultant has pinpointed the nature of the consultee's difficulty, he attempts to remedy this through helping the consultee gain a mastery of the significant issue by means of a discussion of the problems of the client and the consultee's contribution to their solution.

There are four major categories of difficulty that interfere with a consultee's ability to deal adequately with the mental health problems of his client and may stimulate him or his administrative superiors to invoke consultation help. These are (a) lack of understanding of the psychological factors in the case; (b) lack of skill or resources to deal with the problems involved; (c) lack of professional objectivity in handling the case; and (d) lack of confidence and self-esteem due to fatigue, illness, inexperience, youth or old age.

(a) Lack of understanding.   In this type of difficulty the consultee either has not learned during his preprofessional or in-service training enough about psychology and psychopathology to realize what factors are operating in this case, or he has learned the general laws of mental functioning but does not see how they apply to the idiosyncratic complexities of this client and his psychosocial milieu. The consultant will try to help the consultee by adding to his cognitive knowledge and by clarifying the data about the client, to enable the consultee to see meaningful connections between parts of the psychosocial pattern. In doing this, it is important for the consultant to know a good deal about the professional subculture of the consultee so that the information he imparts will be consonant with the type and level of psychological understanding of the consultee's profession. Consultants should guard against trying to turn such consultees as nurses, clergymen and pediatricians into "proxy" psychiatrists or "junior" psychologists. This implies the need, not only to use the terminology of the consultee's profession or else words with a nonspecialized meaning, but also to avoid dealing with concepts such as penis envy, castration fears and pregenital fantasies, the proper understanding of which demands the conceptual framework and style of thinking of a mental health specialist.

Mental health consultation on an individual basis is an expensive way of teaching the facts of human behavior to professional workers. When a particular agency or community makes many requests for this type of consultation, consultants would be well advised to consider organizing preprofessional or in-service training courses in mental health, since systematic group instruction is a more economical way to achieve comparable results.

(b) Lack of skill.   The difficulty here is not lack of understanding of the client's problems, but either lack of professional skill on the part of the consultee, including how to make professional use of the self in dealing with the psychological complications of clients, or else lack of knowledge of appropriate specialist resources in the community or of how to invoke their help for the benefit of the client. The consultant deals with this by assisting the consultee to choose a suitable plan of action. He will therefore be sensitive to the consultee's level and rate of professional development, and, as in the previous category of consultation, he will ensure that the various action possibilities, among which he is helping the consultee to choose, are drawn from a range of actions consonant with the consultee's professional subculture and are not plans specific to mental health specialists. To prevent endangering the professional integrity of the consultee, a consultant who uses this technique must have a great deal of knowledge about the details of role functioning in the consultee profession.

This type of consultation, which fosters the development of professional skills, is rather similar to technical supervision. Many categories of consultees, such as family doctors, clergymen and pediatricians, have no institutionalized system of technical supervision, and in these cases mental health consultation may be the only way of getting help with skill development, although group instruction should always be considered as a useful supplement to individual consultation. Whenever an institution or a profession does provide supervisors, such as in schools, kindergartens and nursing and social agencies, the mental health specialist should avoid suggestions that imply prescriptions for action by line workers; he should substitute methods to increase the knowledge of supervisors so that responsibility for action can remain undisturbed within the system of the consultee agency. In all the caregiving professions the mental health specialist should attempt to influence preprofessional training to insure that these skills are learned more effectively. Any consultant who encounters many instances of lack of skill in consultees should ask himself whether he might not get results more cheaply by thus deploying some of his efforts "upstream."

(c) **Lack of objectivity.** Experienced, well-trained and well-supervised consultees will occasionally meet situations that are beyond their knowledge and skills, and may call for one of the two previous categories of consultation; more commonly, when such a person asks for consultation help, it is because he is unable for various reasons to exploit his knowledge and skills with the particular client. This is usually manifested by a disorder in his professional objectivity due to the distortion of his functioning by subjective factors. His professional empathy for the client and other actors in the client's life situation may be replaced by identification and personal involvement leading to partisanship, or he may turn away from the client's situation because it stimulates in him some personal sensitivity. In either case there is likely to be a distortion of perception and judgment and a lowered effectiveness in utilizing professional knowledge and skills.

My colleagues and I at Harvard School of Public Health have for some years been particularly interested in this category of consultation, and we have formulated the consultee's difficulty as being due to the intrusion into his professional functioning of an interfering problem theme. The latter is derived either from some long-standing personality difficulty made salient by a symbolic trigger in the client's case, or from a current situational conflict in the consultee's home life, or from some problem in the work field—either a role conflict of the consultee or a more general social system disequilibrium, acute or chronic, involving the authority structure or communication pattern within the institution or between it and its surrounding community. Whatever the proximate or ultimate underlying causes, the final common path leading to the work difficulty and the request for consultation is usually a so-called theme interference, that is, a symbolic inhibition of free perception and communication between consultee and client and a concomitant disorder of objectivity. This is usually accompanied by some degree of emotional upset in the consultee, ranging from a relatively mild rise of tension, when he thinks about certain aspects of the client's case (which we call "segmental tension"), to a well-marked crisis response, in which the consultee's general professional functioning and emotional equilibrium are temporarily upset. The consultee usually ascribes his current discomfort to his difficulties with the client, onto whose case he displaces feelings of anxiety, hostility, shame and depression, which can be seen by the consultant to be partly or even primarily originating in his personal life or in his involvement with the social system problems of his institution.

The following example illustrates the operation of theme interference:

A teacher spoke with hopelessness about a ten-year-old girl in his class, who he felt was mentally retarded. He had spent much time in vain trying to teach the child to read so that she would not get too far behind the others in the class. He felt that unless he succeeded she would inevitably become an outcast in society and that others would exploit her weakness. The consultant realized that the teacher was identifying with the child, whom he was perceiving in a stereotyped way as a "mental defective" who must inevitably come to a bad end unless "rescued" by him through greatly augmenting her ability to achieve. The teacher was not perceiving the child's assets, namely, that she was quite popular among her peers, and had nonverbal skills that might one day help her make a useful place for herself in society. He was also exaggerating the likelihood that more intelligent people would exploit her because of her backwardness—in fact, he felt that this was inevitable.

The teacher was currently worrying about his own ability to achieve in a new school to which he had come after an unsatisfactory experience elsewhere as a principal. He was particularly sensitive in his relationship with the headmaster, a driving man who demanded high standards from his teachers. The theme of "mental retardation" was also important in the teacher's past life, because he had been backward himself as a child, and had only begun to improve at the age of ten.

This example illustrates a general characteristic of interfering themes; they can be formulated as preconscious syllogisms that mould the consultee's expectations. In this case the parts of the syllogism are:

This girl is mentally retarded.
All mentally retarded people inevitably fail in life and are exploited by
    more intelligent people.
Therefore, this girl is doomed, despite everything I will do to rescue her.

The stereotyped expectation—*all mentally retarded are doomed to exploitation and failure*—applies equally to himself and to the girl, both of whom are defined by him as fitting into this category. In such instances the consultee stereotypes the perception of the client into a symbol having a personal meaning for the consultee, and this leads to a fixed expectation of some sort of doom for the client, which inhibits the consultee's professional efforts because of a feeling of hopelessness.

In handling this type of situation, our approach is to respect the separation of the consultee's personal life from his work difficulty, and not to investigate the causes of the theme interference, but to focus upon defining the nature of the theme by a careful examination of its manifestations in the work context. The consultant then reduces the theme interference by influencing the consultee to adopt a more reality-based expectation for the client.

In effect, the consultee is defending himself against direct confrontation of a personal problem by working with it vicariously in the client. Irrational fantasies, which prevented him from dealing directly with his own problem, are also hampering him in helping the client. He communicates these to the consultant via the latent content of his descriptions of the client's predicament. The consultant attacks the irrational elements in these fantasies by in turn talking about the client in such a way that he conveys a corrective message through the use of the same symbolism as the consultee uses. The result is that the consultant deals with the consultee's problems without interfering with his defenses, and therefore without arousing anxiety and resistance. Because of this, and because he does not need to uncover the personal sources of the theme in the consultee's current or past life, this type of consultation is most economical. Successful cases usually need only two or three sessions. The effect on the consultee seems to depend upon the degree of his personal involvement with his client. This is evidenced by the degree of interference with his customary professional objectivity and also by the intensity of his emotional upset in handling the difficulties of his client.

As an example of the reduction of theme intereference, let us return to the case of the teacher who asked for consultation with the "mentally retarded" girl. In this particular case, the consultant by chance learned enough about the consultee to realize the personal source of the theme interference. This knowledge was not necessary for his consultation, and consultants usually do their utmost to prevent such personal material entering the content of their discussions with the consultee. When the consultee nevertheless does bring such issues into the consultation, the consultant does not comment directly about them, but turns the discussion back to a consideration of some aspect of the client's problem. In this case, the consultant accepted the consultee's contention that the girl was backward, but he then attacked the inevitability of a bad end for her by involving the teacher in a joint examination of those aspects of her current life from which predictions about her future might validly be made. This was not an entirely intellectual process, since the consultant delayed this discussion until he had encouraged the building up of a supportive relationship between himself and the teacher. On the basis of this relationship he was able to influence the latter to pay attention to such items as the girl's nonverbal skills and her social poise and popularity, which introduced some hope that she might not be entirely useless and unhappy in her future life. The crux of the consultation, however, was a message that the consultant conveyed by implication—by the way he spoke about the girl, and by the way he took it for granted that others would deal with her—namely, that even though it might be recognized that she was mentally dull, the more intelligent people in her environment would not necessarily exploit her.

The invalidation of such a fixed expectation about a personally meaningful issue in the client has an effect not only on the consultee's feelings of hopelessness about this client, but also on similar feelings about himself. It also prepares him in the future to be able to handle, with his customary professional objectivity and skill, other clients who may be correctly or incorrectly perceived as fitting into the first part of the preconscious syllogistic proposition. Incidentally, in this type of consultation it is important not to unlink the client from the first statement of the syllogism—in this case, the perception, *this girl is mentally retarded*. Such an unlinking might be possible with the help of the influence of the consultation relationship. For instance, the consultant might have pointed out that the girl's nonverbal skills indicated a higher level of intelligence, and that she was not really mentally retarded, just slow in the use of words, or else that perhaps she had emotional blocks in reading because of certain past experiences. Had the teacher accepted this possibility, his worry about this girl would have dissipated, but he would have come away from the consultation with no reduction in his theme problem, either in regard to himself as mentally retarded or in regard to future pupils who might appear mentally retarded. In fact, he would very likely search for some other child to take the place of the girl as a displacement object for his personal problem.

It is of interest to point out that, had this case been misdiagnosed by the consultant as due not to theme interference but to lack of understanding of the signs and meaning of mental retardation, the consultation might have been conducted in just such a manner.

(d) Lack of confidence and self-esteem.   This type of difficulty is usually easily identified. The consultee's functioning is interfered with in a nonspecific way by illness, fatigue or infirmity, or else by lack of confidence due to inexperience or youth. What is demanded from the consultant is nonspecific ego support. The only technical difficulty is that this should be tactfully given so as not to weaken the consultee further by the explicit recognition of his personal difficulties in a context that may lead to a further loss of self-esteem.

Professional workers who have the benefit of adequate technical and administrative supervision will rarely need this type of consultation, but for those who work on their own, mental health consultation may be a useful source of support in times of human need.

TYPE B2.   CONSULTEE-CENTERED ADMINISTRATIVE CONSULTATION

As the name implies, the primary goal of this major category of consultation is to help consultees develop an improved capacity to master problems in the planning and maintenance of programs for the prevention and control of mental disorders, and in the interpersonal aspects of the operations of their agencies. As with program-centered administrative consultation, this method is often applied in group situations and is directed toward helping a group of administrators improve their functioning; also it is not infrequently invoked on an individual basis by an administrator. Since a specialist's assessment of the administrative problem by the consultant is not demanded, it is quite feasible to operate with an individual administrator and to restrict consultation help to the circumscribed area of the institutional life that is his province. This type of consultation is very similar to consultee-centered case consultation, with the major exception that few mental health consultants have as thorough a knowledge of administrative problems as they have of the psychosocial complications of an individual client, and they must be careful to restrict their help to those factors in the administrative situation, such as the interpersonal and group dynamic aspects, concerning which they do have special competence. Most mental health specialists who act as administrative consultants make a serious study of administration and social science to augment the traditional knowledge of their own profession. In successful cases the resulting amalgam leads to a "clinical" approach to administrative problems that many administrator consultees find peculiarly helpful, and characteristically different from the kind of help they are accustomed to derive from specialists in their own field.

As with case consultation, individual consultee-centered administrative consultation may be invoked on an *ad hoc* basis to deal with occasional current problems that may necessitate a short block of sessions for their mastery. Because of the great complexity of the administrative situation, consultees will almost always be burdened with some problem, and regularly scheduled meetings with a consultant may be set up on a long-term basis to deal with whatever is uppermost at the moment. With this pattern of operation, consultants must guard against allowing their role unintentionally to slip into one of supervision or nonspecific emotional support, or into psychotherapy.

Consultee-centered administrative consultation in a group setting is a more complicated operation than the above, and its intricacies still await adequate clarification. It is almost invariably carried out in the form of regularly scheduled meetings over a lengthy period. At these meetings the consultees raise for discussion with the consultant any administrative problem of current concern, and this may be the central topic of one or several meetings. The simplest role for the consultant is to help the group clarify the complexities of the problem and for him to contribute to the discussion on the basis of his specialized knowledge of intrapersonal motivations and interpersonal relations, as well as of the human needs of personnel and clients. He may facilitate the acquiring by the consultee group of group dynamic skills, and also help them explore new patterns of actions in dealing with administrative complexities. The main technical difficulty is how to handle theme interference when the consultant identifies this in an individual group member, or when it occurs as a group manifestation.

The techniques of theme interference reduction as practiced in case consultation are often hazardous when handling an individual member in the presence of the group, since, if the consultees are psychologically sophisticated, one of the individual's colleagues may realize his subjective involvement and make a defense-destroying interpretation before the consultant can stop it. Such a situation may rapidly slide into group psychotherapy, in which the separation of personal and work problems is set aside, with the usual arousal of anxiety and resistance. To avoid this, the group consultant must structure the ground rules to prevent the airing of personal problems, and he must maintain a tight control over the direction of the discussion, so that he can steer away from a focus upon theme interference in an individual member. Sometimes this is relatively easy because that member is really acting as spokesman for the group, and his individual theme interference is the presenting example of an issue common to the group as a whole. He may have been stimulated by other members to act as their mouthpiece through a process that Fritz Redl has picturesquely called "role suction." In this situation the consultant can actively refocus the issue as a group problem, and he can thus turn the spotlight away from the individual member.

Such a maneuver raises the technical question of how to deal with theme interference at the group level. In other words, how does the consultant handle the discussion of a program or policy question when he identifies as a major source of difficulty unstated personal conflicts among group members or between the group and other people, usually administrative superiors or high-status figures in some other division of the organization? Are such issues to be opened up for explicit discussion, and if so how does the consultant differentiate such an approach from analytic group psychotherapy? The answer is not too clear, but the differentiation appears to lie in restricting the content of consultation discussions to role conflicts, and minimizing the discussion of private and personal factors. This is not easy, since personality idiosyncrasies and incompatibilities are a frequent source of role clashes. A useful rule of thumb is to avoid discussing the personality of any member of the consultee group, apart from alluding to fundamental aspects of human nature that are common to everyone, the consultant included.

Altrocchi, Spielberger, and Eisdorfer describe a case-seminar method of mental health consultation with groups of consultees. The conception of consultation which they present is broader than Caplan's and they take issue with Caplan regarding some limitations of the consultant-consultee relationship. They discuss the group process aspects of their technique and relate it to approaches such as teaching, sensitivity training, and group therapy. They also point out some advantages and disadvantages of group consultation as opposed to individual consultation. Emphasizing participation and conceptualization, the article demonstrates the way in which practice contributes to innovations in technique.

mental health consultation with groups[1]

John Altrocchi, Charles D. Spielberger, and Carl Eisdorfer

The growing interest in prevention of psychological disorders and promotion of mental health has led mental health professionals to engage in a wide variety of activities which may be collectively labeled mental health consultation. Developments in consultation theory, however, have not kept pace with practice and have been concerned with interactions between a consultant and an individual consultee (Bindman, 1959; Caplan, 1964), with only a few exceptions (Kevin, 1963; Parker, 1958; Rieman, 1963). The aim of this paper is to describe mental health consultation with groups of consultees.

Mental health consultation generally refers to one aspect of a program for the promotion of mental health and the prevention and treatment of psychological disorders. More specifically, mental health consultation is "a helping process, an educational process, and a growth process achieved through interpersonal relationships" (Rieman, 1963, p. 85). The goals are to assist the key professional workers of a community to carry out their professional responsibilities by becoming more sensitive to the needs of their clients and associates and more comfortable and adept in their relationships with them. Members of certain professional groups, such as ministers, teachers, public health nurses, and welfare caseworkers are likely to be called upon by

[1]We appreciate the cooperation of C. B. Davis, Director of the Consolidated Health Department of Wilmington and New Hanover County, N.C. and of Robert F. Young, Director of the Halifax County, N.C., Health Department. We are also grateful to Irving Alexander, Lloyd Borstelmann, Gerald Caplan, Louis D. Cohen, J. Edward Connors, Saul Cooper, and Norman Garmezy for stimulating discussions about consultation and to the Scripps Clinic and Research Foundation, La Jolla, California, where early drafts of this paper were written while the first author was on sabbatical leave.

Reprinted from the *Community Mental Health Journal*, 1965, **1**, 127-134, with the permission of Behavioral Publications, Inc. and the authors.

their clients in times of personal and interpersonal crises; it is assumed that such crises provide particularly opportune times for influencing the clients' emotional growth (Caplan, 1964).

Group mental health consultation is similar in some respects to group supervision, seminar teaching, sensitivity training, and group psychotherapy; but it is also discriminably different from each of these other methods, all of which may have a role in a comprehensive mental health program. While this form of consultation closely resembles group supervision in its emphasis upon the consultees' understanding of the general principles and technical procedures essential to working effectively with their clients, group mental health consultation differs from group supervision in that the consultant typically enters the consultees' social system from the outside and is often from another profession, and each consultee's supervisor retains the usual administrative control.

In its educational goals and emphasis on discussion methods, group mental health consultation resembles seminar teaching, but goes beyond it in attempting to make use of group processes and the consultees' affective involvement in their work problems. Group mental health consultation resembles sensitivity training (when applied to groups of coworkers, Bradford, 1964) in its use of group process and consultees' personal involvement; it diverges in its greater degree of structure and the limitation of content focus to work-related problems of the consultees.

A group method of consultation is similar to group psychotherapy in its attempt to increase personal growth, sensitivity, and effectiveness by applying group processes to individual affective and intellectual learning; but it is distinct in several important ways: (a) the implicit psychological contract in consultation (Caplan, 1964; Parker, 1958) involves a relationship between professionals in which the consultee is free to apply what he learns or not as he sees fit; (b) the relative emphasis is on educational goals rather than on the modification of a disorder; and, especially, (c) the content focus is on the professional rather than the personal problems of the consultee. The consultees' affective involvements with clients are considered only in their relation to current work problems. For example, as Parker (1958, p. 2) has suggested in reference to group consultation with public health nurses, "When an emotional reaction of the nurse destroys her objectivity about some aspect of her job, that reaction is a suitable subject for group discussion, but the intrapsychic conflict which may have helped to generate the reaction should not be considered. . . ." Nevertheless, many of the mechanisms observed in group therapy—acceptance, universalization, intellectualization, reality testing, interaction, spectator therapy, and ventilation (Corsini and Rosenberg, 1955)—may also be observed in group mental health consultation. Thus, while the primary goals of mental health consultation are educational rather than therapeutic, some phases of group consultation resemble some kinds of group psychotherapy and corrective emotional experiences do take place. Although group consultation is not therapy, it may have therapeutic effects.

A CASE-SEMINAR METHOD OF GROUP MENTAL HEALTH CONSULTATION

For varying periods since 1958, each of the authors has been engaged in part-time group mental health consultation in one of two North Carolina counties. One of these is rural and the other is a small metropolitan seaport area. The absence of mental health facilities and the considerable interest of a large number of key professionals in each community made group consultation more appropriate for serving the needs of these communities than working with individual consultees or attempting to work directly with clients. Moreover, time restrictions (only one to three scheduled days a month were spent in these distant counties) rendered "on-call" response to individual consultee crises impractical. For these reasons, we focused on group consultation and selected a case-seminar approach as the principal consultation procedure.

For each case-seminar meeting, a member of the group was asked to present a problem case for which he (or she) had responsibility, and was encouraged to select one of general interest to the group. In order to obtain firsthand contact with the client (patient, student, or parishioner), the consultant, whenever practicable, either interviewed or observed the client interacting with the consultee. This served as a safeguard against missing crucial diagnostic information (e.g., suicidal tendencies) of which the consultee was as yet unaware. Observation of the client also provided the consultant with a better basis for discussing the case with the consultee and for helping the consultee prepare the case for presentation in the group. Actual contact with some clients, when used, permitted the consultant to demonstrate interviewing techniques. In such contacts, the consultant's impact on the client was typically supportive and often therapeutic.

We have used the case-seminar method with public health nurses, ministers, welfare caseworkers, probation officers, policemen, public housing authority personnel, elementary and secondary school teachers, principals, school guidance counselors, and school speech therapists. In these meetings, the etiology and dynamics of the case are discussed in relatively nontechnical terms. The interpersonal relations between client, consultee, and other persons involved in the case, such as the client's family and professional workers from other disciplines, are considered in detail, as is the relevance of the specific case to the roles of the consultee group in the community. Although there are individual differences among our consultation techniques, the general approach which developed is coherent and communicable.

GROUP PROCESSES

The processes that we have observed in the case-seminar method are similar in a number of respects to those more generally observed in the behavior of small groups. During a single session, there are recognizable phases: an introductory phase, a warming-up phase, a problem-focused phase, and an ending phase (Kevin, 1963). Over a series of sessions, we have repeatedly observed a number of characteristics peculiar to the group consultation process, each of which offers opportunities for fruitful problem-solving discussions involving the reactions of clients and consultees.

1. In the early stages of group consultation, when group members are unsure about consultation and are testing the consultant, bizarre or "impossible" cases are often presented (Rieman, 1963). After discussing such cases, reassurance that the consultee is doing all that is reasonably possible (if this is true—and it usually is) helps to establish rapport with the group and provides considerable support for group members, each of whom has some impossible cases. Indeed, an important facet of the consultant's role is helping consultees to recognize impossible cases and the guilt and anxiety associated with them. When a consultee understands that the investment of inordinate amounts of time with such cases is often unwarranted, he is enabled to make better use of his professional time.

2. Consultees tend to present clients from minority or impoverished groups, especially in the beginning stages of consultation. Because they are different and distant from himself, such cases help the consultee avoid examining his own attitudes and behavior (Rieman, 1963). This tendency, like resistance in psychotherapy, needs to be handled carefully. The discussion of attitudes toward minority or impoverished groups, however, often provides an appropriate and useful entree for more specific understanding of the personal reactions of consultees toward their clients (Parker, 1958; Parker, 1962).

3. Those members of professional groups who initially volunteer to present cases, or who are the first to share their reactions, frequently are the least defensive and most competent members of the group. They can be counted on to help move the group into problem solving. Although it is often tempting to move eagerly ahead with them, the consultant must wait until he perceives that the majority of the group can move forward together so as to avoid subgrouping and fragmentation.

4. There are important differences between groups with respect to initial cohesiveness, resistance, and the rapidity with which they proceed from one phase of consultation to the next. Groups with strong cohesiveness and high morale proceed rapidly into the problem-solving phase where they work productively and creatively toward the solution of the problems of individual consultees and their clients. Other groups are simply collections of professionals with similar jobs who may never move beyond the introductory stage of the group consultation process.

DYNAMICS OF GROUP INFLUENCE

In the case-seminar method of group mental health consultation, the consultant attempts to arouse and channel peer influences. Peers have close mutual identifications, share sources of data not available to the consultant, and often provide excellent feedback to each other (Bradford, 1964). If the consultant has been successful in stimulating the development of a group atmosphere which is generally supportive and nonjudgmental, then group members will feel inclined to share problems, anxieties, and guilt. Sometimes this occurs very quickly, sometimes only after a long testing-out period. The hearing of problems establishes meaningful rather than superficial communication between group members and gradually assures each consultee that his problems are not unique. This reduces the consultees' feelings of isolation and inadequacy, permits a more objective evaluation of problems, and leads to the formulation of helpful alternative courses of action. The feedback provided at continuous case seminars also enables group members to observe the practical results of various suggestions made during former sessions.

We have observed that the work requirements of a professional group may dispose group members to develop similar attitudes toward their clients and similar anxieties concerning their professional competence. Also, each profession tends to attract individuals with similar personality characteristics. These factors increase the probability that the problems which come up in group mental health consultation will be shared and work-oriented. In gaining increased awareness of reactions common to the group as a whole, the individual consultee is helped to achieve insight into his own conflicts (Parker, 1962). Occasionally, when there is sufficient group cohesiveness and confidence in the consultant, a nonshared, but still work-connected, personal problem of an individual consultee may be introduced into the discussion. (For instance, discussion of a child who has been neglected by a working mother may stimulate a public health nurse to share her personal guilt about leaving her young children to be cared for by someone else.) When this occurs, we have observed that the group usually deals with it in an understanding and appropriate manner. With regard to the sensitivity of consultee groups in handling the personal problems of group members, our experiences with a number of different professional groups are consistent with Parker's observation:

> In the ten years of my experience as a mental health consultant, not once has a nurse succumbed to the pressure of anxiety and brought before the group personal matters that were inappropriate in kind or degree [1958, p. 18].

Our observations that group members usually handle personal problems with sensitivity and appropriateness contrast markedly with those of Caplan and his colleagues who have focused on mental health consultation with individual consultees. Caplan states:

The techniques of theme-interference reduction as practiced in case consultation are often hazardous in handling an individual member in the presence of the group. If the consultees are psychologically sophisticated, one of the individual's colleagues may realize his subjective involvement and make a defense-destroying interpretation before the consultant can stop it. Such a situation may rapidly slide into group psychotherapy, in which the separation of personal and work problems is set aside, with the usual arousal of anxiety and resistance. In order to avoid this, the group consultant must structure the ground rules to prevent the airing of personal problems and must maintain a tight control over the direction of the discussion, so that he can avoid a focus on theme interference in an individual member [1964, p. 228].

We believe that the forces of group influence in mental health consultation, like other social forces, either can be feared and restrained, or can be put to use.

ROLES AND TECHNIQUES OF THE GROUP CONSULTANT

The mental health consultant who uses the case-seminar approach must function simultaneously in several different roles: teacher, group leader, clinician and facilitator of communication between community groups. As a teacher, the consultant does not necessarily attempt to transmit specialized technical knowledge; but he does convey general principles and knowledge about those techniques which can be used within the range of the consultees' particular professional background. In this capacity, the consultant may function as a seminar leader, a resource person, and a lecturer; the specific techniques will naturally depend upon his own professional background as well as the qualifications, experiences, and needs of the consultee group. In early sessions formal lecturing on personality development and psychopathology, as well as suggestions on interviewing technique, are often appropriate. In later sessions he is more apt to function as a resource person and seminar leader. In the early sessions it is particularly important that the consultant be careful to clarify the limits of his ability to resolve questions raised by the consultees and to dispel any omniscience or omnipotence which may be imputed to him. Since the consultant's primary goal is to help the group and the individual consultees to learn to be able to derive meaningful solutions for work problems on their own, he should gratify demands for him to provide solutions only enough to keep the consultation sessions from becoming unduly frustrating to the consultees.

As a group leader the consultant acts as a catalyst to stimulate members of the group to share experiences and to explore together the problems of their clients, and helps to clarify problems, focus discussion, and conceptualize solutions suggested by consultees. In the roles of group leader and teacher, we have also found it useful to relate the case under discussion to our own clinical experience and to expose to the group our own limitations and continuing efforts to broaden our understanding of human problems. Such personal reflection typically fosters identification with the consultant and emphasizes his humanness and lack of omniscience and omnipotence (Berlin, 1962).

An important technical issue has arisen involving the consultant's teaching and group leader roles. Caplan (1964) has suggested that consultants should employ supportive reassurance and praise with great caution in order to avoid implying that the consultant is judging the consultee and to avoid emphasizing status differences between consultee and consultant. Members of professional groups, however, are aware that they are constantly being judged by their supervisors, colleagues, and clients, and that there are implicit judgments in all interpersonal relationships. Furthermore, consultation implies unequal knowledge and skills in specific areas, and to ignore this is unrealistic. A very crucial task for the consultant is to demonstrate clear respect for the consultee. Only genuine respect, communicated in many subtle ways, can establish a productive working relationship and is, in our judgment, more important than the avoidance of specific kinds of verbal statements.

The mental health consultant's role as group leader often merges with his role as a clinician, especially during the discussion of the feelings of a consultee toward a client. Considerable clinical sensitivity may be required in deciding when to slow down or, instead, to deal directly with affective expression by a consultee. However, as indicated above, we do not concur with Caplan (1964) that the consultant should consistently avoid any direct discussion of the consultee's feelings and should interrupt such discussions if they arise spontaneously in a consultation group. Members of professional groups are not as fragile as patients and therefore do not require the same degree of protection, given the existing protection of the work-group setting. We do draw the line when aspects of the historical development of the consultee's personal feelings enter the discussion. On rare occasions, a brief excursion into a consultee's personal problems may be deemed appropriate because of the centrality of the problem to the role of the particular professional group. Such invasions of the consultee's private life should only be pursued if the consultee has the requisite strength to deal with his problems, commands the respect of the group, and provides the initiative for discussing his personal problems as "a case at point."

As a clinician, the consultant must always be prepared to use his clinical skills and his knowledge of referral resources and procedures in cases of client emergencies. The consultant's experience and ability as a clinician is a particular asset when consultees are interested in "practical approaches" and not merely theoretical approaches to their problems.

Finally, an additional important role of the consultant becomes clear in his interaction with different community agencies. Case presentations often reveal the frustrations of consultees who must work with personnel from other agencies. Complaints range from individual ineptitude on the part of other professionals to red tape, gross obstructionism, and glory seeking. On more than one occasion, workers from two agencies competing for the management of a client presented the same case in their respective seminar groups. This presents the mental health consultant with an ideal opportunity for facilitating interagency communication by helping members of different professional groups to appreciate the role of other professionals. Thus the mental health consultant who works with groups on a community-wide basis has the role of a facilitator of communication between various community caretakers and the professional groups they represent.

A central feature of this method involves clarifying the relationship between the feelings and attitudes of consultees and their work with clients. As Kevin (1963) has pointed out, there are three different foci which the consultant may take in working toward such clarification. If the consultant focuses on the mutual interchange of affectively involved problems and solutions by consultees, group movement and breadth of learning are likely to occur; but this focus can be very frustrating for inexperienced group members who feel that they have little to contribute. If the consultant focuses on the interaction between himself and individual consultees, or if the consultant focuses primarily on the feelings and reactions of individual consultees in response to clients, individual learning at depth is possible; but the consultant must be especially alert to the possibility that such procedures may be sufficiently threatening to some group members to cause them to withdraw from group discussions and he must be constantly aware of the important differences between consultation and psychotherapy. Either of these latter two approaches may provide more direct help with specific problems but also tend to increase the dependency of an individual consultee upon the consultant and to generate competition among the consultees. Some consultants may prefer to use one of these three approaches as a primary approach, despite its potential disadvantages. We have found that the use of all three techniques at appropriate times tends to result in meaningful and rapid progression by the group from the early phase of consultation to the later problem-solving phase. Any approach or combination of approaches, however, can be overused and carried so far that it is disadvantageous to the successful growth of the group and the individual consultees who comprise it. The consultant must always appreciate the difference between consultation and meddling in the affairs of the consultee. Not all of the consultee's work problems are appropriate for discussion in group consultation and not all of the client's problems are the business of the consultee. It is important that the consultant remember that his long-range goal is to help the consultee to be more self-reliant and independent; the consultee in turn learns to help his clients to become more able to help themselves. In other words, what works for the consultant-consultee relationship ought to work for the consultee-client relationship.

CONSULTATION WITH GROUPS AND CONSULTATION WITH INDIVIDUALS

The choice of group or individual methods for consultation will depend on many factors. Group methods have the advantage of efficiency; they provide more cues and hypotheses for the consultant and more support to group members. A group focus musters the forces of group influence on individual members and helps to break through intragroup and intergroup communication barriers. In group consultation, members of different agencies can be included in the same group; this often serves to bring about a more complete understanding of a case while contributing to better cooperation between agencies.

On the other hand, group consultation may have a number of disadvantages: (1) attendance at group sessions takes members of the group away from performing their usual services (Kevin, 1963) and requires more coordination of consultees' schedules; (2) problems that involve delicate personal matters, or in which the confidentiality of case material is critical, may be more appropriately dealt with in individual consultation; (3) insecure consultees are often unwilling to expose to their peers work problems which they might discuss alone with the consultant; (4) group consultation is not as adaptable as individual consultation for meeting individual consultee-client crises; (5) if group cohesiveness is lacking, the case-seminar method of group consultation may not be effective. For example, in group consultation with the principals of schools scattered over a large rural county, there was a defensive tendency on the part of some group members to regard the problems presented to the group as idiosyncratic to other schools and not characteristic of their own. Consequently, it became necessary for the consultant to focus upon specific informational content rather than on the cases introduced by the group members. Although this resulted in requests for consultant visits to a number of the schools and opened the door for individual consultation with several principals, such initial nongroup or antigroup spirit might well present a technical limitation to the case-seminar consultation technique.

Individual and group consultation each appear to have particular advantages and disadvantages. A combination of approaches, such as was noted above with school principals, may prove to be optimal for some professional groups. In group sessions, the individual consultee becomes familiar with the professional competence of the consultant, develops respect for him as a person, and learns to trust him. Subsequently, the consultee may seek consultation on problems that he might feel reluctant to discuss in the group. As a function of such individual consultation, the consultee may ultimately become more comfortable in bringing up his special problems within the group context. Creative exploration of a variety of consultation techniques with many different professional groups by consultants with diverse backgrounds is needed.

While there is as yet no objective evidence of the effectiveness of mental health consultation either with individual consultees or with groups, there is impressive agreement concerning many aspects of group consultation by those who have compiled and recorded their observations (Maddux, 1953; Berlin, 1962; Parker, 1958; Parker, 1962; Rieman, 1963). Our own experiences have indicated that group consultation consistently improves communication, group cohesiveness, and morale among consultees, and gives the consultees increased sensitivity to the dynamics of interpersonal relations. We have also been impressed with consultees' reports of the beneficial influence of consultation on their relationships with their clients. However, objective data, derived from carefully controlled research, will be required to evaluate the effectiveness and usefulness of group consultation procedures and to establish consultation theory.

REFERENCES

Berlin, I. N. Mental health consultation in schools as a means of communicating mental health principles. *Journal of the American Academy of Child Psychiatry*, 1962, **1**, 671-679.

Bindman, A. J. Mental health consultation: Theory and practice. *Journal of Consulting Psychology*, 1959, **23**, 473-482.

Bradford, L. P. Membership and the learning process. L. P. Bradford, J. R. Gibb, and K. D. Benne, eds., *T-Group theory and laboratory method: Innovation in re-education*. New York: Wiley, 1964. Pp. 168-189.

Caplan, G. *Principles of preventive psychiatry*. New York: Basic Books, 1964.

Corsini, R. J., and Rosenberg, Bina. Mechanisms of group psychotherapy: Processes and dynamics. *Journal of Abnormal and Social Psychology,* 1955, **51**, 406-411.

Kevin, D. Use of the group method in consultation. Lydia Rapoport, ed., *Consultation in social work practice*. New York: National Association of Social Workers, 1963. Pp. 69-84.

Maddux, J. F. Psychiatric consultation in a rural setting. *American Journal of Orthopsychiatry*, 1953, **23**, 775-784.

Parker, Beulah. Psychiatric consultation for nonpsychiatric professional workers. *Public Health Monograph No. 53*. Washington, D.C.: Department of Health, Education, and Welfare, 1958.

Parker, Beulah. Some observations on psychiatric consultation with nursery school teachers. *Mental Hygiene, New York*, 1962, **46**, 559-566.

Rieman, D. W. Group mental health consultation with Public Health Nurses. Lydia Rapoport, ed., *Consultation in social work practice*. New York: National Association of Social Workers, 1963. Pp. 85-98.

Drawing upon their experiences in mental health consultation in a rural area, Eisdorfer, Altrocchi, and Young offer 20 principles of community mental health practice. The principles deal with the role of a consultant in the community, the ways in which the consultant can obtain sanctions, and the ways in which programs can be developed. Obviously, the principles have general value that is not limited to the rural setting in which they were developed. Only by testing principles such as these in a variety of environments will the community psychologist be able to amass a body of fundamental knowledge.

principles of community mental health in a rural setting: the halifax county program[1]

Carl Eisdorfer, John Altrocchi, and Robert F. Young

Mental health centers have typically been established in regions of high population density, often the site of training for mental health clinicians. Thus, rural settings, which usually have a paucity of specialized services, tend to become even more relatively deprived. A solution to this dilemma may lie in the development of part-time consultation programs. Our experiences in such a setting have led us to elucidate certain principles that we feel may maximize the effectiveness of any new mental health program.

Halifax County in north central North Carolina is 722 square miles in size with a population of approximately 60,000. The largest city has a population of 12,000 and is the center of the county's paper and textile industries. The county lies in a farming region with cotton, peanuts, and tobacco as the major crops and is considered to be a borderline poverty area with the mean income per family slightly more than $3,000 per year.

In 1958 the health director of Halifax County, accepting the fact that mental health would be an important function of a public health department, participated in a week-long community mental health workshop sponsored by the North Carolina State Health Department. As a result of this experience he and at least one other health director became convinced of the need for and feasibility of such a program in their counties.

Principle I: Workshops sponsored by state, regional or local agencies can play a significant role in preparing for the development of mental health

[1]The authors wish to thank the many individuals whose participation made this program particularly stimulating, Irving Alexander (IA) and the trainees who shared many of these experiences with us, the people of Halifax County, and their officials for their continued cooperation and support.

Reprinted from the *Community Mental Health Journal*, 1968, **4**, 211-220, with the permission of Behavioral Publications, Inc. and Drs. Eisdorfer and Altrocchi.

*programs, especially when the participants are in a central position in pro-
gram development in the community.*

During the next year, the health director paved the way for community
acceptance of a mental health program. The three school superintendents in
the county were asked to estimate the number of students requiring services
of a mental health professional. After polling the teachers in the schools, they
estimated that 600 children needed help. Similar data was obtained from the
County Medical Society, the ministerial association, the police, and key citizens throughout the county. Statistics, such as the number of people estimated to need help, number of suicides, admissions to state institutions, cost
to the county of such losses as well as cost of services and potential benefits,
are essential in presenting a program to a local governing body (e.g., Board
of County Commissioners). These officials are typically active businessmen
or successful farmers who take a critical look at such data to evaluate the
importance of any action in terms of available funds.

*Principle II: The support of community leaders is crucial for the
development of a mental health program. While a key individual may play
the central role in starting a program, he must depend upon the support of
other community figures for long-range development.*

*Principle III: An accurate appraisal of community needs, supported by
data, is extremely helpful in approaching community agencies, especially
those with fiscal responsibility.*

The county commissioners voted to establish the position of a clinical
psychologist on the staff of the Health Department. A psychologist was designated because they felt that such a person could offer diagnostic as well as
certain therapeutic help, especially in the schools. The position could not be
filled and in 1959 the health director asked the Mental Health Section of the
State Board of Health for assistance in obtaining part-time support. They
arranged for the first of the mental health consultants (CE) to visit Halifax
County. The health director and consultant held a series of discussions and,
for reasons that have now been amply discussed (Caplan, 1964; Kiesler,
1965), they agreed that a program organized toward consultation with key
caregivers in the community would be most appropriate. Such a program
was particularly advisable in Halifax County because of the distance from
any mental health service (95 miles) and because of the difficulty in attracting
full-time personnel of a suitably high caliber to such a rural community.

*Principle IV: Given a paucity of skilled mental health professionals, the
best way of initiating a mental health program is through consultation with
people in the community who are already responsible for handling mental
health problems as an integral part of their routine professional functioning.*

This principle implies that part-time consultative help from skilled
mental health professionals is superior to the regular participation of minimally trained professionals. It follows that effective use of the consultant's
time is of paramount importance. In the present instance, the consultant and

the health director together met in individual planning sessions with each of the school superintendents in the county, the chief public health nurse, the director of the county Welfare Department, and the leaders of the local ministerial association. The physicians were not included because there was some ambivalence among members of the group and their overtaxed time and commitments precluded regular meetings. The principals, public health nurses, county welfare workers, and ministers were all receptive to the idea of consultation on a regular basis.

The consultant began to visit the county for two or three one-day visits every month. It was apparent that Caplan's (1964) crisis intervention consultation techniques could not be made the central feature of this program. Furthermore, the attempt to provide a mental health service for the entire county through such limited contact would render extensive individual consultation inefficient. These factors suggested the usefulness of a group consultation method (Altrocchi, Spielberger, and Eisdorfer, 1965). The consultant and the community leaders decided that the consultant would meet twice a month with the public health nurses and monthly with the welfare workers, the ministerial association members, and three groups of principals.

Although the group consultation method predominated, the consultant and the health director agreed that it would be important to program into each visit some unscheduled time for individual and family crises. The health director could schedule such emergencies that arose in the community even when these involved straightforward requests for clinical service, if the situation had achieved notoriety, had potential contagion or epidemic qualities, or involved individuals with key roles in the community. We found it extremely important to provide such brief but specific help to individuals, especially during the early phase of the program. As a result of dealing with a number of such clinical situations, valuable support was gathered for the program from additional community agencies (such as a police department) and from individual citizens who vigorously supported the annual appropriations for the program from the county commissioners.

Principle V: Flexibility in meeting community needs is extremely important. Although the consultation program needs protection against inundation by clinical services, it should nevertheless be recognized that in selected instances direct clinical service may be very valuable to the community and to the development of consultation programs.
As a corollary then:

Principle VI: Mental health consultants must not only be expert clinicians (Bennett, Anderson, Cooper, Hassol, Klein, and Rosenblum, 1966), but must be willing to use their clinical skills directly when appropriate.

The early conferences between the mental health consultant and the local community leaders and many of the early visits of the consultant were given adequate press coverage. As community awareness of a new mental health resource increased, additional requests came for the consultant's services in the form of talks to PTA's, fraternal organizations, and other groups. Self-referral of patients to the Health Department and physician's referrals increased rapidly. The consultant had correctly predicted to the health director that the community would soon express its need for some clinical service to supplement the consultation program. After seven months, the health director and the consultant arranged for a senior psychiatric resident to visit the county two days a month.

Principle VII: A new mental health consultation service will increase the community's awareness of mental health problems and the demand for clinical service will increase sharply. Plans should be made for meeting such demands, at least in part, within a relatively short span of time.

The principal role of the psychiatrist was to handle the severe clinical problems that began to come to light in the community and his second role was to develop a closer liaison with the county's physicians whom he met individually. In dealing with groups such as physicians who have heavily overloaded time schedules and who function with considerable independence, group consultation was inappropriate. It was felt that they might best be worked with in a more traditional context, such as individual case consultation and occasional discussions at county medical society meetings. Therefore, all referrals from physicians were accepted, although a limited number of visits per patient was set (usually a maximum of three). Immediate telephone feedback was given to the referring physician and the patient was returned to the physician for continuing management or disposition. The psychiatrist, of course, was able to screen patients who needed intensive treatment or hospitalization but such action too was arranged through the patient's own physician. It should be noted that the model established with the physicians was not a mental health consultation model but much more the traditional model of a physician referring patients to a medical specialist colleague.

Principle VIII: In dealing with different professionals, it should be understood that each profession has its own mores and, when appropriate, such patterns should be respected.

The psychiatrist requested and the program was able to obtain the help of a clinical psychologist to visit the county on a twice-a-month basis.

Principle IX: In a new program where people are not oriented toward mental health problems, it is better for the mental health professionals to come to the community than to have the patient travel a long distance.

Having the professionals come into the community enhances the role of the sponsoring agency in its program development and keeps the clinical process as close as possible to the patient's home (Joint Commission on Mental Illness and Health, 1961). A close relationship between the clinician and the public health or other caregiving personnel is essential, especially when short-term, rapid therapy or environmental manipulation is involved. In addition, this arrangement gives the clinician a different and perhaps more valid view of the patient and the forces that impinge on him.

By the second year the program was considered to be successful by the criteria of community acceptance and participation, and the budget of the program was supported by the commissioners without difficulty. Consultation was expanded to include other groups such as the police department of the largest city and visits were made directly to the schools where the consultant met with "problem children" and "problem classes" and then discussed these with the faculty.

A key feature of the Halifax County mental health program is that students, residents and colleagues have been invited to accompany the consultant and to participate in every activity as much as their level of experience and training allowed. For effective training in community mental health consultation, it is essential that the trainee be given the opportunity to observe and collaborate closely with the consultant in his regular routine. A similar program had been organized elsewhere in the state (Spielberger, 1967) and the excitement of the new programs and the enthusiasm of the consultants naturally communicated to students and colleagues. This informal teaching was one of the factors that sparked continual growth and interest in training in community mental health at Duke University.

Principle X: The development of new programs should be inseparable from training. An excellent way to assure continued enthusiasm, development of manpower, criticism and the challenge of new ideas is to include mental health consultants-in-training in the program from its inception.

One result of such training is to provide a ready manpower pool to man new services when these are desired by the community. A colleague of the consultant had accompanied him on several visits and was ready to accept certain independent consultation responsibilities in one of the school systems.

Principle XI: A liaison between a mental health training center and a community agency can be a mutually beneficial arrangement. It affords the community a pool of highly trained talent not otherwise available and provides the training center with training and research opportunities at many levels.

While it is ordinarily not possible for a university-based professional to devote a major portion of time to a community program, the community is usually in a position to offer part-time consultation roles for some faculty members. This not only brings talented manpower to the community but also continually confronts the faculty members with issues of practical significance (Bennett, et al., 1966). Other advantages generated by such a liaison include the availability of advanced students who can perform supervised clinical work at minimal expense to the community, the use of the community as a laboratory, the mutual benefits of an ongoing research program, and the interest of well qualified job-seeking professionals when full-time positions become available.

A major unexpected event occurred in the third year of the program. The original consultant (CE), on fairly short notice, had to take a leave of absence and for a few months the consultation program did not exist. There are probably several reasons why the program did not fold at this point. One was that the psychiatric services continued and another was that the Health Director did not give up. The consultant, though he could not visit the community, was able to maintain contact and did assist with a number of clinical emergencies by telephone. Furthermore, the community caregivers' interest continued. After a few months, a colleague (JA) of the first consultant, who had been present at several consultation visits, was able to rearrange his schedule and reopen the consultation program.

As the new consultant toured the schools with the Health Director, he became aware of the growing ferment for services beyond consultation with the caregivers. He arranged to visit the schools in the county on a rotating basis and tried to adapt his service to the needs of each school. These needs sometimes involved group or individual consultation and sometimes direct but brief clinical services to students. Regular group consultation sessions were scheduled with two new emerging groups of caregivers in the county school system, speech therapists and guidance counselors.

This second consultant had already arranged for a sabbatical leave for the coming academic year but he was able to interest another colleague (IA) in replacing him. As in the previous instance, the interest resulted in part because the colleague had accompanied the second consultant on one of his visits. Again, the threats to the program of a key person leaving were probably great but since a replacement from the same institution was available and since the Health Director and school officials remained as important local stabilizing forces, the program continued.

A year later, the second consultant returned from sabbatical and, later in the year, the original consultant returned from his leave of absence. As each consultant returned, even after a three-month summer vacation, he found increased interest in and depth to the consultation program. All of the consultants observed independently that they experienced much more rapid progress in the second year of their particular programs. As in intensive individual psychotherapy, it often takes time for trust and a relationship to develop.

Principle XII: A long-standing relationship is most meaningful for community consultation and for training in consultation. A consultant-in-training should spread his hours over the longest calendar time possible. Two days a month for a year is far more effective than every day for six weeks.

Acceptance of the program by the county had been strong enough so that after six years two long-awaited opportunities presented themselves:

initiation of research and programmatic approaches to major problems such as mental retardation, illegitimacy, and suicide. A collaboration was arranged with one school system to perform an intellectual assessment of each of the 325 entering first graders. During the summer prior to his admission each was administered the Illinois Test of Psycholinguistic Abilities. This effort has resulted in a focused consultation program with the first-grade teachers, a plan to experimentally reorganize certain elementary schools to include an upgraded primary experience, and a research project involving the assessment of the long-range effects of consultation.

One of the consultants assisted the administrators, teachers, teachers' aides, and family counselors involved in Project Headstart during the summer. From the data on families and homes that were obtained routinely for each of the almost 1,100 children involved in the Project, it was also possible to begin planning for epidemiological research in mental health in the county.

Principle XIII: Although a mental health program usually starts on a service basis, research opportunities do present themselves and it is the sign of a stable program that such an opportunity is grasped. Every mental health program should aim to incorporate a research feature (Smith and Hobbs, 1966).

It was a further sign of acceptance for two of the consultants to be invited by superintendents to assist school officials in solving problems of desegregation. School desegregation is associated with enormous tension in the rural south. One consultant, assisted by a psychology intern, has worked with administrators and a school board and has on several occasions actively intervened in school crises. Needless to say, the consultants have maintained their position as outsiders helping the community to solve its own problems (Maddux, 1953; Caplan, 1964). Thus far, the desegregation process in this town has proceeded without any major upheaval, a result that may be particularly significant because this community is a center of political activity on the part of both civil rights and conservative groups.

Principle XIV: A mental health consultant may be consulted on even the most delicate issues if the relationship he has established with the community is a long-standing and trusting one and if he can keep his private attitudes from unduly affecting his role as consultant.

One of the functions of a consultation program is to help the members of the community become more aware of mental health problems. It became apparent very early that a significant problem in the county was mental retardation. The consultants saw many retarded children and twice arranged to provide testing for a large group of children which revealed numbers of retarded children in some areas far in excess of the three to five percent expected. These figures and recommendations for action were discussed with the community in small groups, such as PTA meetings, and over the past few years there has been a striking increase in the number of special education classes in the county.

The problem of pregnancy and birth without marriage has been a source of much concern in the county. Negro and white subcultures handle this problem quite differently but both solutions are generally conceded to be unsatisfactory from a mental health point of view. The lower-class Negro culture does not include a strong social pressure for marriage when a girl is pregnant and a significant incidence of births out of wedlock results. The white culture strongly presses for marriage, and the illegitimacy rate is very much smaller but these unwanted children are raised in tense and angry homes and often come to our attention as school problems. The approach of one consultant has been to work with groups of junior high and high school students in various kinds of relatively free discussions. From these meetings, it became clear that not only is there a strong interest in sex, marriage, and family life, but an appalling amount of misinformation about these topics among these students (e.g., regular sexual activity is necessary after puberty to prevent insanity). The consultants are in the process, therefore, of aiding the schools in adding to their curriculum a course on family relations, marriage, and sex. Another consultant is helping the ministers to work on developing alternatives to enforced marriage in the case of out-of-wedlock pregnancy. A consultant-in-training is working with groups of pregnant and postpartum young women to investigate local attitudes toward contraception as an adjunct to the county's maternal and child-care program.

Principle XV: One of the foremost functions of a consultant is to help the community recognize widespread mental health problems and assist the proper agents in the community in identifying and dealing with them.

Halifax County has a relatively high suicide rate which the Health Director and the consultants readily identified as an important problem. It was necessary, however, to wait until community interest was evoked in order to help plan an effective and sustained program. Perhaps as a result of expressions of interest by the consultants and the publicity accorded the suicides of several prominent people in the county, the Mental Health Association, the ministers and the physicians of the county began themselves to express an active interest in the problem of suicide prevention. When these signs of readiness occurred, the consultants mobilized their efforts to provide information and advice in planning for the development of a suicide prevention service. A county-wide committee now has taken the responsibility for organizing and staffing the program. The consultants then acted as resource people and provided consultation in selection, training and ongoing supervision to the lay staff of the suicide prevention service.

Principle XVI: Timing and patience are very important in helping a community develop an effective program and consultants should wait until the community is prepared to accept the responsibility for action before initiating plans.

A variety of approaches have been used in the Halifax County mental health program: public talks, lectures, group and individual case consultation, administrative consultation, program planning, crisis intervention, diagnosis and brief therapy, and research. Some approaches have been more effectively used by one consultant than another.

Principle XVII: The personality and style of the consultant comprise an important variable in choice of consultation method. The program should be flexible enough to allow for individual differences in consultation style.

Other variables that play a part in the choice of method are more general. For instance, the combined didactic-seminar method has been most effective with school personnel. Teachers and at least one group of principals responded to this approach more than to group consultation sessions in which they seemed reluctant to participate meaningfully because of explicit and implicit status hierarchies within their system.

There are other situations in which didactic methods may prove useful. Contact was initiated with the nurses at the largest hospital in the county to provide better liaison with the medical and hospital services and to prepare for the development of a mental health center in conjunction with the hospital. It was felt that initiation of a general hospital psychiatric service should be preceded by orienting the nurses to psychiatric and psychological principles and attitudes. What has developed is a somewhat didactically oriented series of group meetings with all of the supervisory nurses in the hospital. The nurses requested that they first be allowed to achieve a sufficient understanding of basic psychodynamic principles so that later they may better profit from patient presentations. Another principle is implied and has been noted by Maddux (1953).

Principle XVIII: The use of a consultant as a lecturer can be a valuable way to establish a reasonable social distance and to enable groups to test him out before more experiential methods evolve.

When the administrative authority is open to consultation in a relatively undefensive manner, a most effective use of the consultant's time is to build a relationship and consult with the administrative officials. Sometimes their vigorous support has been important in averting serious problems that could have resulted in damage to or even rejection of the program (Cumming and Cumming, 1957). In one instance, a consultant talked to a group on the theme that we tend to get what we ask for from other people. The talk was well received, the discussion afterwards was active, and the program seemed successful. The next day one of the men who had been at the meeting committed suicide. A day or two later a rumor was circulated that the man's suicide may have been triggered by the consultant's presentation. A prominent public figure, who knew that the suicide was not related to the consultant's speech, was successful in stopping the rumor by directly confronting several persons known to be spreading it.

Principle XIX: Consultants coming into a community from the outside stand in danger of false rumors and a host of potential difficulties which can best be combated by the presence of powerful and vigorous allies in the community.

One of the virtues of a consultation program is that the consultant, although not visible to the patient community, rapidly becomes known to the professional community. Thus, our consultants, in the community for two or three days a month, are in much closer contact with the caregivers than a full-time clinician who stayed in the clinic and performed traditional clinical services.

Our final observation involves an overriding principle that we feel may be crucial to the success of any mental health program.

Principle XX: The most appropriate attitude of the consultant is one of eagerness to learn from the community.

The citizens in a rural community often manifest an exquisite understanding of the dynamics of their social structure, a kind of knowledge that can enormously expand a consultant's vision. This knowledge can be used for maximum effectiveness by a receptive consultant and will enable him to utilize his specialized skills for service of the community without imposing his ideas and beliefs.

These principles are presented as hypotheses that should be subjected to continual examination. With our ongoing participation in the Halifax County program, we look to the elaboration and modification of the program and principles.

REFERENCES

Altrocchi, J., Spielberger, C. D., and Eisdorfer, C. Mental health consultation with groups. *Community Mental Health Journal*, 1965, **1**, 127-134.
Bennett, C. C., Anderson, Luleen S., Cooper, S., Hassol, L., Klein, D. C., and Rosenblum, G. *Community psychology: A report on the Boston conference on the education of psychologists for community mental health.* Boston: Boston University Press, 1966.
Caplan, G. *Principles of preventive psychiatry.* New York: Basic Books, 1964.
Cumming, Elaine, and Cumming, J. *Closed ranks: An experiment in mental health education.* Cambridge, Mass.: Harvard University Press, 1957.
Kiesler, F. Programming for prevention. *North Carolina Journal of Mental Health,* 1965, **1**(2), 3-17.
Joint Commission on Mental Illness and Health. *Action for Mental Health.* New York: Basic Books, 1961.

Maddux, J. F. Psychiatric consultation in a rural setting. *The American Journal of Orthopsychiatry* 1953, **23**, 775-784.

Smith, M. B., and Hobbs, N. The community and the community mental health center. *American Psychologist,* 1966, 21, 499-509.

Spielberger, C. D. A mental health consultation program in a small community with limited professional mental health resources. E. L. Cowen, E. A. Gardner and M. Zax, eds., *Emergent approaches to mental health problems.* New York: Appleton-Century-Crofts, 1967. Pp. 214-236.

suggested additional readings

Caplan, G. *Principles of preventive psychiatry.* New York: Basic Books, 1964.

Newman, R. *Psychological consultation in the schools: A catalyst for learning.* New York: Basic Books, 1967.

four   planned change

Given his commitment to prevention, how will the community psychologist most effectively achieve this goal? It should be obvious that the better able the psychologist is to influence the provision of what Caplan terms "basic supplies" and the delivery of services, the more effective the community psychologist will be in fostering prevention. Similarly, the better able he is to reduce the pathogenic conditions which exist in the environment, the better able he will be to further his cause. This line of reasoning leads inevitably to one conclusion: Although the community psychologist can work effectively at a variety of levels, his most significant endeavors will be to bring about social system innovation and constructive change. By their very definition, social systems impinge on the lives of groups of individuals. The various social systems found in any community are inextricably bound with the lives of the community members and have potential for either satisfying human needs or producing social and personal disorganization, maladaptation, and deviance. Think for a moment about the effect one social system, a school system, has upon the people of the community: A school system may function in such a way as to meet human needs—or frustrate the lives of many.

It may be true that intervention at the organizational and social system level is a priority activity for the community psychologist, but it is also true that most professionals are ill-prepared to deal with the change issues involved. Organizations and social systems are "communities" in their own right and are exceedingly difficult to understand. Community psychologists and community mental health workers have much to learn from the people who have been working in the organization/social system area, namely, those interested in industrial psychology, organizational consultation, and management. The first two papers in this section are directed at a justification for a commitment to social system and organizational change activities. The third article based on work outside of the community psychology and community mental health areas, presents some important thoughts on theoretical and methodological aspects of planned organizational change.

Sylvain Nagler and Saul Cooper, in the following article, offer a conceptual framework for understanding community mental health interventions and services. They suggest that mental health services can be described in terms of the target of the service, the goal of the service, the means employed, and the locus of operation. These concepts encompass three levels of social and community change ranging from a concern for an individual client or patient to a concern with a social system. Using the example of high school dropouts, the authors discuss how the model can be used to categorize change issues at each level of concern. They argue for a community (social system level) approach to the delivery of mental health services.

Their model is a kind of social systems analysis (see Section six) turned inward on the mental health agency that attempts to systematically categorize and clarify agency goals and functions. In addition, this schema highlights some available options. The model also suggests the basis for systematic record-keeping to describe the various activities of the agency, relative investments in terms of time and resources, and possibilities for evaluation research.

influencing social change in community mental health

Sylvain Nagler and Saul Cooper

One prominent characteristic of mental health's "third revolution"[1] has been the shift away from a nearly exclusive concern with the treatment of individual patients and a move toward including more and more indirect and nonclinical services. This shift to community focused planning, the product of a growing acceptance of the community mental health movement, has required a reordering of program priorities and a redistribution of mental health manpower resources. The most conspicuous concrete change in regard to this shift of orientation has been the growing emphasis on extramural activities, resulting in a significant increase in the time spent by mental health practitioners outside the clinical setting. At present, the most common of these extramural activities is mental health consultation.

Clearly, mental health consultation did not wait for the "revolution"; it has been practiced for many years. However, consultation has recently achieved far greater prestige and acceptance than ever before. It is no longer viewed by mental health administrators as an insignificant ancillary service, peripheral to the primary operations of an institution. Indeed, in several mental health programs, at least in this country, consultation is a *primary* service.[2,3]

Gerald Caplan and the Laboratory of Community Psychiatry at Harvard have had a major impact on the growth and development of mental health consultation in the U.S., both in terms of training and theorizing. Caplan[4] has conceptualized consultation as falling into four categories of

---

The superscript numbers refer to the References found at the end of this article—Ed.

Reprinted from *Canada's Mental Health* (bimonthly journal of the Department of National Health and Welfare, Ottawa, Canada), September-October 1969, **17**, 6-12, with the permission of the journal editor and the authors.

action, depending on whether it is client or consultee centered and whether it is case or administrative in content. Despite this seeming broad frame of reference, Caplan remains rather conservative and narrow in his approach, stressing that "however much we widen our focus, we retain the sick individual as our primary point of reference; the questions we ask, whether in research or practice, deal with issues that relate directly to him."[5]

Caplan's model is limited in another respect, in that it deals with only one mental health service, i.e., consultation, in effect isolating it, at least theoretically, from intramurally based clinical services. Thus, while his enthusiastic support of consultation has significantly contributed to elevating it to its present position of prestige, at the same time this effort may have overshadowed—perhaps even suppressed—a similar potential emanating from within the operations of the mental health institution.

Historically, mental health centers have been regarded as sources of planned change only in terms of the patients they serve and the personnel they train. However, a mental health center has the potential for broader impact. It too, like a consultative service, can become an instrument of social and community change.

CONCEPTUAL FRAMEWORK FOR LEVELS OF CHANGE

We propose to conceptualize both the clinical functions and the consultative service of a mental health center within the same theoretical framework and model, thereby providing a breadth unmatched by Caplan's approach. This model includes three possible levels of intervention, i.e., three levels of attempt at change. Each level, in turn, is defined in terms of three variables: the target, the goal, and the means of change. Thus each level has its own related *target,* its own related *goal* and its own related *means.*

The variables are defined as follows: The target at Level I is defined as a client or patient; at Level II the target is defined as a community caretaker; and at Level III the target is defined as a social system.

At Level I the goal is producing appropriate behavior change and psychological well-being in the client (the client being the target at this level). At Level II the goal is enhancing the functioning efficiency of a community caretaker (the caretaker being the target at this level). At Level III the goal is institutional change (the social system being the target at this level).

A major premise underlying the basic framework of this model is that the target, goal and means at each level, are inextricably bound together. That is, given any one, the other two variables are fixed. Thus it is not functionally possible to combine variables from the different levels.

Figure I presents the interrelationship of the target and goal with the

Figure I Interrelationship of Target, Goal and Means

LEVEL	TARGET	GOAL	Locus of Operation INTRAMURAL MEANS	EXTRAMURAL MEANS
I	Client or patient	Behavior change	Client-focused clinical service	Case-centered consultation
II	Community caretaker	Enhanced functioning efficiency	Case conferences with community involvement	Educational consultation and inservice training
III	Social system	Institutional change	Program delivery management	Program and/or administrative consultation

means. The specific means needed to achieve the various goals depend on the locus of operation, whether it is intramural, i.e., originating from within the institution (clinical services), or whether it is extramural, i.e., originating outside the institution (consultation services).

Figure I illustrates that at Level I both intra- and extramural interventions can be directed at changing the behavior of a client or patient. The mental health institution achieves this *goal* by *means* of clinical service; the consultant by *means* of case-centered consultation. However, regardless of whether the origin of the change is intra- or extramural, the extent of the change, i.e., the *goal,* will be limited at this level to the individual client. To put it another way, when a consultant engages in case-centered consultation, or when a mental health institution offers treatment, it is unrealistic to expect any major change in other than the single client. Thus both intra- and extramural *means* at Level I produce only limited change.

If on the other hand, the strategy is to be directed at enhancing the functional efficiency of the caretaker, Level II, different techniques need to be employed. From a consultative approach this would involve, as the *means,* educational consultation or in-service training. Or on a parallel level, the same *goal* could be achieved intramurally by *means* of case conferences at which the caretaker is invited to participate. These conferences would highlight certain aspects of a problem in an attempt to further sensitize the caretaker and thereby improve his day-to-day functioning. Thus, the conference would not be for the primary purpose of seeking a way to change the behavior of the particular client being discussed; rather, the client would be seen as illustrative of a class of clients and the discussion used as a training exercise.

Finally, at Level III it may be possible to bring about institutional change within a given social system. Extramurally, this is accomplished by *means* of administrative or program consultation with appropriate personnel who have the power to effect change within the system in which they function. Here the focus is neither on a clinical case nor a caretaker, but on the system as a whole. Such changes can be attempted by the consultant in a variety of ways: sensitizing the administrator to some organizational weakness in his system and helping him to consider possible options to correct them; suggesting a trial of new programs to be introduced when they have proven their worth; helping to examine the communication pattern within the system, etc.

But such change can also be brought about by altering the way an institution delivers its services. For example, by changing the treatment policies for a certain category of patients, the institution stimulates the outside community to make adjustments and find alternative means of caring for this particular target group of persons. But as long as a psychiatric institution is available and willing to care for certain kinds of patients—e.g., those whose behavior causes unrest in the system unless they are cared for, the community will make little effort, if any, to discover its own ways of dealing with the problem.

EXAMPLES OF APPROPRIATE INTERVENTION

To be more specific. Consider the problem of high school dropouts. At Level I, the effort would be directed primarily at getting the youngster back to school (the *target* is the student, the *goal* is changing his truant behavior). The extramural *means* would include case consultation with the school officials and other agency personnel, in an attempt to uncover the source of the problem confronting these students which is causing their truancy. Given some understanding of the problem, the consultant would offer practical suggestions aimed at changing the student's behavior (e.g., home visits by various school personnel, conferences with the parents, referrals to the court, etc.) A mental health institution might approach the problem similarly. It might try to engage the youngster (and relevant members of the family) in some form of treatment that would help him and the family resolve the difficulties that are contributing to his truancy.

It is possible to intervene at a higher stage (Level II) where the *goal* would be directed at a different *target*. Here the effort would be to enhance the functioning of those community caretakers who are involved in the case and are likely to get involved in similar cases in the future. These might include school attendance officers, guidance counselors, principals, social workers, policemen, probation officers, judges, etc. By *means* of educational consultation, the consultant might review with them possible reasons why such behavior occurs, how to discover it in its incipient stage, what kinds of corrective action generally works with what type of youngster, and so on. The student in question would be used as an example of the general problem, serving to illustrate relevant aspects of this kind of difficulty. In this way, the consultees would hopefully be better prepared to cope with similar problems in the future. Again, as in the previous example, the mental health institution could approach the problem in a similar way. Case conferences designed to present the significant facts in such kinds of cases would be employed as a teaching device to further educate the community caretakers, the first-line service agents for such problems.

Finally, one could view the problem more generically (Level III). Here the *goal* of intervention would not be to directly change either the client (the truant student) or the community caretakers (the involved school personnel, policemen, probation officers, etc.), but rather aim at those aspects of the social system that may be contributing to the problem. In this case, the problem may be an irrelevant and boring course of study which becomes so irritating that eventually some students prefer to drop out. Beginning with occasional class "cuts," it develops into an attendance problem, from there to truancy, and finally to a dropout problem. In discussing this with school officials (who have power to effect changes in the system) the consultant would endeavor to help the school to understand a possible relationship between curriculum and motivation, between motivation and attendance, and between attendance and truancy. Once the problem has been identified in this way the consultant, in collaboration with school personnel can then recommend appropriate actions to correct such defects in the system.

Another approach to the same problem would be for the mental health center involved to inform the school that it would be willing to develop a treatment program for such high school dropouts, on the understanding that the school examine how its policies may be a contributing factor. Or perhaps the center might refuse to treat or deal with the dropout problem for the moment and instead raise the issue in the community and force the school and/or some other agencies to seek solutions of a preventive nature.

RELATIONSHIP BETWEEN DIFFERENT LEVELS OF INTERVENTION

At this point, the relationship between the various levels needs to be made more explicit. It should be obvious that the various *means* for effecting change have inherent restrictions and limitations. For example, administrative consultation is not directed at a client or his problem; likewise, focusing on a client will have little or no impact on the system as a whole. This is not to say that the impact of any intervention is entirely limited to that level, since residual benefits may accrue to adjacent levels. For example, consulting with a school teacher about a particular case will, hopefully, also have some impact on her future interaction in similar cases. Similarly, a problem-focused case conference will provide some specific help for the case under discussion, in addition to its designed purpose of assisting the caretaker to better understand the problem. But residual benefits such as these, since they are indirect and not planned, cannot be very reliable. To maximize both reliability and impact, intervention must be at the appropriate level, for it is unrealistic to expect institutional changes by way of efforts directed solely at caretakers or clients. For reliable changes to be brought about in the social system, one must intervene at the system level; to occur in a patient, at the case level.

Thus a consultant's frustration at not being able to effectively influence institutional change may not be due to an inherent flaw in the system, but rather to his selection of an inappropriate level of intervention, and to his use of methods and techniques that are relevant to effect change in clients and caretakers, not in systems. Furthermore, the longer the consultant uses a particular approach or method, the more difficult it will be to make a future shift to a different level. Thus if a consultant begins his work in the system focusing primarily on a case-centered approach (as most mental health consultants seem to do), the content of his future consultative service will quickly narrow, more and more, to include only problems at the clinical case level. Similarly, if a mental health agency restricts its activities only to clinical care, it reinforces the perception that this is its only purpose, thereby reducing the likelihood that the community will request other services (such as training or program development). For these reasons, great caution must be exercised in determining an initial strategy level (case, caretaker, or system) for both intra- and extramural functions.

While either intra- or extramural *means* can be used successfully to bring about change, the nature of the desired *goal* determines which of the two can be more effective. As a general rule, intramural *means* are more effective at the case level. In other words, individual treatment, generally speaking, will have a greater and quicker impact than case consultation—when the *goal* is to change the client's behavior. On the other hand, administrative consultation, in most cases, will be more effective than program delivery management when the *goal* is to change the system. Thus each approach has unique attributes which make it the most appropriate for a specific circumstance.

TO ASSURE THE GREATEST RETURNS

This kind of a model can cause discomfort to mental health planners and administrators, for it requires them to make priority decisions about the distribution of resources—intra- or extramural, and between the three levels of intervention: client, caretaker or system. On what basis can these decisions be made? Which will likely assure the greatest returns?

The answer to these questions will depend on two considerations: Who are identified as the client(s) or constituency? How are social problems viewed? In regard to the former, if it is held that mental health services should be primarily directed to serve those who, voluntarily or otherwise, come to the mental health center and are considered eligible for help, then clearly the greatest return will be obtained from a heavily case-oriented operation. On the other hand, if the community is seen as the agency's primary responsibility, and institutional change is to be the primary focus, then it is equally clear that significant and meaningful impact can be achieved *only* through a system-focused approach that might also include a caretaker, but to a lesser extent.

BIAS TOWARD THE COMMUNITY FOCUS OF LEVEL III

From our point of view, the choice is clear. We are—or must become—the servants of the community and must set priorities in response to its needs, rather than functioning primarily for those individuals who, for a variety of reasons (many of a non-psychiatric nature), reach our doors. This does not imply the abolition of clinical services; rather, it means that planners and administrators need to place a much higher priority on the establishment of programs that will have an impact on the community as a whole. If we continue to serve only those who come for psychiatric help, we will be helping only a very select population (even excluding, perhaps, many who are in great need of change) and not directly helping our primary client—the community.

This bias for a community (system level) approach to mental health services relates rather directly to how one views social problems in general. It has some theoretical roots in the universalistic position advocated by Ryan[6] and the institutional conceptualization developed by Wilensky and Lebeaux.[7] Rather than viewing social problems as "exceptions to the general run of affairs and as accidental, unpredictable, and arising from special individual circumstances," Ryan's universalistic outlook demonstrates how they are historically rooted in societal and structural contradictions, and are general, regular and predictable. Consequently, problems need to be approached "with systematic arrangements that are not dependent on individual agreement but are ordered, canonical, and with the goal of systematic and structural change that can be institutionalized."

Given this definition of the nature of social problems, the system level of intervention remains the most appropriate. Intervention at this level should be stressed, not because of the manpower shortage to provide clinical level intervention, but because social system change is more inclusive, more efficient, and more effective in benefiting the entire community. Here, then, is where to expect the greatest returns.

REFERENCES

1. Hobbs, N. Mental health's third revolution. *American Journal of Orthopsychiatry*, 1964, **34**, 822-833.
2. Hunter, W. F., and Ratcliffe, A. W. The range mental health center: Evaluation of a community oriented mental health consultation program in northern Minnesota. *Community Mental Health Journal*, 1968, **4**, 260-269.
3. Eisdorfer, C., Altrocchi, J., and Young, R. F. Principles of community mental health in a rural setting: The Halifax County program. Community Mental Health Journal, 1968, **4**, 211-221.
4. Caplan, G. *Principles of preventive psychiatry*. New York: Basic Books, 1964.
5. *Ibid*. P. 268.
6. Ryan, W. Community care in historical perspective. *Canada's Mental Health*, Supplement No. 60, March 1969.
7. Wilensky, H. L., and Lebeaux, C. N. Industrial society and social welfare. New York: Free Press, 1965.

In the article that follows, Seymour Sarason states, ". . . any theory which purports to explain behavior and which does not come to grips with man-system relationships is a naive, incomplete, and mischief-producing theory." Writing from his experiences at the Yale Psycho-Educational Clinic and elsewhere in New Haven, he emphasizes the need in psychology to understand social systems, organizational change, and innovation and to recognize the factors that inhibit change. He discusses the role of the advice-seeker and the advice-giver and presents a case as an illustration.

toward a psychology of
change and innovation[1]

Seymour B. Sarason

There is an increasing number of psychologists who are interested in how
organizations or social systems work and change. One of the factors in this
development is the realization that all psychologists, like the rest of humani-
ty, are affected by the different social systems of which they may be a part.
This realization is frequently not due to considerations of theory or training
but an awareness forced on one by virtue of day-to-day living. I suppose it is
possible for a psychologist to live his days unaware that his thinking, teaching, practices, and relationships (personal or professional) bear in some way
the stamp of his past and present immersion in what may be termed organizations or social systems. It is possible, and it may even be that such a person
is involved as a psychologist with problems upon which this unawareness has
no particular effect. Such a psychologist would likely be a researcher who at
the same time that he views his research as unaffected by the workings of
social systems—such as the particular department or university of which he
is a member—can usually talk loud and long about how the conduct of his
research has in some measure been affected by grant-giving agencies which
are, after all, organizations or social systems. There are probably no important facets of a psychologist's existence which do not reflect the influence of
his relationship to one or another type of organization.

I have not made the above comments because I happen to think that

[1]Psi Chi (National Honor Society in Psychology) invited address at American Psychological
Association, New York, September 1966.

psychologists should have a keen sensitivity to the world in which they live. That would be as presumptuous as it would be ineffective. My comments were by saying that as psychological theorists move in the direction of stating comprehensive formulations about the determinants of human behavior they will become increasingly concerned with the nature of social organizations, the ways in which they change, and the consequences of these changes. This development will not be a matter of choice but rather of necessity in that in reality the relationship between the individual and "organized settings" is not a matter of choice. The problem for theory is how to go beyond token gestures to these relationships, how to study and understand the extent of variations in these relationships, and how to begin to formulate generalizations which do justice to the complexities involved.[2]

Several years ago a number of colleagues and myself became interested in the processes of change in a certain social system. In the course of studying this system we became aware, as might have been predicted, how complex the processes of change were to understand and how little there was in psychological theory and practice to guide us. The complexity of the problem would have been more tolerable were it not for the fact that we had no conceptual framework which could serve, however tentatively, as a basis for thinking, planning, and action. It has been said that there is nothing more practical than a good theory. There are times when we would have settled for the illusory comfort of a bad theory. In any event, what follows in this paper is no more than a variety of thoughts which may serve only to convince others that the problem is important and requires thoughts better than our own.

[2]It is important to note that the problem which I am stating generally is one quite familiar to the industrial psychologist, as Stagner (1966) has made clear. "Industrial psychology has since its inception dealt with problems of man in an organization, but in its early stages gave consideration only to part of the man, and took the organization for granted. . . . Decided changes began to appear after 1950. . . . Only within the past ten years, however, has this transformation of industrial psychology been completed. People like Haire and Simon began to write about the total organization as a network of human interactions; Likert and McGregor applied new ideas of psychodynamics to the managerial role. The Survey Research Center and other research institutes began to pile up empirical evidence for the reciprocal effects of organizations and individuals.

"A look at a clutch of recent books dealing with the behavior of human beings in industrial organizations confirms my feeling that industrial psychology is no longer the step-child of theoretical and research efforts. Instead there is a good deal of sophisticated work in both theory and data-gathering. Undoubtedly some industrial psychologists of what we may call 'the old school' will protest that this new baby is no legitimate offspring of their speciality. Certainly its parentage is in doubt. Social psychology, sociology, and anthropology have made important genetic contributions; even a few psychoanalytic genes seem to have been incorporated. I would hold, nevertheless, that this new growth is truly industrial psychology to the understanding of human behavior in industrial settings." It is my point that the need for, and the problems involved in, conceptualizing comprehensively man-system relationships is not a necessity for one kind of psychologist (e.g., school, industrial, etc.) but for any psychologist concerned with human behavior.

THE PSYCHO-EDUCATIONAL CLINIC

Several years ago a Psycho-Educational Clinic was started at Yale as an integral part of our clinical training program. The origins, purposes and activities of the Clinic have been described in detail elsewhere (Sarason, Levine, Goldenberg, Cherlin, and Bennett, 1966). For the present paper it is necessary to state very briefly two of the purposes which have increasingly become the focus of our interest and concern. The first of these purposes is to describe and understand the educational setting as a social system, i.e., to view and study this setting as a subculture possessing a distinctive pattern of traditions, dynamics, and goals (Sarason, 1966). We are quite aware that this is a task far beyond the capacities of any single group of investigators. We are acutely aware that it is a task which involves almost every important problem and field in psychology. The complexity of the task in part reflects the fact that in the educational setting these problems have to be conceptualized in a way which erases artificial or arbitrary distinctions (e.g., learning, social psychology, clinical psychology, child development, etc.) and which truly reflects actual relationships. For example, it apparently (but inexplicably) makes sense to some people to talk of "curriculum" independent of who teaches it, why he teaches it, to whom he teaches it, his conceptions of children and the nature of learning, and whether or not he has had any voice in its selection or is given the freedom to depart from it. Elsewhere (Sarason, 1966) I have illustrated and discussed this problem in relation to the "new math," emphasizing the point that how a curriculum is introduced to (and even foisted upon) teachers affects children, teachers, supervisors, and the "curriculum." What I am saying is obvious to any thinking graduate student, i.e., any graduate course is a function not only of the formal curriculum for that course and the particular instructor but also of the particular department, relationships within it, and characteristics of the particular university.

The second purpose which I must briefly discuss is that we are interested in two kinds of change: that which is introduced and executed by those indigenous to the school, and that which represents primarily forces outside the social system we call a school. We know far more about the latter than the former kind of change and this is symptomatic not only of our lack of knowledge about what goes on in a school but also of the implicit assumption that it is a static and not particularly complicated kind of setting. There are many people, including most psychologists who should know better, who view the school as they do (or would) a so-called primitive society, i.e., life in it is simple, the people in it relatively uncomplicated and easy to understand, and the surface appearance of order and purpose can be taken pretty much at face value. There are times when those of us at the Psycho-Educational Clinic wish that such a view of the school setting could indeed be justified because the more we have gotten into the problem the more impressed we have become with its complexity. We sometimes look back nostalgically at the days when we could think of studying the school in terms of what seemed to be discrete problems such as learning, socialization, intellectual development, the process of teaching, the formal curriculum, and the like. This is not to say that one cannot study these discrete problems in a profitable way, but one runs the risk of becoming a prisoner of one's limited theories and methodologies. It is not always made clear that theories—containing as they do a defined but limited set of variables and their presumed relationships—constrict one's scope at the same time that they expand it. Nowhere is this more true than in the literature on the school setting.

But the school is only one of several settings in which we have been able to observe processes of change. In relation to all these settings we have also been in the role of "advice-givers," a role which illuminates not only the processes of change as they are reflected in the "advice-seeker" but in the advice-giver as well. The remainder of this paper contains observations and thoughts about processes of change as we have seen them in the role of observer and advice-giver.

CHANGE AND IMPLEMENTATION

Some of the most interesting and important aspects of the processes of change are revealed before the point of implementation of proposals for change. The importance of these aspects resides not only in how they affect implementation *but in the degree to which they result in no implementation at all.* It is not enough for the person interested in processes of change in various types of organizations or social systems to focus on ongoing or planned changes, although there is no question that such a focus can be a productive one. It is my contention, however, that an equally important part of the problem is the frequency of, and the contexts which surround, proposals for change which either do not get a hearing or never reach the stage of implementation. I have no doubt that these instances are far more frequent than those which reach the stage of implementation. Organizations—such as a university department, a professional school, a social agency—vary tremendously among and between themselves in the degree to which proposals and ideas for change never reach the stage of discussion or implementation.

In recent months I have taken to asking members of various types of organizations what their estimate was of the relationship between proposals made and proposals implemented. The most frequent response was embarrassed silence. In some instances the embarrassment stemmed from the feeling that the question touched on something which, if pursued, would be quite revealing of that organization, and the revelation would not be very pleasant. In other instances the embarrassment was a consequence of the realization that the individual had never been aware of what was implied in the question, although I tried to ask the question without stating what I thought its implications were.

The significance of the question I have been putting to individuals may be gleaned in the following opinion: The greater the discrepancy between the frequency of proposals for change which are never implemented, and the number of proposals which are implemented, the more likely that the implemented changes over time will increasingly lose whatever innovative characteristics they may have had or were intended. In other words, the more things change on the surface the more conditions remain basically the same.

The basis for this opinion brings us back to one of the major interests of the Psycho-Educational Clinic, i.e., the culture of the school and the processes of change. It has been in relation to our work in various school systems that we have become acutely aware of how implemented changes quickly lose their innovative intent.[3] Elsewhere (Sarason, 1966) I have indicated that one of the major reasons for this self-defeating process is the tendency for change proposals to emanate from on high without taking into account the feelings and opinions of those who must implement the changes, i.e., the teachers. What I emphasized was the interpersonal turmoil which such tendencies engender and its effect on the content and goals of change. My comments, however, were in relation to the history and consequences of a single proposal for change (e.g., new math, bussing, etc.) and neglected what I now think is the more general characteristic of the system: the marked discrepancy between the number of proposals to change the system and the number of proposals actually implemented. Put in another way: The fate of any single proposal for change will be determined in part by the number of changes which have been proposed but never implemented. If this is true, my observations suggest that it is because those who have to implement any single proposal for change react to it in terms of their knowledge of and experiences with other proposals (implemented or not) for change in the system. If they are aware, rightly or wrongly, that there is a discrepancy between proposals made and implemented, and particularly if this awareness is associated with feelings of dissatisfaction, it often affects the implementation of the single proposal for change in a way so as to fulfill the prophecy that the more things change the more they remain the same. The fate of a single proposal for change cannot be understood apart from all other proposals for change if only because those who do the implementing do not understand or react to it in that way—and any theory of change and innovation must face this inescapable fact.

The above observations and formulations stemmed in part from repeated experiences in the role of advice-giver in relation to personnel in the

---

[3]A colleague, Albert Myers, has well characterized urban school systems as the "fastest changing status quos."

school system. More candidly, they stemmed from a variety of frustrating and failure experiences in which, as I look back over them, I underestimated how much of an advice-seeker's behavior reflected the system of which he was a part. I could, of course, be criticized as naive. The point is that my naivete reflects well the naivete of psychological theories (e.g., learning, psychoanalytic) which do not face the fact that individual behavior always takes place in the contexts of organizations or social systems. I am not maintaining that social systems "cause" behavior. I am only maintaining that any theory which purports to explain behavior and which does not come to grips with man-system relationships is a naive, incomplete, and mischief-producing theory.

THE ADVICE-SEEKER AND ADVICE-GIVER

The behavior of advice-givers, like that of advice-seekers, reflect man-system relationships. With increasing frequency, in ours as well as other societies, the advice-giver is outside the system of the advice-seeker, a fact which can markedly influence change and innovation. Put in its most concrete form the question which I would like to raise is: If somebody is interested in studying a social system (e.g., a school, a company, police department, etc.) with the intent of devising ways of changing it in some ways, and that somebody comes to you for advice and guidance, how would you go about deciding how to respond? Let us assume that you are relatively unfamiliar with the particular setting the individual wishes to study and ultimately change in some large or small way. This assumption provides an easy out for many people who feel uncomfortable thinking about problems with which they are not familiar. It may well be that these are the kinds of people who discourage students and others from getting into unfamiliar territory. I do not intend this as an *argumentum ad hominem* but as a way of stating that an unfamiliar problem—be it unfamiliar to a single advice-giver or to the field at large—tends to engender reactions which serve to change the problem or to discourage the advice-seeker. It is not all necessary for the unfamiliar to be threatening in some personal way to the establishment. It is often sufficient that the proposal be unfamiliar, i.e., not capable of being assimilated by prevailing attitudes toward "important" problems.

Am I straying from the question by focusing initially on the response of an individual advice-giver or field to an unfamiliar problem? There are at least two reasons why I do not think I have strayed. The first reason is that the fate of any proposal for change is not unrelated to the prevailing attitudes of the field to which the advice-giver belongs. Although these attitudes may not always be decisive—the situation is much too complicated to permit one to focus exclusively on a single source or variable—they can or do play a role well before the time when the proposal for change reaches the point of implementation. It needs hardly to be pointed out that these prevailing attitudes can abort the proposed change even though the change involves a setting different from that in which the prevailing attitudes are found. The second reason I do not think I have strayed from the original question is, I think, less of a glimpse of the obvious than is the first reason. The relationship between the advice-seeker, on the one hand, and the advice-giver or field, on the other hand, is frequently identical to the relationship between the advice-seeker and the setting which is the object of change. The point here is that a proposal for change far more often than not encounters an obstacle course and its ultimate fate, by whatever criteria this may be judged, must be viewed in terms of how the proposal changed as a function of each hurdle. We are far more aware of what happens once a proposal reaches the stage of implementation than we are of what happens to the proposed change (and changer) before that stage. A psychology of change and innovation cannot neglect these preimplementation events which, in my experience, frequently have the effect of insuring that changes will take place in a way so as to preclude innovation.

AN ILLUSTRATIVE CASE

A number of years ago in New Haven an organization was started the major aim of which was to develop programs and services for the inner city or poverty population. The name of this organization is Community Progress Inc. (CPI). Anyone familiar with community action programs is well aware that CPI was one of the first of such programs and is regarded as one of the, if not *the,* most successful and comprehensive of these ventures. CPI antedates many of the Federal programs and, in fact, a number of Federal programs are modeled on what CPI has done. In our recent book (Sarason et al., 1966) we described two of CPI's most pioneering and intriguing programs and the relationship of our clinic to these programs. One of these programs is the Neighborhood Employment Center and the other is the Work Crew Program for school dropouts. Most of the employees in these programs are nonprofessional personnel who are indigenous to the area and the population served. With very few exceptions no employee had previous experience in or training for the job he was doing. It is obviously impossible for me here to describe in any detail the nature of and rationale for these programs. Suffice it to say that the titles "Neighborhood Employment Center" and "Work Crew Programs" are distressingly ineffective in communicating the seriousness, variety, and complexity of the human problems which these programs encounter, cope with, and effectively handle. By "effectively handle" we mean that there is no reason to believe that the rate of success is any less than that in more traditional helping agencies. Our opinion is that when one takes into account the nature of the population served, the rate of success is somewhat short of amazing. It sometimes has offended some of our colleagues in the mental health professions when we have said that these two programs are truly mental health programs. But how can you call them mental health programs if they do not employ psychiatrists, clinical psychologists, and social workers? The obstacles to change or innovation—both in thinking and action—are many, and words and categorical thinking will be found high on the list.

How did these programs, reflecting as they do change and innovation, come about? Before answering this question I must tell you two things about CPI. First, the mental health professions had nothing to do with the beginnings of CPI. It would be near correct to say that CPI was begun and developed by a small group of individuals who had no previous formal training to do what they subsequently did. The second fact I must tell you is that today, a few years after CPI's existence, there is not a single mental health agency in New Haven whose thinking and practices have not been changed by what CPI has developed. This is not to say that these agencies have changed in a fundamental way but rather that to a limited extent they have adapted their way of thinking to new problems and new settings. This is not true for the Psycho-Educational Clinic and I hope it will not be taken as an expression of arrogance or presumption when I say that as in the case of those at CPI we at the Clinic are involved in problems and settings in ways which represent a deliberate break with our own pasts and professional training—as a result of which we have become quite knowledgeable about the interactions among the unfamiliar, anxiety, and resistances to change in self and others. I must add that the consequences of resistance are much less lethal to change, by which I mean here engaging in an activity one has not done before, than they are to innovation by which I mean sustaining the spirit or intent of change so that one recognizes that one has unlearned part of one's past and that the direction of one's future has thereby been influenced.

Now let us return to the original question via a fantasy I have sometimes had. Reformulated, the question is: What if CPI, as an advice-seeker, came to me as an advice-giver to respond to their initial plans to develop programs and services for the school dropouts and poverty population? In point of fact CPI did circulate a document containing a general statement of its aims in relation to its view of the problems with which it was to deal. This document was sent to me and I confess that I saw a lot in there that I considered presumptuous, if not grandiose, particularly in light of the fact that a program in "human renewal" was going to be attempted by people possessing no particular expertise in the dynamics of human behavior and the ways in which one goes about helping problem people. The fantasy I have had centers around the situation in which CPI learns that I think what they are planning to do is probably for the birds and that I was not prepared to give them my blessings. (In reality, of course, nobody was asking for my blessings or anything else I had to give them.) CPI comes running to my door and says, "O.K., you don't like what we want to do. You don't like the way we are thinking about the problems. What would *you* do?" That would have been the polite way they would phrase the question. The more legitimate way of phrasing the question —and fantasy is not noted for its close relation to reality—would have been: "What do you or your mental health colleagues who have not been involved with the poverty population have to suggest to us?" It is not important to relate in detail what I would have told them. Suffice it to say that what I would have recommended would have been an instance of translating an unfamiliar problem into familiar terms. I would have told them about clinics, diagnostic and treatment services, mental health professionals, and research and evaluation. The result, of course, would have been quite different from what they intended and subsequently implemented. Had they taken my advice some innovative programs which have had a pervasive and sustained effect around the country would have been scuttled, to the detriment of the populations served *and* the mental health fields.

SOME CONCLUDING COMMENTS

Social systems, large or small, are fantastically complicated. To describe and understand a single school, let alone a school system, presents staggering problems for methodology and theory. What I have attempted to do in this paper is to suggest that the complexity of these systems as well as some of their distinctive characteristics become quite clear as one focuses on how these systems change over time, particularly in relation to innovations which are sustained, or aborted, or in one or another way defeating of the aims of change. Perhaps the major import of this view is that at the same time that it illuminates features of the system it also makes clear how understanding of the behavior of the individual requires, in fact demands, conceptualization of man-system relationships. This is as true for the individual we call a psychologist as it is for anyone else. I tried to illustrate the point by focusing on the psychologist in the role of advice-giver not only because the psychologist is so frequently related to processes of change in individuals or groups but because he so often is the contact point between different social systems or organizations, i.e., he illustrates the fact that processes of change frequently (if not always) involve interacting systems. An additional factor in focusing on the psychologist is that it is too easy to overlook that whatever conceptualizations we develop will have to be as relevant for psychology and psychologists as for any individual in any other social system.

At the beginning of this paper I ventured the opinion that there are probably no important facets of a psychologist's existence which do not reflect the influence of his relationship to one or another type of organization. I would at this point venture the additional hypothesis that there is not a single psychologist who has not at some time or another been involved in initiating or administering proposals for change in some organization. Whatever his role, I would predict that if we ever studied the psychologist in relation to processes of change in various types of organizations we would be impressed by two findings. First, psychologists are as good as anybody else in initiating change and as bad as everybody else in sustaining it in a way such that "the more things change the more they remain the same." Second, in relation to these changes the behavior of most psychologists will be found to be remarkably uninfluenced by knowledge of or concern for relationships between change and innovation, on the one hand, and complexity of social systems, on the other.

The distinction between processes of change and innovation as they occur in organized settings is fundamental to understanding how these settings work. It is a distinction which has profitably occupied the thinking of those interested in child development, e.g., the concept of stages implies a distinction between change and innovation. As this distinction is applied to the most important social systems with which we are or have been related, our understanding of these systems *and* the individuals in it will take on an innovative characteristic. I have no doubt that this will be particularly true in the case of the social system we call a school.

The last point brings me, finally, to a consideration to which I have only alluded earlier in this paper. One can characterize our society as one in which massive and deliberate attempts are being made to change aspects of the nature of groups, settings, and regions within as well as beyond our society. The schools, the Negro, the poverty population, Appalachia, the public mental hospital—these are only some of the more important objects of change. Being, as most of us are, for virtue and against sin we applaud and support these programs for change. We know something is being done because billions are being spent. For what it is worth, it is my opinion, based on some extensive observations, that much is being done but little of it in a way calculated to bring about changes which sustain the intent to innovate. I do not say this in the spirit of criticism, but rather as a way of suggesting that, among many reasons, two of them are: the absence of a psychology of change and innovation, and the tendency within psychology to develop molecular theories about molecular-sized problems. In relation to the latter reason it is necessary to state that however necessary it may be at times to restrict the scope of theorizing by grasping a part of the problem and sticking with it, there is the distinct danger that over time the part unwittingly becomes the whole of the problem.

REFERENCES

Sarason, S. B. The culture of the school and processes of change. Brechbill Lecture, University of Maryland School of Education, January 1966.

Sarason, S. B., Levine, M., Goldenberg, I. I., Cherlin, D., and Bennett, E. *Psychology in community settings: Clinical, educational, vocational, social aspects.* New York: John Wiley & Sons, 1966.

Stagner, R. Book review. *Contemporary Psychology*, 1966, **11**, 145-150.

Warren Bennis' article, the last in this section, is an interesting and stimulating paper dealing with "Theory and Method in Applying Behavioral Science to Planned Organizational Change." It explains what is meant by the "change agent." Some would include the application of an activist orientation, protest techniques, and advocacy in addition to the role as it is presented in the article. Bennis discusses the emergence of the action role, the lack of a viable theory of social change, some requisites for planned change, eight different types of change programs and their limitations, and programs that implement planned organizational change (including training, consultation, and applied research). He discusses two different strategic models for change used in industrial settings and a variety of aspects of the change agent's role. The question of a systems approach will be considered again in Section six in the articles on systems analysis. The present article provides many important concepts and definitions for the community psychologist. It casts some light on questions such as: What is a change agent? What is the difference between planned organizational change, action research, and operations research? Do fields outside of community psychology and community mental health have something to offer? The answer to this last question is affirmative. The community psychologist needs to be familiar with the existing knowledge in this area; otherwise, he is ill-equipped to work at the organizational and systems level.

theory and method in applying behavioral science to planned organizational change[1]

Warren G. Bennis

What we have witnessed in the past two or three decades has been called the "Rise of the Rational Spirit"—the belief that science can help to better the human condition (Merton and Lerner, 1951). The focus of this paper is on one indication of this trend: the emerging role for the behavioral scientist and, more specifically, the attempts by behavioral scientists to apply knowledge (primarily sociological and psychological) toward the improvement of human organizations.

THE EMERGENCE OF THE ACTION ROLE

Many signs and activities point toward an emerging action role for the behavioral scientist. The *manipulative standpoint,* as Lasswell calls it, is becoming distinguishable from the *contemplative standpoint* and is increasingly ascendant insofar as knowledge utilization is concerned.[2] Evidence can be found in the growing literature on planned change through the uses of the behavioral sciences (Bennis, Benne, and Chin, 1961; Freeman, 1963; Zetterberg, 1962; Gibb and Lippitt, 1959; Leeds and Smith, 1963; Likert and

[1]Drawn from keynote address presented at International Conference on Operational Research and the Social Sciences, Cambridge, England, September 1964.
[2]For an excellent discussion of the "value" issues in this development, see A. Kaplan. *The conduct of inquiry,* San Francisco: Chandler, 1964, Chapter 10; and K. D. Benne and G. Swanson, eds. Values and social issues. *Journal of Social Issues,* 1960, **6**.

Reprinted from the *Journal of Applied Behavioral Science,* 1965, **1**, 337-360, with the permission of the NTL Institute for Applied Behavioral Science and the author. Copyright © 1965 by the NTL Institute for Applied Behavioral Science Associated with the National Education Association.

Hayes, 1957; Glock, Lippitt, Flanagan, Wilson, Shartle, Wilson, Croker, and Page, 1960) and in such additions to the vocabulary of the behavioral scientist as action research, client system, change agent, clinical sociology, knowledge centers, social catalysts. The shift is also reflected in increased emphasis on application in annual meeting time of the professional associations or in the formation of a Center for Research on the Utilization of Scientific Knowledge within The University of Michigan's Institute for Social Research.

It is probably true that in the United States there is a more practical attitude toward knowledge than anywhere else. When Harrison Salisbury (1960) traveled over Europe he was impressed with the seeming disdain of European intellectuals for practical matters. Even in Russia he found little interest in the "merely useful." Salisbury saw only one great agricultural experiment station on the American model. In that case professors were working in the fields. They told him, "People call us Americans."

Not many American professors may be found working in the fields, but they can be found almost everywhere else: in factories, in the government, in underdeveloped countries, in mental hospitals, in educational systems. They are advising, counseling, researching, recruiting, developing, consulting, training. Americans may not have lost their deep ambivalence toward the intellectual, but it is clear that the academic intellectual has become *engagé* with spheres of action in greater numbers, with more diligence, and with higher aspirations than at any other time in history.

It may be useful to speculate about the reasons for the shift in the intellectual climate. Most important, but trickiest to identify, are those causative factors bound up in the warp and woof of "our times and age" that Professor Boring calls the *Zeitgeist*. The apparently growing disenchantment with the moral neutrality of the scientist may be due, in C. P. Snow's phrase, to the fact that "scientists cannot escape their own knowledge." In any event, though "impurity" is still implied, action research as distinguished from pure research does not carry the opprobrium it once did.

Perhaps the crucial reason for the shift in emphasis toward application is simply that we know more.[3] Since World War II we have obtained large bodies of research and diverse reports on application. We are today in a better position to assess results and potentialities of applied social science.

Finally, there is a fourth factor having to do with the fate and viability of human organization, particularly as it has been conceptualized as "bureaucracy." I use the term in its sociological, Weberian sense, not as a metaphor *à la* Kafka's *The Castle* connoting "red tape," impotency, inefficiency, despair. In the past three decades Weber's vision has been increasingly scrutinized and censured. Managers and practitioners, on the one hand, and organizational theorists and researchers on the other, are more and more dissatisfied

[3]For a recent inventory of scientific findings of the behavioral sciences, see B. Berelson and G. A. Steiner. *Human behavior*. New York: Harcourt, Brace & World, 1964.

with current practices of organizational behavior and are searching for new forms and patterns of organizing for work. A good deal of activity is being generated.

THE LACK OF A VIABLE THEORY OF SOCIAL CHANGE

Unfortunately, no viable theory of social change has been established. Indeed it is a curious fact about present theories that they are strangely silent on matters of *directing* and *implementing* change. What I particularly object to —and I include the "newer" theories of neo-conflict (Coser, 1956; Dahrendorf, 1961), neo-functionalism (Boskoff, 1964), and neo-revolutionary theories—is that they tend to explain the dynamic interactions of a system without providing one clue to the identification of strategic leverages for alteration. They are suitable for *observers* of social change, not for practitioners. They are theories of *change,* and not of *changing.*

It may be helpful to suggest quickly some of the prerequisites for a theory of changing. I am indebted here to my colleague Robert Chin (1961, 1963):

a. A theory of changing must include manipulable variables—accessible levers for influencing the direction, tempo, and quality of change and improvement.
b. The variables must not violate the client system's values.
c. The cost of usage cannot be prohibitive.
d. There must be provided a reliable basis of diagnosing the strength and weakness of conditions facing the client system.
e. Phases of intervention must be clear so that the change agent can develop estimates for termination of the relationship.
f. The theory must be communicable to the client system.
g. It must be possible to assess appropriateness of the theory for different client systems.

Such a theory does not now exist, and this probably explains why change agents appear to write like "theoretical orphans" and, more important, why so many change programs based on theories of social change have been inadequate. This need should be kept in mind as we look at models of knowledge utilization.

THE NOTION OF PLANNED CHANGE

Planned change can be viewed as a linkage between theory and practice, between knowledge and action. It plays this role by converting variables from the basic disciplines into strategic instrumentation and programs. His-torically, the development of planned change can be seen as the resultant of two forces: complex problems requiring expert help and the growth and via-bility of the behavioral sciences. The term "behavioral sciences" itself is of post-World War II vintage coined by the more empirically minded to "safe-guard" the social disciplines from the non-quantitative humanists and the depersonalized abstractions of the econometricists. The process of planned change involves a *change agent,* a *client system,* and the collaborative attempt to apply *valid knowledge* to the client's problems.[4]

Elsewhere I have attempted a typology of change efforts in which planned change is distinguished from other types of change in that it entails mutual goal setting, an equal power ratio (eventually), and deliberateness on both sides (Bennis et al., 1961, p. 154).

It may further help in defining planned change to compare it with another type of deliberate change effort, Operations Research. I enter this with a humility bordering on fear and a rueful sense of kinship in our mutual incapacity to explain to one another the nature of our work. There are these similarities. Both are World War II products; both are problem-centered (though both have also provided inputs to the concepts and method of their parent disciplines).[5] Both emphasize improvement and to that extent are *normative* in their approach to problems. Both rely heavily on empirical science; both rely on a relationship of confidence and valid communication with clients; both emphasize a *systems* approach to problems—that is, both are aware of interdependence within the system as well as boundary mainte-nance with its environment; and both appear to be most effective when work-ing with systems which are complex, rapidly changing, and probably science-based.

Perhaps the most crucial difference between OR and planned change has to do with the identification of strategic variables, that is, with those fac-tors which appear to make a difference in the performance of the system. Planned change is concerned with such problems as (1) the identification of mission and values, (2) collaboration and conflict, (3) control and leadership, (4) resistance and adaptation to change, (5) utilization of human resources, (6) communication, (7) management development. OR practitioners tend to select economic or engineering variables which are more quantitative, mea-surable, and linked to profit and efficiency. Ackoff and Rivett (1963), for example, classify OR problems under (1) inventory, (2) allocation, (3) queuing, (4) sequencing, (5) routing, (6) replacement, (7) competition, (8) search.

[4]For a fuller discussion, see R. Lippitt, J. Watson, and B. Westley. *The dynamics of planned change.* New York: Harcourt, Brace & World, 1961; and Bennis et al., 1961.

[5]For a brilliant exposition on the contributions of applied research to "pure" theory, see A. Gouldner. Theoretical requirements of the applied social sciences. Bennis et al., eds. 1961. Pp. 83-95.

A second major difference has to do with the perceived importance of the relationship with the client. In planned change, the quality and nature of the relationship are used as indicators for the measure of progress and as valid sources of data and diagnosis. Undoubtedly, the most successful OR practitioners operate with sensitivity toward their clients; but if one looks at what they *say* about their work, they are clearly less concerned with human interactions.

A third major difference is that the OR practitioner devotes a large portion of his time to research, to problem solving. The change agent tends to spend somewhat more time on implementation through counseling, training, management development schemes, and so forth. Fourth, planned-change agents tend to take less seriously the idea of the *system* in their approaches. Finally, the idea of an interdisciplinary team, central to OR, does not seem to be a part of most planned-change programs.

One thing that emerges from this comparison is a realization of the complexity of modern organization. Look through the kaleidoscope one way, and a configuration of the economic and technological factors appears; tilt it, and what emerges is a pattern of internal human relations problems. It is on these last problems and their effects upon performance of the system that practitioners of planned organizational change tend to work.

A FOCUS OF CONVENIENCE

To develop what George Kelley refers to as a "focus of convenience" for planned organizational change, I want to make two key aspects clearer: the notions of "collaborative relationships" and of "valid knowledge." I see the outcome of planned-change efforts as depending to some considerable extent on the relationship between client and agent. To optimize a collaborative relationship, there need to be a "spirit of inquiry," with data publicly shared, and equal freedom to terminate the relationship and to influence the other.

As to valid knowledge, the criteria are based on the requirements for a viable applied behavioral science research—an applied behavioral science that:

a. Takes into consideration the behavior of persons operating within their specific institutional environments;
b. Is capable of accounting for the interrelated levels (person, group, role, organization) within the context of the social change;
c. Includes variables that the policy maker and practitioner can understand, manipulate, and evaluate;
d. Can allow selection of variables appropriate in terms of its own values, ethics, moralities;

e.   Accepts the premise that groups and organizations as units are amenable to empirical and analytic treatment;
f.   Takes into account external social processes of change as well as interpersonal aspects of the collaborative process;
g.   Includes propositions susceptible to empirical test focusing on the dynamics of change.

These criteria must be construed as an arbitrary goal, not as an existing reality. To my knowledge, there is no program which fulfills these requirements fully. In this focus of convenience, I have arbitrarily selected change agents working on organizational dynamics partly because of my greater familiarity with their work but also because they seem to fulfill the criteria outlined to a greater extent than do other change agents. My choice of emphasis is also based on the belief that changes in the sphere of organizations—primarily industrial—in patterns of work and relationship, structure, technology, and administration promise some of the most significant changes in our society. Indeed it is my guess that industrial society, at least in the United States, is more radical, innovative, and adventurous in adapting new ways of organizing than the government, the universities, and the labor unions, who appear rigid and stodgy in the face of rapid change. If space permitted, however, I would refer also to change agents working in a variety of fields—rural sociology, economics, anthropology—and in such settings as communities, hospitals, cultural-change programs.

Let us turn now to some of the "traditional" models of knowledge utilization.

EIGHT TYPES OF CHANGE PROGRAMS[6]

It is possible to identify eight types of change programs if we examine their strategic rationale: exposition and propagation, elite corps, human relations training, staff, scholarly consultations, circulation of ideas to the elite, developmental research, and action research.

I should like to look at each of these programs quickly and then refer to four biases which seem to me to weaken their impact.

Exposition and propagation, perhaps the most popular type of program, assumes that knowledge is power. It follows that the men who possess "Truth" will lead the world.

Elite corps programs grow from the realization that ideas by themselves do not constitute action and that a strategic *role* is a necessity for ideas to be implemented (e.g., through getting scientists into government as C. P. Snow suggests).

[6]For a fuller exposition of these ideas, see my paper, A new role for the behavioral sciences: Effecting organizational change. *Administrative Science Quarterly,* 1963, **8,** 125-165.

Human relations training programs are similar to the elite corps idea in the attempt to translate behavioral science concepts in such ways that they take on personal referents for the men in power positions.

Staff programs provide a source of intelligence within the client system, as in the work of social anthropologists advising military governors after World War II. The strategy of the staff idea is to observe, analyze, and to plan rationally (Myrdal, 1958).

Scholarly consultation, as defined by Zetterberg (1962), includes exploratory inquiry, scholarly understanding, confrontation, discovery of solutions, and scientific advice to client.

Circulation of ideas to the elite builds on the simple idea of influencing change by getting to the people with power or influence.

Developmental research has to do with seeing whether an idea can be brought to an engineering stage. Unlike Zetterberg's scholarly confrontation, it is directed toward a particular problem, not necessarily a client, and is concerned with implementation and program. (I would wager that *little* developmental research is being done today in the behavioral sciences.)

Action research, the term coined by Kurt Lewin, undertakes to solve a problem for a client. It is identical to applied research generally except that in action research the roles of researcher and subject may change and reverse, the subjects becoming researchers and the researchers engaging in action steps.

These eight programs, while differing in objectives, values, means of influence, and program implications, are similar in wanting to use knowledge to gain some socially desirable end. Each seems successful or promising; each has its supporters and its detractors. Intrinsic to them all, I believe, is some bias or flaw which probably weakens their full impact. Four biases are particularly visible.

RATIONALISTIC BIAS: NO IMPLEMENTATION OF PROGRAM

Most of the strategies rely almost totally on rationality. But knowledge *about* something does *not* lead automatically to intelligent action. Intelligent action requires commitment and programs as well as truth.

TECHNOCRATIC BIAS: NO SPIRIT OF COLLABORATION

Change typically involves risk and fear. Any significant change in human organization involves rearrangement of patterns of power, association, status, skills, and values. Some may benefit, others may lose. Thus change typically involves risk and fear. Yet change efforts sometimes are conducted as if there were no need to discuss and "work through" these fears and worries (e.g., F. W. Taylor's failure to consider the relationship between the engineer

with the stopwatch and the worker, or Freud's early work when he considered it adequate to examine the unconscious of his patients and tell them
what he learned—even to the extent on occasion of analyzing dreams by
mail).

INDIVIDUALIST BIAS: NO ORGANIZATION STRATEGY IS INVOLVED

This refers to strategies which rely on the individual while denying the organizational forces and roles surrounding him. There is, however, simply no
guarantee that a wise individual who attains power will act wisely. It may be
that *role corrupts*—both the role of power and the role of powerlessness. In
any event, there is no guarantee that placing certain types of people in management—or training them or psychoanalyzing them or making scientists of
them—leads to more effective action. Scientists act like administrators when
they gain power. And graduates of human relations training programs tend
to act like nonalumni shortly after their return to their organizational base.

The staff idea, proposed by Myrdal, is limited by the unresolved tensions in the staff-line dilemma noted by students of organizational behavior
and by the conflicts derived from the role of the intellectual working in
bureaucratic structures. The elite strategy has serious drawbacks, primarily
because it focuses on the individual and not the organization.

INSIGHT BIAS: NO MANIPULABILITY

My major quarrel here is not with the formulation: insight leads to change,
though this can be challenged, but with the lack of provision of variables
accessible to control. It is not obvious that insight leads directly to sophistication in rearranging social systems or making strategic organization interventions. Insight provides the relevant variables for planned change as far as
personal manipulation goes, but the question remains: How can that lead
directly to the manipulation of external factors?

THE ELEMENTS OF PLANNED ORGANIZATIONAL CHANGE

In the October 7, 1963, edition of the *New York Times,* a classified ad
announced a search for change agents. It read:

> WHAT'S A CHANGE AGENT? A result-oriented individual able to
> accurately and quickly resolve complex tangible and intangible problems.
> Energy and ambition necessary for success . . .

The change agents I have in mind need more than "energy and ambi-
tion." They are *professionals* who, for the most part, hold doctorates in the

behavioral sciences. They are not a very homogeneous group, but they do have some similarities.

They are alike in that they take for granted the *centrality of work* in our culture to men and women in highly organized instrumental settings; in their concern with improvement, development, and measurement of *organizational effectiveness;* in their *preoccupation with people* and the process of human interaction; in their interest in changing the relationships, perceptions, and values of *existing personnel.* They may be members of the client system, arguing that inside knowledge is needed, or external agents, arguing that perspective, detachment, and energy from outside are needed. They intervene at different structural points in the organization and at different times.

Though each change agent has in mind a set of unique goals based on his own theoretical position and competencies as well as the needs of the client system, there are some general aims. In a paradigm developed by Chris Argyris (1962), bureaucratic values tend to stress the rational, task aspects of work and to ignore the basic human factors which, if ignored, tend to reduce task competence. Managers brought up under this system of values are badly cast to play the intricate human roles now required of them. Their ineptitude and anxieties lead to systems of discord and defense which interfere with the problem-solving capacity of the organization.

Generally speaking, the normative goals of change agents derive from this paradigm. They include: improving interpersonal competence of managers; effecting a change in values so that human factors and feelings come to be considered legitimate; developing increased understanding among and within working groups to reduce tensions; developing "team management"; developing better methods of "conflict resolution" than suppression, denial, and the use of unprincipled power; viewing the organization as an organic system of relationships marked by mutual trust, interdependence, multi-group membership, shared responsibility, and conflict resolution through training or problem solving.

PROGRAMS FOR IMPLEMENTING
PLANNED ORGANIZATIONAL CHANGE

TRAINING

Discussion here will focus on three broad types of change programs that seem to be most widely used, frequently in some combination: training, consultation, and research. Training is an inadequate word in this context, as its dictionary meaning denotes "drill" and "exercise." I refer to what has been called laboratory training, sensitivity or group dynamics training, and most commonly, T-Group training.[7] The idea originated in Bethel, Maine, under the guidance of Leland Bradford, Kenneth Benne, and Ronald Lippitt, with initial influence from the late Kurt Lewin. The T-Group has evolved since 1947 into one of the main instruments for organizational change. Bradford has played a central role in this development as director of the National Training Laboratories. Growth has been facilitated through the active participation of a number of university-based behavioral scientists and practitioners. Tavistock Institute has played a similar role in England, and recently a group of European scientists set up a counterpart to the National Training Laboratories.

The main objective at first was *personal change* or *self-insight.*Since the fifties the emphasis has shifted to *organizational development,* a more precise date being 1958, when the Esso Company inaugurated a series of laboratories at refineries over the country under the leadership of Blake and Shepard (Shepard, 1960).

Briefly, laboratory training unfolds in an unstructured group setting where participants examine their interpersonal relationships. By examining data generated by themselves, members attempt to understand the dynamics of group behavior, e.g., decision processes, leadership and influence, norms, roles, communication distortions, effects of authority on behavioral patterns, coping mechanisms. T-Group composition is itself a strategic issue. Thus the organization may send an executive to a "stranger laboratory" which fills a "seeding" function; "cousin laboratories" may be conducted for persons of similar rank and occupational responsibilities within the company but from different functional groups; "diagonal slices" may be composed of persons of different rank but not in the same work group or in direct relationship; and "family laboratories" may be conducted for functional groups. The more the training groups approach a "family," the more the total organization is affected.

CONSULTING

The change agent *qua* consultant, perhaps best exemplified in the work of the Tavistock Institute, operates in a manner very like the practicing physician or psychoanalyst: that is, he starts from the chief "presenting symptom" of the client, articulates it in such a way that causal and underlying mechanisms of the problem are understood, and then takes remedial action. Heavy emphasis is placed on the strategy of *role model* because the main instrument is the change agent himself. Sofer (1961) reveals this when he suggests that

[7] For a popular account of laboratory training, see C. Argyris. T-groups for organizational effectiveness. *Harvard Business Review,* 1961,**42**, 60-74. For a theoretical background, see L. P. Bradford, J. R. Gibb, and K. D. Benne, eds. *T-group theory and laboratory method.* New York: Wiley, 1964; and E. H. Schein, and W. G. Bennis. *Personal and organizational change via group methods.* New York: Wiley, 1965.

psychotherapy or some form of clinical experience is necessary preparation for the change agent. Argyris, as consultant, confronts the group with their behavior toward him as an analogue of their behavior *vis-a-vis* their own subordinates.

If the role of the consultant sounds ambiguous and vague, this probably reflects reality. Certainly in the consultant approach the processes of change and the change agent's interventions are less systematic and less programmed than in training or applied research programs. A word about the latter.

APPLIED RESEARCH

I refer here to research in which the results are used systematically as an *intervention*. Most methods of research application collect information and report it. Generally, the relationship ends there. In the survey-feedback approach, as developed primarily by Floyd Mann (1957) and his associates at The University of Michigan's Institute for Social Research, this is only the beginning. Data are reported in "feedback" meetings where subjects become clients and have a chance to review the findings, test them against their own experience, and even ask the researchers to test some of their hypotheses. Instead of being submitted "in triplicate" and probably ignored, research results serve to activate involvement and participation in the planning, collection, analysis, and interpretation of more data.

Richard Beckhard, too, utilizes data as the first step in his work as change agent (in press). In his procedure the data are collected through formal, nonstructured interviews which he then codes by themes about the managerial activities of the client for discussion at an off-site meeting with the subjects.

It should be stressed that most planned-change inductions involve all three processes—training, consulting, researching—and that both agent and client play a variety of roles. The final shape of the change agent's role is not as yet clear, and it is hazardous to report exactly what change agents do on the basis of their reports. Many factors, of course, determine the particular intervention the change agent may choose: cost, time, degree of collaboration required, state of target system, and so on.

STRATEGIC MODELS EMPLOYED BY CHANGE AGENTS

More often than not, change agents fail to report their strategy or to make it explicit. It may be useful to look at two quite different models that are available: one developed by Robert Blake in his "Managerial Grid" system, and one with which I was associated at an Esso refinery and which Chris Argyris evaluated some years later.

Blake has developed a change program based on his analytic framework of managerial styles (Blake, Mouton, Barnes, and Greiner, 1964). Figure 1 shows the grid for locating types of managerial strategies. Blake and his colleagues attempt to change the organization in the direction of "team management" (9, 9 or high concern for people and high concern for production).

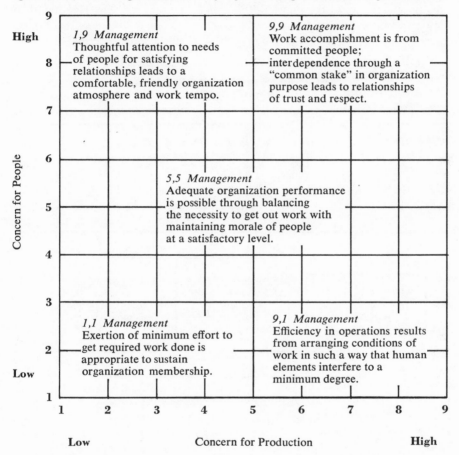

Fig.1. The managerial grid®. [From The Managerial Grid *by Dr. Robert R. Blake and Dr. Jane S. Mouton. Copyright 1964, Gulf Publishing Company, Houston, Texas. Used with permission.]*

Based on experience with 15 different factories, the Blake strategy specifies six phases: off-site laboratory for "diagonal slice" of personnel; off-site program focused on team training for "family" groups; training in the plant location designed to achieve better integration between functional groups; goal-setting sessions for groups of 10 to 12 managers.

Blake and his colleagues estimate that these four phases may require two years or longer. The next two, implementing plans and stabilizing changes, may require an additional two years.

Figure 2 (Argyris, 1960) presents another strategy: a change program used in a large oil company to improve the functioning of one of its smaller refineries. A new manager was named and sent to a T-Group training session to gain awareness of the human problems in the refinery. The Headquarters Organizational Development staff then conducted a diagnosis through a survey and interview of the managerial staff (70) and a sample of hourly

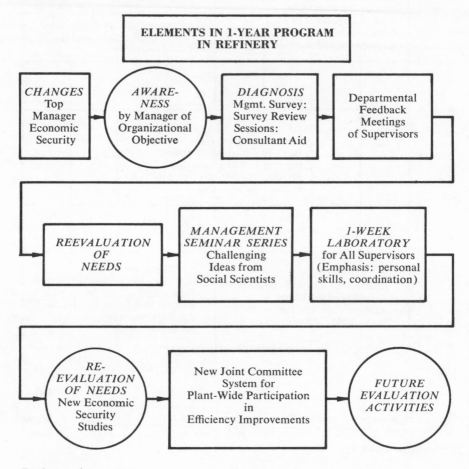

Fig.2. A change program

employees (40/350). About that time the author was brought in to help the headquarters staff and the new manager.

It was decided that a laboratory program of T-Groups might be effective but premature, with the result that weekly seminars that focused on new developments in human relations were held with top management (about 20). A one-week laboratory training program followed for all supervisors in diagonal slices, and then another reevaluation of needs was undertaken. Some structural innovations were suggested and implemented. During the last phase of the program (not shown in the figure), the Scanlon Plan was adapted and installed (incidentally, for the first time in a "process" industry and for the first time that a union agreed to the Plan without a bonus automatically guaranteeed).

Though it cannot be said with any assurance that these two strategies are typical, it may be helpful to identify certain features: (a) *length of time* (Blake estimates five years; the refinery program took two years up to the Scanlon Plan); (b) *variety of programs* utilized (research, consulting, training, teaching, planning); (c) *necessity of cooperation* with top management and the parent organization; (d) approaching the organization *as a system* rather than as a collection of individuals; (e) *phasing program* from individual to group to intergroup to overall organization; (f) intellectual *and* emotional content.

POWER AND THE ROLE OF THE CHANGE AGENT

How and why do people and organizations change, and what is the nature and source of the power exerted by the change agent? We have to make inferences because change agents themselves tend to be silent on this. It is not *coercive power,* for the change agent generally does not have the ability to reward or punish. Moreover, he would prefer, at least intellectually, not to wield power at variance with his normative goals. Further, there is some evidence that coercive power is less durable than are other kinds of power, except under conditions of vigilant surveillance.

Traditional power? Almost certainly not. The change agent is, in fact, continually working without legitimization. *Expert power?* Possibly some, but it is doubtful whether his knowledge is considered "expert" enough—in the sense that an engineer or doctor or lawyer is seen as expert. *Referent* or *identification power?* Apparently so. Sofer, for example, attributes some influence to the client system's ability and desire to emulate the change agent. Still, this will vary from a considerable degree to not at all.

This leaves us with *value power* as the likeliest candidate of the possible sources of power. Most change agents do emit cues to a consistent value system. These values are based on Western civilization's notion of a scientific humanism: concern for our fellow man, experimentalism, openness and honesty, flexibility, cooperation, democracy. If what I have said about power is correct, it is significant (at least in the United States) that this set of values seems to be potent in influencing top management circles.

CHARACTERISTICS OF CLIENT SYSTEM

For the most part, the client systems appear to be subsystems of relatively large-scale international operations who find themselves in increasingly competitive situations, in rapidly changing environments, subjected to what have been called "galloping variables." Often the enterprise was founded through an innovation or monopolistic advantage which is thought to be in jeopardy.

Then there is some tension—some discrepancy between the ideal and the actual—which seems to activate the change program.

Finally, there is some faith in the idea that an intermediate proportion of organizational effectiveness is determined by social and psychological factors and that improvement here, however vague or immeasurable, may improve organizational effectiveness.

THE MEASUREMENT OF EFFECTS

Until very recently, change agents, if they did any evaluation research at all, concentrated almost exclusively on attitudinal and subjective factors. Even so-called "hard" behavioral variables, like absentee rates, sickness and accident rates, personnel turnover, and so forth, were rarely investigated. Relating change programs to harder criteria, like productivity and economic and cost factors, was rarely attempted and never, to my knowledge, successful.

And again, the research that was conducted—even on the attitudinal measures—was far from conclusive. Roger Harrison attempted an evaluation study of Argyris' work and found that while there was a significant improvement in the individual executive's interpersonal ability compared with a control group, there was no significant "transfer" of this acuity to the real-life organizational setting. In short, there was a fairly rapid "fade-out" of effects obtained in T-Group training upon return to the organization (Harrison, 1962). This study also shows that new tensions were generated between those individuals who attended the training program and those who did not—an example of the lack of a *systems* approach. Shepard's evaluation on the Esso organization shows that the impact of laboratory training was greatest on personal and interpersonal learnings, but "slightly more helpful than useless" in changing the organization.

More recently, though, some studies have been undertaken which measure more meaningful, less subjective variables of organizational effectiveness. Blake, Mouton, Barnes, and Greiner (1964), for example, conducted an evaluation study of their work in a very large (4,000 employees) petrochemical plant. Not only did they find significant changes in the values, morale, and interpersonal behavior of the employees, but significant improvements in productivity, profits, and cost reduction. David (in press), a change agent working on a program that attempts to facilitate a large and complicated merger, attributed the following effects to the programs: increased productivity, reduced turnover and absenteeism, in addition to a significant improvement in the area of attitudes and subjective feelings.

While these new research approaches show genuine promise, much more has to be done. The research effort has somehow to equal all the energy that goes into developing the planned-change programs themselves.

SOME CRITICISMS AND QUALIFICATIONS

The work of the change agents reported here is new and occurs without the benefit of methodological and strategic precedents. The role of the change agent is also new, its final shape not fully emerged. Thus it has both the advantage of freedom from the constraints facing most men of knowledge, and suffers from lack of guidelines and structure. Let us touch quickly on problems and criticisms facing the change agents.

PLANNED CHANGE AND ORGANIZATIONAL EFFECTIVENESS

I can identify six dimensions of organizational effectiveness: legal, political, economic, technological, social, and personal. There is a good deal of fuzziness as to which of these change agents hope to affect, and the data are inconclusive. Argyris, who is the most explicit about the relationship between performance and interpersonal competence, is still hoping to develop good measures to establish a positive relationship. The connection has to be made, or the field will have to change its normative goal of constructing not only a *better* world but a more *effective* one.

A QUESTION OF VALUES

The values espoused indicate a way of *behaving and feeling;* for example, they emphasize openness rather than secrecy, collaboration rather than dependence or rebellion, cooperation rather than competition, consensus rather than individual rules, rewards based on self-control rather than externally induced rewards, team leadership rather than a one-to-one relationship with the boss, authentic relationships rather than those based on political maneuvering.

Are they natural? Desirable? Functional? What then happens to status or power drives? What about those individuals who have a low need for participation and/or a high need for structure and dependence? And what about those personal needs which seem to be incompatible with these images of man, such as a high need for aggression and a low need for affiliation? In short, what about those needs which can be best realized through bureaucratic systems? Or benevolent autocracies? Are these individuals to be changed or to yield and comply?

The problem of values deserves discussion. One of the obstacles is the emotional and value overtones which interfere with rational dialogue. More often than not, one is plunged into a polarized debate which converts ideas into ideology and inquiry into dogma. So we hear of "Theory X vs. Theory Y," personality vs. organization, democratic vs. autocratic, task vs. maintenance, human relations vs. scientific management, and on and on.

Surely life is more complicated than these dualities suggest, and surely they must imply a continuum—not simply extremes.

LACK OF SYSTEMS APPROACH

Up to this point, I have used the term "organizational change" rather loosely. In Argyris' case, for example, organizational change refers to a change in values of 11 top executives, a change which was not necessarily of an enduring kind and apparently brought about some conflict with other interfaces. In most other cases of planned organizational change, the change induction was limited to a small, elite group. Only in the work of Blake and some others can we confidently talk about organizational change—in a systems way; his program includes the training of the entire management organization, and at several locations he has carried this step to include wage earners.

Sometimes the changes brought about simply "fade out" because there are no carefully worked out procedures to ensure coordination with other interacting parts of the system. In other cases, the changes have "backfired" and have had to be terminated because of their conflict with interface units. In any case, a good deal more has to be learned about the interlocking and stabilizing changes so that the total system is affected.

SOME GENERALIZATIONS

It may be useful, as peroration, to state in the most tentative manner some generalizations. They are derived, for the most part, from the foregoing discussion and anchored in experience and, wherever possible, in research and theory.

First, a forecast: I suspect that we will see an increase in the number of planned-change programs along the lines discussed here—toward *less* bureaucratic and *more* participative, "open-system" and adaptive structures. Given the present pronounced rate of change, the growing reliance on science for the success of the industrial enterprise, the growing number of professionals joining these enterprises, and the "turbulent contextual environment" facing the firm, we can expect increasing demand for social inventions to revise traditional notions of organized effort.

As far as adopting and acceptance go, we already know a good deal.[8] *Adoption* requires that the *type* of change should be of proven quality, easily demonstrable in its effects, and with information easily available. Its cost and accessibility to control by the client system as well as its value accord have to be carefully considered.

Acceptance also depends on the relationship between the change agent and the client system: the more profound and anxiety-producing the change, the more collaborative and closer relationship required. In addition, we can predict that an anticipated change will be resisted to the degree that the client system possesses little or incorrect knowledge about the change, has relatively little trust in the source of the change, and has comparatively low influence in controlling the nature and direction of the change.

What we know least about is *implementation*—a process which includes the creation of understanding and commitment toward a particular change and devices whereby it can become integral to the client system's operations. I will try to summarize the necessary elements in implementation:

a. The *client system* should have as much understanding of the change and its consequences, as much influence in developing and controlling the fate of the change, and as much trust in the initiator of the change as is possible.

b. The *change effort* should be perceived as being as self-motivated and voluntary as possible. This can be effected through the legitimization and reinforcement of the change by the top management group and by the significant reference groups adjacent to the client system. It is also made possible by providing the utmost in true volition.

c. The *change program* must include emotional and value as well as cognitive (informational) elements for successful implementation. It is doubtful that relying solely on rational persuasion (expert power) is sufficient. Most organizations possess the knowledge to cure their ills; the rub is utilization.

d. The *change agent* can be crucial in reducing the resistance to change. As long as the change agent acts congruently with the principles of the program and as long as the client has a chance to test competence and

[8]See, in particular, E. Rogers. *The diffusion of innovations.* New York: The Free Press, 1962; and M. Miles, ed. *Innovation in education.* New York: Bureau of Publications, Teachers College, Columbia University, 1964.

motives (his own and the change agent's), the agent should be able to provide the psychological support so necessary during the risky phases of change. As I have stressed again and again, the quality of the client-agent relationship is pivotal to the success of the change program.

REFERENCES

Ackoff, R. L., and Rivett, P. *A manager's guide to operations research.* New York: Wiley, 1963. P. 34.

Argyris, C. *Organization development: An inquiry into the Esso approach.* New Haven: Yale University, 1960.

Argyris, C. *Interpersonal competence and organizational effectiveness.* Homewood, Ill.: Dorsey, 1962. P. 43.

Beckhard, R. An organization improvement program in a decentralized organization. D. Zand, ed., *Organization development: Theory and practice,* in press.

Bennis, W. G., Benne, K. D., and Chin, R., eds. *The planning of change.* New York: Holt, Rinehart & Winston, 1961.

Blake, R. R., Mouton, Jane S., Barnes, L. B., and Greiner, L. E. Breakthrough in organization development. *Harvard Business Review,* 1964, **42**(6), 133-155.

Boskoff, A. Functional analysis as a source of a theoretical repertory and research tasks in the study of social change. G. K. Zollschan and W. Hirsch, *Explorations in social change.* Boston: Houghton Mifflin, 1964.

Chin, R. The utility of system models and developmental models for practitioners. W. G. Bennis, K. D. Benne, and R. Chin, eds., *The planning of change.* New York: Holt, Rinehart & Winston, 1961. Pp. 201-214.

Chin, R. Models and ideas about changing. Paper read at Symposium on Acceptance of New Ideas, University of Nebraska, November, 1963.

Coser, L. *The functions of social conflict.* New York: Free Press, 1956.

Dahrendorf, R. Toward a theory of social conflict. W. G. Bennis, K. D. Benne, and R. Chin, eds., *The planning of change.* New York: Holt, Rinehart & Winston, 1961. Pp. 445-451.

David, G. The Weldon study: An organization change program based upon change in management philosophy. D. Zand, ed., *Organization development: Theory and practice,* in press.

Freeman, H. E. The strategy of social policy research. *The Social Welfare Forum,* 1963, 143-160.

Gibb, J. R., and Lippitt, R., eds. Consulting with groups and organizations. *Journal of Social Issues,* 1959, 15.

Glock, C. Y., Lippitt, R., Flanagan, J. C., Wilson, E. C., Shartle, C. L., Wilson, M. L., Croker, G. W., and Page, H. E. *Case studies in bringing behavioral science into use.* Stanford, Calif.: Inst. Commun. Res., 1960.

Harrison, R. Chapter 11. C. Argyris, ed., *Interpersonal competence and organizational effectiveness.* Homewood, Ill.: Dorsey, 1962.

Leeds, R., and Smith, T., eds. *Using social science knowledge in business and industry.* Homewood, Ill.: Irwin, 1963.

Likert, R., and Hayes, S. P., Jr., eds. *Some applications of behavioral research.* Paris: UNESCO, 1957.

Mann, F. Studying and creating change: A means to understanding social organization. *Research in industrial relations.* Ann Arbor: Industrial Relations Research Association, 1957, Publication No. 17.

Merton, R. K., and Lerner, D. Social scientists and research policy. D. Lerner and H. D. Lasswell, eds., *The policy sciences: Recent developments in scope and method.* Stanford, Calif.: Stanford University Press, 1951.

Myrdal, G. *Value in social theory.* New York: Harper, 1958. P. 29.

Parsons, R. T. Evolutionary universals in society. *American Sociological Review,* 1964, **29**, 339-357.

Salisbury, H. E. *To Moscow and beyond.* New York: Harper, 1960. P. 136.

Shepard, H. Three management programs and the theory behind them. *An action research program for organization improvement.* Ann Arbor, Mich.: Foundation for Research on Human Behavior, 1960.

Sofer, C. *The organization from within.* London: Tavistock, 1961.

Zetterberg, H. L. *Social theory and social practice.* Totowa, N. J.: Bedminster, 1962.

suggested additional readings

Bennis, W. G., Benne, K. D., and Chin, R., eds. *The planning of change,* Second Edition. New York: Holt, Rinehart, & Winston, 1969.

Sarason, S. B., Levine, M., Goldenberg, I. I., Cherlin, D. L., and Bennett, E. M. *Psychology in community settings: Clinical, educational, vocational, social aspects.* New York: Wiley, 1966.

Schein, E. and Bennis, W. G., eds. *Personal and organizational change through group methods.* New York: Wiley, 1965.

five   mental health manpower

A recent television commercial has implored, "Please, Mother, I'd rather do it myself!" Even if the community psychologist wanted to do everything himself, he could not. Even if one person had all the competencies required, he would not have the time to do what was required. As a result, indirect techniques such as consultation and training are essential. In consultation and training, the community psychologist shares his knowledge and skills to enable other people to make contributions to the adaptation of the community. In other words, the community psychologist does his part to increase competence and fuctional efficiency of community caregivers. This approach is especially significant when considered in terms of the growing shortage of professional manpower. For example, it would take a full work week for a psychologist to work with every child in one elementary school classroom. The classroom teacher, on the other hand, works with all the children for hours each day, five days a week. Through consultation or in-service training with the teacher, the psychologist is able to have an indirect impact on all the children in the class. Thus, "mental health" filters down from the community psychologist to the grass-roots level via the caregiver.

Manpower and training are of interest to the community psychologist for a number of other reasons. In addition to the shortage of mental health manpower, the personnel that now comprise the mental health manpower pool are, by and large, traditionally trained. Are the models in which they were trained relevant to the existing problems? Do the techniques in which they were trained have demonstrated effectiveness? Many conclude that it is necessary to train more people and to train them differently than they have been trained in the past. The community psychologist is, of course, interested in training community psychologists and others to work in the field of community mental health. Through training programs community psychologists can provide a competent corps of nonprofessionals who ordinarily would not be in the mental health-human services field. Thus the mental health manpower pool can be enlarged while, at the same time, new careers can be developed for people who lack profitable careers.

Because of a willingness to innovate, prevent, and act on a wide variety of social issues, some interesting developments have taken place in the training of new manpower. Attempts have been made to train people from the community at large. One example of this is the training of the so-called "indigenous nonprofessionals."

The willingness of professionals to work with nonprofessionals may be the critical factor in the development of sufficient manpower resources to meet human needs. The articles in this section cast some light on the issues involved. What are the implications of the conceptual model under which we operate? What are its manpower requirements? How do we recruit and select people for new training programs? How do we insure a "career ladder" or upward mobility for people in the new career programs? While training nonprofessionals, paraprofessionals, and new professional groups will not be the be-all and end-all for social problems in the community, we can learn from our experiences in the training area and see significant advances in the delivery of human services.

In the first article, Bennett mentioned that the Boston Conference generally rejected the traditional "medical model" for community mental health. George Albee discusses this viewpoint further, with particular reference to the implications models have for the shortage of mental health manpower. If a social learning model is adopted in place of an illness model, unattainable manpower requirements for medical and paramedical personnel are replaced by realistic requirements for other kinds of personnel, at other levels of training. Albee sees psychology as fulfilling the role of the developer of conceptual models and research bases for application.

The ecological model suggested by Kelly in Section one, and the competence model discussed by Phillips in the next section are also extremely attractive alternatives to the traditional mental health models. While these models would require a good deal of rethinking and retooling on the part of the professions, they also are consistent with more realistic and attainable manpower requirements.

conceptual models and manpower requirements in psychology

George W. Albee

It is increasingly clear that the current and the prospective professional manpower shortages in the mental health field derive primarily from a set of interacting considerations that go somewhat as follows:

Disturbed and disturbing human behavior currently is "explained" by a conceptual model which attributes causation to "disease" or to some form of "illness." The content of the explanatory model accounting for these sorts of human deviation dictates the specific kind of institutional structure which society must support for the delivery of care or intervention. And the nature of the institution in turn dictates the kind of manpower required for its staffing. So we are confronted with a desperate shortage of medical and paramedical professionals required to staff hospitals, clinics, and centers. This shortage is going to worsen in the years ahead as the institutional demands proliferate while the manpower supply does not.

Because of the primacy of the disease explanation for disturbed behavior, the largest share of available funds for training and for research is funneled into biomedical programs. These training programs are producing professionals who, after being trained at public expense, do not work primarily with these serious, chronically disturbed people who are the responsibility of tax-supported institutions (Arnhoff and Shriver, 1967). And, further, the biomedically oriented research programs demanded by the disease model support complex laboratory research studies that have little relevance to the real etiological problems of disturbed people.

There is a current, popular platitude which says that the social and behavioral sciences seriously lag the physical and biological sciences in knowledge. If only, it is opined, we could make faster progress in behavioral science, if only we could learn as much about the human being as we know already about germs and atoms, then more effective programs could be developed to deal with man's problems with himself and with his fellows.

This reading of the knowledge situation is far from accurate. We *do* know a great deal in the behavioral sciences, but many of the things we know are threatening to the mental health Establishment and therefore to the status quo. For example, we know very well that *the nature of the social world of the infant and child in the family* are of primary importance as determinants of subsequent rates of disturbed behavior. In our Western culture the stable family is the best bulwark against later behavioral and emotional disturbance. Efforts at prevention of mental disorder should be directed to those social institutions that affect family stability directly or indirectly, positively or negatively. For hopelessly disrupted families we should seek new ways of providing the best possible alternatives for the children affected—whether in foster homes or specially designed institutions like kibbutzim.

When eventually alternative explanatory models for disturbed behavior are widely tolerated, and institutions based on them supported with public funds are available, there will still be real mental illness to keep busy the organically oriented psychiatrist. All of the emotional problems associated with serious central nervous system malfunctioning, seizure states, toxic and endocrinologically induced psychoses, and the problems of organically induced behavioral disturbances in general will be left. But of course these are not the conditions that interest contemporary psychiatry, perhaps in part because there is so little token reinforcement with these kinds of cases! Psychotherapy is the primary professional activity in psychiatry, and mild neurotics are the preferred cases.

The mental health establishment has made so many promises to so many groups in our society that it is beyond the wildest manpower dream that it can begin to supply these services (Albee, 1967). Let me just mention some of these new demands without elaborating them.

The labor unions, particularly the United Auto Workers, have negotiated contracts for outpatient psychiatric care for their members and families —more than two and a half million UAW people suddenly have become eligible for outpatient mental health care. Other unions actively are establishing their own mental health clinics. Once one union does these things other unions must begin to do them too, and all of these new plans require scarce professional manpower.

Perhaps the single most important recent legislative act in this whole field, so far as manpower demand is concerned, was Medicare. Without going through all of the different components of Medicare, it can be said for sure that an enormous new group of users of mental health services suddenly is eligible for prepaid or insured care. One of the most important parts of Medicare is Title 19, under which anyone defined as "medically indigent," along with their children, is eligible for outpatient psychiatric care and other mental health services. There will be very large new demands for professional mental health care under this law.

Nor need we dwell long on the 2,000 new comprehensive mental health centers that the National Institute of Mental Health promises will be built by 1980 with Federal, state, and local funds. The demand for professional medical and paramedical care in these centers is beyond all hope of realization. How can the 2,000 centers be staffed when two thirds of our existing 2,000 psychiatric clinics are without a single full-time psychiatrist, and when little psychiatric care is available in at least one third of our state hospitals (National Committee against Mental Illness, 1966)?

There is no point in discussing the Appalachian program, although it contains more extensive blueprints for programs in mental health than the whole Comprehensive Community Mental Health Centers Act!

Nor need there be further elaboration on current manpower shortages in all the other professions represented in the 2,000 existing "psychiatric" clinics, the VA hospitals, the state hospitals, in higher education, etc. The point I hope to leave with you in this recitation of the growing demand for mental health services is this: All of the plans for increasing professional services for the aged, for the union members and their families, for the medically indigent, for the inner-city poor, and for all the others lining up for care—all of these programs are going to fail because we do not have enough of the *kind* of manpower demanded by the disease model of mental disorder.

It is so simple. The explanatory model dictates the kind of professional manpower needed to staff the institutions. This means a current and future need for nonexistent medical and paramedical professionals. Since 1958, when the Bane report was made to the Secretary of Health, Education, and Welfare (Bane, 1959), it has been the consensus of all manpower experts that we should be producing at least 11,000 physicians a year in this country, if we are only to stay even in the ratio of physicians to population! But we are not training this number. Currently we are training only 7,500 annually—so, year after year, we fall at least 3,500 new MDs farther behind the number that would be required just to keep our ratio of physicians to population constant. The only possible conclusion is that physicians, and, as a consequence, psychiatrists, are going to be in even shorter supply, while all of these service demands I sketched a moment ago are mushrooming everywhere.

Elsewhere I have argued that the future available supply of clinical psychologists and social workers is at least as inadequate as the prospective supply in psychiatry (Albee, 1967). The demands for academicians in psychology, for example, can absorb most of the PhDs we produce over the next decade or two. Because psychology is a relatively young profession there has not been a large replacement demand for faculty members in this field. In other academic fields this replacement figure approaches 6% a year. As psychology professors continue to age we will need to hire replacements in addition to those needed for the expanding student enrollments.

Any manpower planning for mental health care as now conceived must confront explicitly these prospective chronic shortages of professionals. If we continue to use the illness model of mental disorder, we cannot produce a fraction of the medical and paramedical people the model demands. This would not be a sufficient reason for abandoning the illness model, if it were supported firmly by research evidence. But the evidence supporting it is thin indeed. What I am suggesting is that we are in a manpower *cul de sac* because of the conceptual model we use. The development of alternative models could lead to new manpower solutions because they would allow for new institutional solutions requiring manpower more easily recruited and trained.

Eventually the demands of society will prevail. The times are ripe for new models, for new ideas. We cannot push along this social change unless we develop a new set of concepts, a new conceptual armamentarium, a new language, a new delivery system for service.

This reconceptualization must follow rejection by psychology of the illness model. But it is not simply a matter of blowing a trumpet and seeing the walls collapse! The illness model is supported by powerful forces. There are many reasons for its persistence in the field of functional behavior disorder (Albee, 1967).

The model was developed, and it has persisted, because it was more convincing than the sin, taint, or demonic explanations. Also, the early success in finding the spirochete to be the cause of paresis led to hopes that other mental "illnesses" also had similar causes. Further, it seemed more and more as though genetic factors were important. The illness explanation also supported the practice of putting victims out of sight in plague houses until "a cure" was found. Money could be spent on chemical and biological research, without upsetting the value hierarchy in the society. Finally, both family and society could avoid personal responsibility for mental disorder. They could blame *Fate*.

Perhaps, however, the most compelling reason of all for the persistence of this model has been the absence of any alternative model. A scientific model will persist until a more valid and more convincing model appears.

Over the past 20 years there have begun to emerge out of psychotherapy, experimental work in the learning laboratory, cultural anthropology, and social work, to name just a few sources, elements of an explanatory model for disturbed behavior which might be called the *social learning theory*. This theory argues that most disturbed behavior consists of learned operant anxiety-avoiding responses. The origins of the anxiety to be avoided are to be found in traumatic social interaction of infants and children with the parents or parent surrogates. Evidence to support this explanatory model is accumulating in the research literature.

I suggest that as psychologists we have played the illness game for 20 years and this is long enough. The rules of the illness game are such that there will never be enough professional people available to provide care except to selected members of the middle and upper classes. As long as the illness model occupies the center of the stage, all of the planning, all of the action is going to deal with psychiatric treatment, mental hospital beds, and the Team. Psychology must create its own institutional structure for developing methods for the delivery of service, because only in its own structure can it begin to elaborate this new conceptual model—the dimensions of which I have sketched so briefly—together with the language and the intervention methods that eventually will permit people with a bachelor's degree (or even less education) to be the line workers in the field of behavioral disorders.

Let me emphasize that I do *not* see psychology as the care-delivery field. We can never have the manpower to meet the demands. Rather, we must create the theory and show how it is applicable, to enable care to be given by bachelor's level people in habilitation centers that they themselves administer. Psychology can only be the developer of the conceptual models and of the research underpinning. The parallel with the field of education is evident. Intervention in the educational system is by bachelor's level teachers who are supported by more highly trained research workers from several fields. Only when institutions are built in which BA people can work with disturbed or retarded children and adults (perhaps Project Re-ed is the best example of what I have in mind) will we begin to meet the demand.

Frankly, I find it astonishing that all of us as parents, and as citizens, are willing to send our children to the daily ministrations of school teachers trained essentially at the bachelor's level, and yet we insist that professionals dealing with our emotionally disturbed and mentally retarded children and adults must have far more training than teachers for their face-to-face intervention.

Let us start developing an institutional structure where the rules and language are based on research findings in behavior modification. Let us develop centers where technicians, nonprofessionals, rehabilitation workers of all kinds can be used to maximize human potential. Until we have a conceptual assessment system that uses indications of strength we will still be playing the illness game. The new model which I think we must develop will stress the maximization of human effectiveness. I have argued that this model will not be built until psychology develops it in its own service delivery setting from which we can also go out into those community agencies where the real problems are.

Once society accepts the position that most, if not all, functionally disturbed behavior represents learned patterns of anxiety avoidance, the institutions developed to deal with these conditions may well be *educational* in nature.

Albert Bandura (1967) has said it well:

> The day may not be far off when psychological disorders will be treated not in hospitals or mental hygiene clinics but in comprehensive "learning centers," when clients will be considered not patients suffering from hidden psychic pathologies but responsible people who participate actively in developing their own potentialities [p. 86].

Unless psychology assumes leadership in developing alternatives to the illness model, the mental health manpower picture is going to continue to get worse. We cannot train enough medical and paramedical professionals to meet the manpower needs of hospitals and clinics, but, more important, we cannot use knowledge already available to deal with the pressing problems of our urbanized, automated antihuman existence.

REFERENCES

Albee, G. W. The relation of conceptual models to manpower needs. E. Cowen et al., eds., *Emerging approaches to mental health problems.* New York: Appleton-Century-Crofts, 1967.

Arnhoff, F. N., and Shriver, B. M. A study of the current status of mental health personnel supported under National Institute of Mental Health training grants. United States Department of Health, Education, and Welfare, Public Health Service Publication No. 1541. Washington, D. C.: United States Government Printing Office, 1967.

Bandura, A. Behavioral psychotherapy. *Scientific American*, 1967, **216** (3), 78-86.

Bane, J. Physicians for a growing America. United States Public Health Service Publication No. 709. Washington, D. C.: United States Government Printing Office, 1959.

National Committee against Mental Illness. *What are the facts about mental illness?* Washington, D. C.: Author, 1966.

It is unfortunate that in professional training very little, if any, attention is given to training people how to train others. As has already been pointed out, the community psychologist needs to be concerned with issues of manpower and training. Frank Riessman has helped to develop the notion of the "indigenous nonprofessional." Here he offers observations on the training of nonprofessionals based upon the experiences of the Lincoln Neighborhood Service Center Project. The Lincoln Project has had a significant influence in breaking down some of the rigid professional barriers related to new manpower and to the delivery of mental health services to the community. Riessman discusses several kinds of situations in which nonprofessionals can be used and a number of factors which have to be considered in training nonprofessionals. His ten suggestions for training nonprofessionals illustrate the complexities involved and affirm that such training does, indeed, require special consideration.

strategies and suggestions for training nonprofessionals

Frank Riessman

Approximately one hundred and fifty thousand nonprofessional positions have been established in the United States as a result of the antipoverty and related legislation. If the nonprofessional revolution is to create more than jobs, if it is to develop genuine careers for the poor, moving them up the ladder, step by step, authentic training is the key (Pearl and Riessman, 1965). Trainers must be trained in how to evaluate nonprofessionals; how to encourage participation; how to listen; how to supervise in new ways; how to provide functional on-the-job learning.

Nonprofessionals are being utilized in a number of different structures. One major model is the neighborhood service center. This may be a storefront, employing 5 to 10 nonprofessionals with one or two supervisors, which was the pattern at the Lincoln Project (Hallowitz and Riessman, 1966), or the larger multiservice neighborhood centers, which may include anywhere from 30 to 200 nonprofessionals with a professional staff of 5 to 30 supervisors.

This model is characterized by a high ratio of nonprofessionals to professionals and a base of operation in the community, on the "home turf," so to speak, of the nonprofessional. The character of the involvement of the NP is likely to be quite different from the second model. Here the NP is attached to a service agency, such as the Welfare Department or the Health Department. He is not in the majority and his base of operations is not in the community but rather in the agency itself. Some of these agencies may be committed to an ideology emphasizing the value and significant new role of the nonprofessional, but in other cases they may simply be utilizing the new

Reprinted from the *Community Mental Health Journal,* 1967, **3**, 103-110, with the permission of Behavioral Publications, Inc. and the author.

manpower because of the assistance it provides to professionals or because funding was available for NP positions.

Thus the variables to be considered are: the ratio of professionals to nonprofessionals; the base of operation, whether it be in the community or in the traditional agency; and the ideology or lack of it connected to the utilization of this new type of personnel. Training and supervisory staff should consider these three dimensions as they have implications for training methodology and supervision and for the development of the nonprofessional, the role he can play, his participation, and his power.

In the Lincoln setting it is interesting to note that nonprofessionals function both in neighborhood-based centers, where they are in the majority, and in a multipurpose clinic, where they are in the minority. At joint staff meetings the professionals have the opportunity to observe all the nonprofessionals (16-32) functioning at a meeting in which there are approximately 25 professionals present. Initially, these meetings included only 5 nonprofessionals. Marked differences in participation took place at the point where the percentage of nonprofessionals significantly increased.

Frequently, professionals assume that NP's identify with the poor and possess great warmth and feeling for the neighborhood of their origin. While many NP's exhibit some of these characteristics, they simultaneously possess a number of other characteristics. Often, they see themselves as quite different from the other members of the poor community, whom they may view with pity, annoyance, or anger. Moreover, there are many different "types" of nonprofessional: some are earthy, some are tough, some are angry, some are surprisingly articulate, some are slick, clever wheeler-dealers, and nearly all are greatly concerned about their new roles and their relationship to professionals.

It is most important to note then that NP's are frequently quite competitive with professionals. In essence, many NP's think they are different from the poor and would be more effective than professionals if they had a chance. Many are aware of the new ideology regarding nonprofessionals that calls attention to the special properties (style, etc.) that enable the NP to communicate with the low-income community in an effective manner. They feel this gives them something of an edge over professionals, and when combined with the training and knowledge they are acquiring in the professional structure, they will be "double smart."

While nonprofessionals may be selected because of certain characteristics they possess, such as informality, humor, earthiness, neighborliness—in other words some of the "positive" characteristics of the resident population —the other side of the coin cannot be ignored. That is, they may possess characteristics of low-income populations that interfere with effective helper roles. For example, they may possess considerable moral indignation, punitiveness, suspicion, or they may be so open and friendly on occasion that the significance of confidentiality escapes them. Thus, while the training staff will want to build on their positive helping traits and potential skills, to some extent there must be an effort to either train out or control some of these other negative characteristics (negative in playing the helping role in a social service framework).

ROLE AMBIGUITY: WHO AM I?

One of the greatest problems experienced by the nonprofessional is role ambiguity or lack of role identity: He does not know who he is or who he is becoming. He is no longer a simple member of the community—if he ever was one—nor is he a professional. Actually, he is a highly marginal person, just as the new community action programs he frequently represents are also highly marginal and lacking in a clear identity.

"Nonprofessional" describes what he is *not,* but does not clearly indicate what he is. He is not simply a citizen nor a volunteer participating in the organization, although the desire to have him represent the feelings of the neighborhood produces some similarity with the citizen advisory board role of the local resident. He is not the traditional kind of employee because his participation, neighborhood know-how, and advice are sought; yet he is also an employee. He is not a professional, even though he does represent the agency and many people in the community may see the aide as a new kind of social worker. He is not a political action organizer, even though he does develop groups in the community concerned with various types of change. He is an amalgam of all these various roles, and his trainers and the leaders of the community action programs must understand and try to clarify this new role. But to repeat, the role itself has strains and contradictions, and the nonprofessional must be assisted to live within the framework of these dilemmas. He is the new marginal man. He must be selected with this in mind, trained and supervised in this fashion, and assisted in forging this new role. Perhaps he will become the new integrated man for the "Other America."

Finally, the ambiguity is also related to the unclarity of goals and programs in the rapidly developing community action programs. The newness of the programs, the vagueness of many of the goals, and the fact that the tasks for nonprofessionals are only beginning to be defined contribute to the total atmosphere of amorphousness and produce confusion and anxiety. The programs are new, the jobs are new, and the personnel are new. Clearly, flexible and innovative supervisors and trainers are required to function in this difficult, rapidly evolving situation. All staff members, supervisory and nonprofessional, should be made honestly aware of the character of the situation; that is, the fact that it is rapidly changing and not highly structured and traditional. Some tolerance has to be built up for this climate and some structure has to be provided as quickly as possible. To some extent, structure can be achieved by attempting to define as specifically as possible the job function, and the description of it should be provided in as much detail as possible without sounding overwhelming.

PHASED TRAINING

The relationship of training to job performance for the nonprofessional is different than it is for other types of employees. Perhaps the main reason for this is the general lack of skill possessed by the nonprofessional and, more particularly, the lack of certain requisite skills for the new jobs (e.g., record-keeping).

The traditional principle that long periods of training are necessary before an individual can be employed must be reversed; the motto should be "Jobs First—Training Built In."

It has become axiomatic that most of the training of the nonprofessional will take place on the job itself. This requires that job functions be phased in slowly and that the NP's receive ample time to master the required tasks at each stage before going on to more advanced tasks.

Prejob training (to be distinguished from core training or the training in basic knowledge which can take place throughout the program) should be oriented primarily to enabling the NP to perform the simplest entry features of the job in a fairly adequate fashion. Moreover, the job itself must be broken down and phased in, so that in the initial stage the nonprofessional will be required to perform only limited aspects of the job itself. Further skills will be learned on the job itself, through on-the-job training and systematic in-service training.

The preservice period should be short lest anxiety be built up and the aide become threatened by the anticipated job. The learning should be active; the aide should be doing things, and knowledge and concepts should be brought in around the discussion of his activities.

As quickly as possible the aide should be placed on the job itself for a part of the day under close professional supervision. The sooner the aides can get their feet wet, the better they will feel. Thus, in the Lincoln Project, the aides were placed on the job in the Neighborhood Service Center for one half a day in this prejob period (after a three-week period spent in job simulation, practice, etc.). The half day in which they were not working was utilized to discuss the specific experiences they were having.

Beyond this point, the really significant training and learning will occur on the job itself and in carefully planned discussion about the work they are doing. It is not to be assumed, unlike many other positions, that the NP knows his job when he begins it. Rather, in the early stages of this on-the-job experience, he is actually involved in continuous training, and the first job operations are to be considered preliminary aspects of the position that he will ultimately fulfill. He is really still in training on the job itself.

ON-THE-JOB TRAINING

On-the-job training, then, becomes decisive, and different types of on-the-job training should be considered. The aides will learn from simply performing some of the tasks—that is, they will learn from their own experience; the aides will learn from each other (utilizing peer learning and the helper principle); the aides will learn from their supervisor, who will support them and correct their mistakes and provide assistance at any time on request. The aides will also learn from a special series of group meetings that can be held. One such group can be concerned with systematic training introducing, for example, further skills in interviewing. There can also be group discussions about general problems being experienced: on-the-job problems with professionals, problems with other agencies, problems about their own marginality, problems stemming from competition with each other or annoyance with the type of supervision they are receiving. These discussions should be task centered, with personality and individual components coming in as relevant (the traditional sensitivity training—T-group—experience seems to require considerable modification if it is to be used with the nonprofessional population).

Another very significant type of informal training can be developed as the program of the agency moves forward. In the Lincoln NSC Program the initial phase was concerned with providing and expediting service. After a number of months, the program moved toward the development of groups, committees, community action, campaigns (voter registration, etc.). At this point the program had to be discussed with the aides, and this provided an excellent opportunity for the introduction of new training with regard to concepts and skills. Thus, in order to involve clients in a community meeting, it was necessary to discuss with the aides plans for calling such a meeting, how to conduct the meeting, how to bring the client population to the meeting, how to develop committees, and so on.

The discussion, which was program-centered for the most part, brought in training in what might be described as an informal but highly functional fashion. But it is exactly in this fashion that the aides seemed to learn best. They needed to know how to conduct a meeting, develop participation in committees, and the like, and consequently their motivation was high and the learning was sensitive and highly directed. Moreover, issues about how fast can we move, what kinds of action can we take, what is our relationship to the community became commonplace discussion, and the concepts and goals of the program were easily introduced in this context. For example, one of the aides asked why we couldn't use an Alinsky-type TWO program approach. Other aides suggested that if we did, we wouldn't have our jobs long. The leader indicated that there were target populations among the poor whom the Alinsky groups did not influence easily but that our agency, because of its legitimacy, might be able to work with and involve in various types of nonmilitant activity. A great deal of excited discussion took place and apparently much concrete understanding regarding the agency's viewpoint emerged.

To take another example: At one of the community meetings that was called, where over 100 people from the neighborhood attended, the combined enthusiasm of the aides who led the meeting and the client-citizens who attended it went into the formation of eight different committees. In a discussion after the meeting the aides were able to understand fairly easily that they had really run ahead of themselves; that they had taken on more work than the agency could handle. Various methods for consolidating the committees and developing volunteers were then discussed in a highly meaningful fashion. Thus the fact that the programs of the new neighborhood service centers are not fully developed can be used to good advantage in the phasing of the training of the nonprofessionals. As these programs develop, new training appropriate to the program phase can be introduced, and this is a most meaningful way for the aides to learn.

The Howard Community Apprentice Program provides another illustration of functional learning. Initially the functionally illiterate research aides in the Howard Program interviewed each other with a tape recorder and learned only the simplest principles of interviewing in order to perform this task. Before long, they recognized that they needed to know something about how to record this information and categorize it, and later they needed some statistics in order to analyze it appropriately. As each of these needs became apparent, the appropriate training was introduced to develop the requisite skills. This can be done either formally or informally, through systematic inservice training and/or through informal discussions related to the problem.

HOW TO UNIFY TRAINING AND SUPERVISION

When possible, it seems useful to have one person responsible for selecting the aide (interviewing him either individually or in a group), training him, and supervising him in the actual program. This was the model developed by Mary Dowery at the Mobilization for Youth Parent Education Program. It allowed for identification by the aides with one person and prevented the confusion that develops when there are multiple leaders. The limitations in this type of model relate to the fact that one person cannot encompass all the required skills that are to be imparted to the NP's. This difficulty can, to some degree, be minimized by introducing a number of different consultants as assistants to the trainer at various points. However, the trainer has to utilize this information selectively and interpret to the aides what the consultant is offering. The consultant does not become the leader.

However, in the larger agency model, it will not be as easy for one person to play the multiple roles of selector, trainer, and supervisor. For this model a number of adaptations are recommended.

NP's can be introduced in a circumscribed sphere of the agency—in one department, for example, where the selection, training, and supervisory responsibilities are delegated to one person or to a team of two or three individuals working closely together.

Another possibility is to permit professionals in the larger agency to volunteer to select and work with a nonprofessional assistant, in a sense, functioning as selector, trainer, and supervisor. While some general suggestions can be offered as to how the professionals might use the nonprofessionals, in general it would seem best at this stage to permit the professionals to define the assignments and working relationships. Some professionals will want the NP's, at least at first, to do fairly menial tasks, simply serving as assistants. Others may suggest fairly early that nonprofessionals perform new and meaningful assignments, really discussing things with clients, for example, rather than merely serving as translators. It should be especially valuable for the nonprofessional to work with the professional on a one-to-one basis initially, rather than being involved in a team in which the professionals are the majority.

The professionals who self-select themselves might meet together from time to time with an individual in the organization or a consultant who has responsibility for the development of the use of nonprofessionals—this could be a trainer or other program developer. In these discussions, some of the experiences of the professionals would be exchanged and discussed, problems would be raised, and the specialist or consultant would offer advice, bring in experience from other settings, suggest problems that might arise, indicate different roles that nonprofessionals could play.

This way of involving professionals might be an excellent way in which to introduce the nonprofessionals into a particular institution and establish the tradition of using NP's. The resistance on the part of the professionals who did not self-select themselves for working with nonprofessionals might be dissipated after they observed some of the initial (hopefully) positive experiences of the professionals who volunteered.

In the multiservice centers where large numbers of NP's are to be employed, it will not be possible to integrate the selection, training, and supervisory functions in one individual or small team. To obtain a more full and systematic training product, it is probably best to have the training done by a special training agency. Even though a large part of the training will have to be on the job itself, the training organization can dispatch its senior trainers to the service agency in order to provide the initial on-the-job training. (The training institution can provide prejob training at its own base.) The training agency will, of course, have to work very closely with the service organization and plan to phase out its own role, leaving in its place a training and supervisory capability.

RECOMMENDATIONS

1. Trainers should not expect or demand deep identification with the poor on the part of nonprofessionals, and they should anticipate competitive feelings toward professionals (often professionals other than themselves, but not always).

2. Constant support and assistance must be provided; supervisors should be available for assistance at all times, and it should be clear to the NP that he can request help without any negative implications regarding his evaluation. (Frequently NP's confuse supervisors with factory foremen.) On the other hand, opportunity for considerable initiative and flexibility on the part of the NP must be established. He wants both the flexibility and the support. He is a new kind of employee, and reflecting the developing anti-poverty ideology, he wants more of a say, or at least wants to be consulted, regarding the operation of various programs and rules.

3. The process of obtaining the job must be made as simple and short as possible. Every effort should be made to reduce the competitive feelings that the recruits may develop in relation to other candidates for the position. Long delays between the original time of the job application and later interviews are likely to produce considerable anxiety for the candidate. This attitude may be carried over in the training and on the job itself, thus producing competitive difficulties with other aides and anger toward the program and the staff.

4. The group interview can be used very successfully in selecting applicants. Aside from the fact that it is economical in time, the group process permits the selector to observe how the candidates relate to other people in a group; who influences whom; who listens; who is sensitive; who is overwhelmed by group pressure; who has leadership potential, etc. It is also possible to produce an excellent group atmosphere and develop the beginnings of later camaraderie, *esprit de corps,* group feeling, teamwork, etc. The danger, however, lies in the competitive setting in which the applicants observe that they have to compete against others for a limited number of jobs.

The competitive troubles can be reduced by establishing an informal, friendly setting; coffee and cake should be supplied from the beginning, even before the group forms and starts to talk. A leisurely pace of discussion can be established by the leader or the co-leader. Everybody should be introduced. Plenty of time for warming up should be available. The group should be no larger than 10 people and should be sitting fairly close together in a circle or around a table. But the selectors must make perfectly clear that evaluation is taking place and that it will be difficult to assess people unless they participate and have something to say. Otherwise "quiet ones" will be penalized by this group selection process. The group session itself should stress interaction and not go around the circle having each person announce his interests or goals.

5. Nonprofessionals frequently expect magic from the training process; that is, they expect to learn how to do everything they are supposed to do quite perfectly. To the degree that this is not achieved, they blame the training process. To some extent this reflects a naive view about training, education, and learning. The training staff should be aware that it probably will receive this reaction and insofar as possible should try to explain to the trainees that many dimensions of the job will take some time to learn fully in practice. Fundamentally, of course, the trainees' reaction reflects their anxiety about the new job and role and this has to be dealt with in other ways as indicated below. Trainers also sometimes expect too much from the training; sometimes their expectations of nonprofessionals are initially too high and their appraisal of adequate progress is based on experience with more experienced professional learners. While NP's have some surprising knowledge and understanding of a variety of issues, there are areas of their knowledge that are unbelievably remiss. They often have great gaps in their knowledge or know-how about the system—how to fill out forms, how to make outlines, how to take tests, how to read effectively. Because they are frequently very sensitive and bright in their understanding of people and the neighborhood, the tendency (in halo fashion) is to assume that their understanding is equally good in areas removed from their previous experience. Thus, it is a shock to discover that a nonprofessional who has conducted an excellent interview with a client records the interview inadequately. Constant training and emphasis must be built in to improve report-writing skills, etc.

6. Nonprofessionals have quickly learned that part of the ideology of the antipoverty movement is directed toward developing, not merely jobs for nonprofessionals, but career lines as well. It is therefore extremely important that the agency establish these lines so that there can be aides, assistants, associates, supervisory positions, and possibly assistant neighborhood service center director positions available to the nonprofessional through career development and education. The training staff must clarify these career lines, indicating the relationship of education to them and further indicating the time involved before individuals can expect to "move up." If this is not done

appropriately, aspirations may develop very rapidly and may outstrip possibilities.

7. Nonprofessionals should be encouraged as soon as possible to form their own groups or unions. (We would predict that organization and unionization of the aides will progress fairly rapidly in the coming period.) Aides at Harlem Hospital have been encouraged to meet by themselves, but these meetings have been recorded and utilized by the research staff there. The Lincoln aides meet independently at an "aides-only" meeting, not under the surveillance of their professional supervisors. These groups are very important in developing the power of the aides and a feeling of identification as a group and should contribute greatly to the formation of role identity and job identity. In the Lincoln Project, aides also met off the job on their own time. These meetings led to the development of leadership among the aides, to powerful group identity vis-a-vis the professionals on the staff, and to the raising of a number of highly significant demands: the demand for greater participation in certain aspects of decision making of the organization (this was not an unlimited demand for participation on all decisions); the demand for closer supervision and periodic discussions with the leaders of the program; the curtailment of T-groups (sensitivity training groups, which were highly unpopular among the aides); the demand for career lines to be developed so that nonprofessionals could move up the ladder—the associated demand for education to be provided by the Yeshiva University, of which the Lincoln Project is a part; the demand that if volunteers were to be used, they should be carefully trained; the demand for a greater voice in the selection of delegates to the local Anti-Poverty Community Convention, the request for the aides-only meeting.

8. While much emphasis has been placed on the use of group procedures in training, it should be noted that a great deal of deep learning develops on a one-to-one identification basis. Bank Street College's summer experiment, in which each teacher worked one hour per day with one student, found this one of the most effective learning devices. And Mobilization for Youth's homework helper program, in which one high school youngster worked individually with one elementary school youngster, also supports the value of the one-to-one relationship. This principle can be utilized at a number of points in the training design. As noted above, individual aides can be assigned to professionals in the agency who select themselves for this purpose and volunteer to develop a nonprofessional assistant. We have also found that it is possible to use experienced, trained nonprofessionals to assist in one-to-one work with new trainees; that is, for a period during the day a new trainee can be assigned to work alongside of an experienced nonprofessional. This has to be done selectively or else we will have the "blind leading the blind." But when it is supervised thoroughly, there exists the possibility of utilizing the full advantages of peer learning. Peers learn from each other in very different

ways and sometimes more fully than they learn from "superior" teachers. The "helper principle" notes that the peer teacher (that is, the more advanced aide) learns enormously from imparting information to the trainee; he learns from teaching (Riesman, 1965).

9. While a certain degree of anxiety is useful in stimulating learning, the NP is probably faced by far too much anxiety due to his role ambiguity. Hence, every effort should be made to reduce the anxiety level. This can be achieved by phasing of tasks (not demanding too much too fast), defining the job as carefully as possible, developing group support, providing specific training and evaluation (positive performance should be commended in as detailed a fashion as are weaknesses), providing constant supervisory support and assistance, and holding frank discussions of program and role difficulties. We suspect that the NP's anxiety tolerance is not high and that a learning style that utilizes anxiety stimulation is not characteristic of this population.

10. Many professionals express great concern about nonprofessionals losing their community ties, their feeling for the neighborhood, and their identification with "the people." This is based on the obvious fact that nonprofessionals are no longer simply members of the community but are now employed by an agency. Moreover, since career lines may develop, the NP's can anticipate moving up the ladder and, in some cases, becoming professional.

The issue is not whether the NP identifies with the poor or not, but rather whether he remains committed to them. (Many professionals are committed to the poor without in any way identifying with this population.) What the Anti-Poverty Program needs from the indigenous nonprofessional is his knowledge, his ability to communicate with the poor, and his commitment. It does not need his identification with the poor.

Actually, it generally takes people a long time to lose their knowledge and understanding of the ways, traditions, style, and language of their origin. And if they initially have some commitment, this concern will not fall away overnight. Thus, the commitment and knowledge can remain even if immediate identification diminishes. Moreover, commitment can be maintained by the reinforcement of it by the agency and the training staff. In other words, to the extent that the agency reflects the developing antipoverty ideology, it can reinforce and reward at every turn the nonprofessional's concern for his neighborhood and the poor. The training staff can be critical of any tendency on the part of the nonprofessionals to lose this commitment as they come to identify with the agency or with professionals. In other words, it is possible for nonprofessionals to develop new identifications, at the same time maintaining traditional commitments. In fact, these commitments can be deepened by new systematic understanding regarding the nature of poverty. It is in this context that continuous training can perhaps provide its greatest contribution to the nonprofessional and the antipoverty program.

REFERENCES

Hallowitz, E., and Riessman, F. The role of the indigenous nonprofessional in a community mental health neighborhood service center program. Paper presented at the American Orthopsychiatric Association, San Francisco, April 15, 1966.

Pearl, A., and Riessman, F. *New careers for the poor.* New York: Free Press, 1965.

Riessman, F. The "helper" therapy principle. *Social Work*, (Apr.) 1965, **10**(2), 27-31.

suggested additional readings

Guerney, B. G., ed. *Psychotherapeutic agents: New roles for nonprofessionals, parents, and teachers.* New York: Holt, Rinehart, & Winston, 1969.

Reiff, R., and Riessman, F. *The indigenous nonprofessional. Community Mental Health Journal* Monograph No. 1, 1965.

six   program evaluation and
systems analysis

Most enabling legislation in the health and welfare fields calls for some kind of evaluative research. A high percentage of convention papers, journal articles, and books call for research. Yet very few programs have been systematically evaluated, and very little basic or applied community research has been accomplished. Good theory and good research are inextricably intertwined. The development of a good theory for community psychology and community mental health and the development of a research base are, or should be, the two highest priorities for community psychology. Such endeavors would be other instances of participation and conceptualization. Here the community psychologist's applied and behavioral science backgrounds should converge.

While outcome research is admittedly fraught with many difficulties, community psychologists and community mental healthers are quick to note that existing research fails to demonstrate the success of traditional mental health techniques. When asked if the efficacy of community activities has been demonstrated, the community psychologist is apt to reply, "But the community is so much more complex!" This is a meager excuse for the failure to provide good program evaluation and research on community programs and techniques. It is true, however, that community programs may require us to restructure our thinking about research and evaluation and necessitate the development of new concepts and techniques. The articles in this section reflect a movement in that direction.

There are innumerable community research questions. Some have higher priorities than others when considered in terms of magnitude of the problem—or magnitude of the investment. Some research problems are easier to conceptualize and investigate than others. Historically, there have been several major directions in community mental health research. Epidemiological research has investigated the relationship of various demographic and socioeconomic factors to the incidence and prevalence of a variety of disorders and deviant behaviors. A second trend has been to investigate community information and attitudes regarding mental illness. In recent years, yet a third area of interest has been the assessment of need for services, supply of available resources or lack thereof, and other factors associated with the delivery of services to the mentally ill.

It appears that the epidemiological, ecological, and systems analysis approaches have most to offer both with respect to increasing our knowledge about the community and community mental health and in helping to develop a strong theoretical basis for community intervention and community programs. The papers in this section focus on evaluation of social action and mental health programs. Although some important community mental health research does exist, it is felt that the kind of thinking represented in these four articles will serve to stimulate further research developments in the field. At present we have more questions than answers.

There are many problems inherent in conducting evaluations of social-action programs. In the following article, Peter Rossi discusses these problems and potential strategies for evaluating such programs. His discussion is based, in part, on his survey of research in the Office of Economic Opportunity. All of his comments and concerns are equally relevant for mental health and other kinds of health and welfare programs. (It can be argued that the War on Poverty legislation had the potential for more significant mental health programming than has ever been enacted under the rubric of mental health.) Rossi discusses the practice and theory of evaluation research, design problems, the politics involved in evaluation, and some strategies for evaluation research. Many of the problems that he highlights can be seen as latent consultation problems. Since the community psychologist quite frequently is called upon to be a research consultant or an evaluation consultant, this paper has important implications for the practicing community psychologist, as well as for the further development of community psychology as a behavioral science.

practice, method, and theory
in evaluating social-action programs[1]

Peter H. Rossi

INTRODUCTION

In the thirties, when the New Deal programs got underway, the behavioral sciences were mainly the recipients of program assistance: Works Progress Administration (WPA) and National Youth Administration (NYA) clerical help made it possible to conduct social research on a larger scale than heretofore possible.[2] But little research was conducted on the programs themselves.[3] As a consequence, the effectiveness of New Deal programs is unknown.

In contrast, the behavioral sciences were explicitly invited into the current War on Poverty by the initial enabling legislation, funds being explicitly set aside under the act for evaluation research. Behavioral scientists this time were not to be merely recipients of help in the form of free labor; they were to participate in the policy-making process through the exercise of special skills. As a consequence, one could imagine a considerable flowering of evaluation research and advances in evaluation-research methodology. In some sense, indeed, there has been a flowering: Behavioral scientists throughout the country have been engaged in undertaking evaluations, and new research firms have sprung up to provide the needed services. In another sense, however, the flowering has meant more the encouragement of weeds than of more desirable species. Few of the researches conducted under the Poverty Program have been the best that behavioral scientists could offer (or the best they attempted to offer). Rather, much evaluation can be called research only by the most charitable extension of the meaning of that term. Only a few

The superscript numbers refer to the Notes at the end of this article—Ed.

Chapter 10 of *On Fighting Poverty,* edited by James L. Sundquist with the assistance of Corinne Saposs Schelling, copyright © 1969 by the American Academy of Arts and Sciences, Basic Books, Inc., New York. Reprinted with the permission of Basic Books, Inc. and the author.

delight the connoisseurs: Few have that elegance of design and clarity of execution that would achieve widespread admiration among social researchers.

Nor is this condition a peculiarity of Poverty Program evaluation researches. Research on the effects of educational programs, on the effectiveness of police methods, even on the effectiveness of publicity campaigns, all have the same characteristic of falling far short of the potentialities of currently acceptable research methodology. Evaluating the effectiveness of social-action programs is a depressed area within the realm of behavioral science.

The purpose of this chapter is to explore some of the main reasons why evaluation research has fallen so short of its potential and to suggest some ways in which these difficulties can be overcome. Providing much of the materials on which this chapter has been based have been experiences as director of a university-connected research center[4] and a survey of researches conducted by the Office of Economic Opportunity (OEO). Although these sources of information cover the OEO research program quite well, with the exception of those researches for which no reports have been submitted to OEO, they do not cover the total spread of evaluation researches over the full range of current social-action programs.

The methodological standpoint on which this view of evaluation research rests is that, in principle, the evaluation of social-action programs is best undertaken through the use of experimental designs. All the elements that would strongly recommend such designs are usually present: The program to be tested is some treatment that is either added on to or is designed to supersede some existing treatment. Programs of this sort are under the control of someone or some agency and hence can be fitted into an experimental design if proper steps are taken to set up reasonable experimental and controlled situations. In addition, such programs are usually not designed to cover the entire population to which they are directed, but only some portion, so that withholding treatment from control groups is not radically different from what would ordinarily happen in the administration of such programs. In practice, however, there are many obstacles to the employment of experimental designs, as a later section of this chapter will show.

THE MAIN DESIGN PROBLEM—WEAK EFFECTS

Although a social historian might deplore the lack of good research on the New Deal programs, it may well be the case that research in that instance would have been superfluous. The impact of the Great Depression was so great that any program would help, provided it included some income-maintenance provisions. The problem in the thirties was not conceived so much in terms of rehabilitation as in terms of providing for needs that a weakened economic system had neglected.

In contrast, the present historical period is perhaps the wrong one in which to develop a heavy conscience concerning the poor. The treatments we can devise cannot be expected ordinarily to produce massive results. It appears that we are in much the same situation with respect to social ills as we are with respect to physical ills. The introduction of modern medicine and especially modern sanitation practices into a country that has neither can be expected to produce dramatic results in the forms of reduced morbidity and mortality. But, in the United States of today, each new gain in the reduction of morbidity and mortality can be expected to be smaller and more difficult to achieve. Providing potable water in a community that has used polluted water supplies will achieve dramatic reductions in mortality. Expensive research on lung cancer or attempts to reduce the amount of smoking will not, even if very successful, reduce mortality by very much.

Similarly with respect to our social ills: Dramatic effects on illiteracy can be achieved by providing schools and teachers to all children. Achieving universally a high enough level of literacy to assure that everyone capable of learning is qualified to obtain and hold down a good spot in our modern labor force will be very much more difficult. Hence, the smaller our rates of unemployment, the more difficult it will be to affect the employment status of those who are unemployed. The more social services we have already supplied, the more difficult it is to add to the benefits derived by additional services.

Part of the reasoning behind this pessimism lies in the assumption that affecting the course of a marginal social problem is more difficult than affecting the course of a central one. Thus, affecting the unemployed in a labor force with a high unemployment rate is quite different from affecting the same group under conditions of high employment.

In part, the reasoning flows from the types of effects that are desired. The goals of social programs that are directed toward affecting institutions and hardware are easier to achieve than those of programs directed toward changing the behavior and attitudes of large numbers of individuals. Thus, the armed forces have made stronger progress toward removing discriminatory practices than have government attempts to influence thousands of private employers. Or, the provision of a modern sanitary sewer is easier to achieve than convincing millions of smokers to stop smoking.

Thus, the problem of evaluation in this historical period is that new treatments can be expected to yield only marginal improvements over existing treatments and, hence, that cost-to-benefit ratios can be expected to rise dramatically as target problems and populations constitute smaller and smaller fractions of their universes. When only marginal effects are to be expected, evaluation becomes more difficult to achieve and at the same time program administrators can be expected to be more and more apprehensive concerning the outcome of evaluation research.

To illustrate, consider the case of Project Headstart: We have apparently wrung most of the benefits we can out of the traditional school system. We have learned how to deliver education to every educable child and for the large majority of children succeed quite well in providing sufficient skills to obtain places in the labor force. Everyone would agree that universal schooling for children up to approximately age sixteen has been a huge success, compared with no schooling at all or schooling mainly for those who can pay. Yet, there remains room for improvement, especially in the education of the poor and otherwise disadvantaged. A supplementary preschool program attempting to bring such children into parity with those better off because of family background would appear to be an excellent program. But any such program is not likely to produce as much benefit as did the introduction of elementary schooling. Nor is such a program likely to move underprivileged children into a position of true parity with others because no part-time supplementary program is likely to compensate for what a full-time total institution, the family, was supposed to do.

Effective new treatments that produce more than equivocal results can be expected to be expensive. For example, each trainee at a Job Corps camp costs somewhere between five and ten thousand dollars a year as compared to considerably less than one thousand dollars per year in the usual public high school. Yet, a year in a Job Corps Training Center is not going to be five to ten times more effective than a year in a public high school.[5]

To compound difficulties, the costs of evaluation for programs that are marginally effective are higher (for the same quality) than for programs that are very effective. If effects can be expected to be small, then greater precision is needed in research to demonstrate their existence unequivocally. Thus, we are presented with the paradox that precisely in the cases in which the most powerful research instruments are needed, they are unlikely to be used. It is almost as if we do not want to know whether the social-action programs are really effective.

Although as social scientists we can expect the new social programs to show only marginal effects, the practitioner does not ordinarily share our cautious outlook, at least not when he faces the congressional appropriations-committee hearings. The public claims made for the programs are ordinarily pitched much higher than one could reasonably expect to be able to show. However, although with the best of research we could show only very slight results, with the worst of research we could show anything. Thus it turns out that some of the major obstacles to good research lie in the interests of administrators in program maintenance. The worst of evaluation research is not research at all, but some other type of activity that goes under the name of research.

THE PRACTICE AND THEORY OF
EVALUATION RESEARCH

In order to properly display the range of activities going under the name of evaluation research under OEO, we surveyed a sample of evaluation reports contained in the library of that agency.[6] Some 294 reports were contained in the library as of December 1967, a subsample of a larger group of 1,123 research projects contracted for by OEO as of June 1967.[7] The first 200 reports catalogued form the basis of the discussion that follows.

One hundred and seventy of the reports (or 85 per cent) were primarily descriptive accounts of how many people were being reached by the program in question or descriptions of the activities that took place within the program. They tended to be written in a loosely narrative form, with virtually no systematic observations on the effectiveness of the programs included. Five reports were missing. A remaining 25 reports were judged to be based on procedures sufficiently systematic to be at least considered research. These were read carefully and abstracted for later analysis.

Most of the reports contained what might be called systematic social bookkeeping data. For example, a purported evaluation of the Community Action Program (CAP)[8] involved interviews with residents of areas affected, obtained by sampling in ever-widening circles around the CAP headquarters. The nonresponse rate was more than 50 percent. Data were presented to show how many persons had heard of the programs and participated in them and how many rated each program as effective or ineffective. Or, another report[9] was based on interviews with the personnel of nineteen small-business development centers in operation at the time of the study. Staff members were asked about their backgrounds and the social characteristics of the clientele of the program. Conclusions were drawn concerning whether or not the small-loan program was reaching its presumed target population.

The last example cited above illustrates that such social-bookkeeping studies can be useful. It is on the basis of this study that OEO concluded that its small-business loan program was not effective.[10] At this point, it is useful to distinguish between two meanings of effectiveness: "coverage" and "impact." By coverage is meant the ability of a program to reach the units that it is expected to affect. Thus a small-business loan program that was not giving loans to poor people is obviously having poor coverage and is in that sense ineffective. But, a program may have a proper coverage and not affect the people whom it is reaching. Thus, the same small-loan program even when making loans to the poor may not be helping small business to survive (if that is its goal) beyond what would ordinarily be the case without such a program. This last type of effect may be called a program's impact.

In this sense, most of the studies found in our survey were descriptions of coverage but not impact. Obviously, a program must have some coverage as a necessary but insufficient condition for being judged effective. But even with coverage, impact may be high or low.

Impact studies may be illustrated in the group of reports containing evaluations of Headstart programs. Typically, children are tested before and after participation in the program, and gains in test scores are judged to be the result of the program.[11] About half of the 25 evaluation reports studied in detail contained information designed to measure the impact of programs.

Not a single report contained by the most charitable definition the results of a controlled experiment.[12] At best, individuals exposed to a program (for example, Headstart, Job Corps) were compared with persons who were not exposed to the program, the comparison group presumed to represent an approximation to a control group. The range of quality represented by these researches runs almost the full gamut, from "moseying around" to quasi-experimental designs. But the distribution is weighted toward the poorer quality end of the range; the vast majority of the reports can best be characterized as "moseying around," with the best studies representing estimates of program coverages rather than impact.

This is not the place to lay out in detail the importance of experimental designs in the study of the impact of social-action programs.[13] It is sufficient to state at this point that without such designs it is difficult to unravel the effects of self-selection and other biases from the effects of administered programs. Surveys and quasi-experimental designs have some value, however, as I will attempt to show later on in this chapter.

THE POLITICS OF EVALUATION

The will to believe that their programs are effective is understandably strong among those who conceive and administer them. After all, they have committed their energies, careers, and ideologies to the programs, and it is difficult under such circumstances to take a tentative stance concerning outcomes. Hence, most administrators who have some sort of commitment to their programs have a strong incentive to believe that evaluations will prove their worth. They hope and expect that evaluations will come out with positive, or at least not negative, results.

As long as results come out positive, relationships between the practitioners and the researchers are cordial and perhaps even effusively friendly. But it often enough happens that results are not positive. A dramatic illustration of what occurs under these circumstances helps to underscore the resulting deterioration of relations. A few years ago, the National Opinion Research Center (NORC) undertook research, with the best of sponsorships,[14] on the effects of fellowships and scholarships on graduate study in the arts and sciences. It was the sincere conviction of the learned societies that sponsored the research that the availability of fellowships and scholarships was an important determinant of how many students went on to graduate work and, furthermore, that such stipends affected the distribution of talent among fields within the arts and sciences. The results of the research were nonpositive: It did not appear that financial support had much to do with going on to graduate study nor did the availability of stipends in one field attract students from another. Those who were committed found some way to get their advanced degrees, often relying on their spouses to make investments in their training. It certainly did not appear that stipends were holding back graduate training, but it also did not appear that stipends were doing much more than providing relief to overworked spouses. These results were quite disappointing to the sponsors, whose first reactions were to question the adequacy of the research. Humanists and biophysicists suddenly became experts in sampling and questionnaire construction as they looked for some fault in the study design that would undermine the plausibility of the results. One of the social scientists on the advisory committee obviously spent hours adding up frequencies in statistical tables and cross-checking tables for internal consistency. Some question was raised as to whether or not the results of the study should be published.

Needless to say, the relations between the researchers and the sponsoring learned societies have been relatively cool ever since. The learned societies believe that their problems have been badly researched, and the researchers believe that their research has been badly treated. The findings have affected policy not one whit: The sponsoring groups are still adamantly claiming more and more in the way of financial support for graduate students.

It is difficult to recall any social-action program that was put out of business by a negative evaluation.[15] Why is this the case? Why do negative (or nonpositive) results have so little impact? The main reason is that the practitioners, first of all, rarely seriously entertain in advance the possibility that results may come out negative or insignificant. The rules of the game of evaluation of social-action programs have not yet become institutionalized in the same way that the rules of evaluation for drugs have become institutionalized.

Proper rules for the game of evaluation would require that action alternatives for the contingencies of positive and negative findings be thought through and that administrators and practitioners alike become committed to following through such alternatives. Without commitment to such alternatives, the gamblers usually welch.

The ways in which welching is accomplished are wonderfully varied. It is easy to attack the methodology of a study: Methodological unsophisticates suddenly become experts in sampling, questionnaire construction, experimental design, and statistical analysis, or borrow experts for the occasion.

Apparently, you can always find some expert who will be able to find something wrong with the research.[16]

Further replication may be called for to more firmly establish the findings. The best example here is the long history of research on the effects of class size on learning in which each new generation of educational psychologists attempt anew to find a negative relationship between class size and learning—so far without success. The net effect of the more than two hundred researches finding little or no relationship has been nil on social policy. Every proposal for the betterment of education calls for reductions in the size of classes.

Most often of all, it is "discovered" that the "real" goals of the social-action program were not the goals that were evaluated in the research after all. Thus the important goals of a job-retraining program were not to get jobs for the trainees but to train them in the etiquette of work. Or, the goals of a community organization in an urban renewal area were not really to affect the planning process but to produce a commitment to the neighborhood on the part of residents while planning took place. Or, the goals of a community-action program may not be to produce any specific benefits but to increase the satisfaction of the poor with their lot.

Perhaps the best example of how "real" goals are discovered after goals that were evaluated were found to be poorly attained can be found in the work of a very prominent school-administration group.[17] Fully committed to the educational modernities of the forties and fifties, this group found to its apparent surprise that whether or not a school system adopted innovations it was sponsoring had little to do with the learning levels achieved by the students. Hence, they dropped achievement tests as a criterion of the quality of a school system and substituted instead a measure of the flexibility of the school administration in adopting new ideas, thereby producing an evaluation instrument, which, in effect, stated that a school system was good to the extent that it adopted policies that were currently being advocated by the group in question.

The main point to be made here is that the proper employment of evaluation research requires a commitment *in advance* on the part of the administrators and other practitioners to action based on whichever of the alternative potential outcomes in fact occurs. Without such commitment, it becomes all too easy to brush aside disappointing results, making the research effort a fatuous enterprise.

As mentioned earlier, few evaluation researches employ controlled experiments as their basic research design. It is important to understand that a key reason for this condition lies not so much in the difficulty of designing such experiments as in the impediments to their use in practice. The key feature of a controlled experiment lies in the control exercised by the experimenter over the processes by which subjects are allocated to experimental and control groups. In a well designed experiment, such allocations are made in an unbiased fashion; that is, potential subjects have a known probability of falling into one or the other group. But there are many ways in which a well thought out plan for unbiased allocation can go awry.

Perhaps the major obstacle to the use of controlled experiments in evaluation research is a political one. The political problem is simply that practitioners are extremely reluctant to allow experimenters to exercise proper control over the allocation of potential subjects to experimental and control groups. For example, the proper evaluation of the Job Corps would require that potential trainees be separated into experimental and control groups, the former receiving Job Corps training and the latter receiving either no treatment at all or some sort of training differing in essential respects from Job Corps treatment. The contrasts between the later performance of both groups provide a measure of the effectiveness of Job Corps experiences. The political sore point is that a controlled experiment means that some potential trainees who are otherwise qualified are barred "arbitrarily" from training, an act that public agencies are extremely reluctant to authorize.

In part, the political problem arises because researchers have not thought through sufficiently the problem of what constitutes a control or nonexperimental experience. The logic of experimental designs does *not* require that the control group be completely neglected—not given any treatment. The logic *does* require that the control group not be given the same treatment as the experimental group. One could administer to the control group another type of treatment designed to improve their job skills that was nonresidential and that lacked certain other critical features of Job Corps training. In short, we have not been ingenious enough in inventing *social placebo* treatments that are realistic enough to give public officials who have to authorize such experiments the security that they are not merely slighting individuals at random.

Such social placebos are not difficult to invent. For example, a social-placebo treatment for a job-retraining program could be designed to help men get jobs that do not involve retraining and over which the job-retraining program ought to show some advantage. Perhaps testing and intensive counseling might be an acceptable placebo treatment for a job-retraining program. Or, a placebo treatment for a Headstart program might be traditional nursery-school experience.

Note that the placebo aspect of the control-group experiences suggested above is directed not at the potential subject—as is the case in the usual meaning of placebo—but is designed to placate the administrators and public officials. In other words, control groups have to be given politically acceptable alternatives to the programs being tested.[18]

However, even in the best of circumstances and with the best of sponsors, the carrying out of controlled experiments can run into a number of boobytraps. For example, early in the history of the Job Corps, NORC attempted to set up an experimental evaluation of the Job Corps, but the program did not generate enough qualified volunteers to fill up both experimental and control groups. Under these circumstances, the administrators chose to fill up the experimental groups, abandoning all attempts to segregate qualified volunteers into experimental and control sections.

There is also the example of a well-designed experiment in the effectiveness of certain means of reaching low-income families with birth control information whose design was contaminated when the City Health Department elected to set up birth control clinics in those areas that had been designated as controls.

There is also a special risk that is run by long-range experiments. The world may change the experiences of control groups so that differences between their experiences and that of experimental groups are minimized. For example, an evaluation of the effects of public housing unfortunately took place in a period when the quality of the general housing stock of Baltimore was improving at such a fast rate that differences in the housing conditions between experimental and control groups had greatly diminished by the end of the experimental period. Similarly, a job-retraining program in a period when unemployment rates are declining cannot be expected to show as much of an effect as a treatment for a control group as would be the case in a period in which unemployment rates were either steady or increasing.

STRATEGIES FOR EVALUATION RESEARCH

There are a number of lessons to be drawn from the experiences discussed in this chapter that hopefully could help in devising a strategy for the conduct of evaluation research. Although it is true that in the best of all possible worlds the best of all possible research designs could be employed, in a compromised, present-day real world, full of evil as it is, it is necessary to make do with what is possible within limits of scarce time and resources available to us. The problem facing social scientists and policy makers alike is how to set up conditions for doing the best job we can in producing research that contains powerful enough information to permit making sensible judgments about the worth of social-action programs, without at the same time making political errors and within a time period that makes it possible to modify programs.

Although the idea of evaluation research has gained wide acceptance, we are a long way from full commitment to the outcomes of evaluation research. It is part of the researcher's responsibility to bring to the practitioners awareness of the possibility that in most cases the effects of social-action programs are not going to be spectacular and that there is more than an off-chance possibility of negative or at least nonpositive evaluations. As already indicated, the policy implications of such findings must be worked out in advance, with the practitioner firmly committed to acting on them if evaluation research is not to be turned into either fatuous or just plain irrelevant exercises.

A second lesson to be drawn is that we have a long way to go in divising acceptable ways of applying controlled experiments to evaluation. Political obstacles[19] to the use of controls often make it difficult to get acceptance of such designs. The difficulty of maintaining controls in a nonsterile world makes full-fledged use of experimental designs over long periods of time relatively rare. Earlier in this chapter, I suggested that we take a lesson from medical research and search for the social analogues of placebos to be administered to our control groups.[20] There are other directions in which experimental designs should go: For example, considering that there is a high likelihood that treatments for social ills will have small effects, we need very powerful designs to demonstrate positive results. But, because power costs money, it is worthwhile to consider research designs that evaluate several types of treatment simultaneously, thus increasing the amount of information obtained at a relatively slight increment in cost. To illustrate: It would be considerably more useful in terms of the amount of information gained if OEO were to provide experimental evaluations of several types of Job Corps programs rather than merely a single experiment that regarded all Job Corps centers as a single experimental treatment. Looking at the differential effectiveness of different Job Corps programs would provide information that would make it possible to construct better programs as well as information that would provide estimates of how much difference attendance at any Job Corps camp makes.

This chapter has stressed desirability of the model of the controlled experiment for evaluation research. But it is abundantly clear that controlled experiments are not being used and that they are difficult to employ. Most frequently found are one or another variant on quasi-experimental designs in which control groups are constructed by methods that allow some biases to operate,[21] for example, correlational designs in which persons subjected to some sort of treatment are contrasted with persons who have not been subjected to this treatment, controlling statistically for presumably relevant characteristics.

The important question that faces evaluation researchers is how bad are such "soft" designs? How much credence can be placed in their results, and what are the circumstances under which they can be employed with relatively strong confidence in their outcomes?

When massive effects are both desired and expected, "soft" techniques are almost as good as subtle and precise ones. To illustrate: If what is desired as the outcome of a treatment is the remission of symptoms in each and every individual subject to the treatment in question, then it is hardly necessary to have a control group. Thus, if a birth control technique is to be judged effective *if and only if* it completely eliminates any chance of conception, then the research design is vastly simplified. The question is not whether those who use the method have fewer children than a control group, but whether they have any children at all, a question that can easily be decided by administering the technique to a group and counting whether any conceptions appear at all.

Of course, with respect to social-action programs one is rarely confronted with the evaluation of a technique that is expected to accomplish complete remission of symptoms in every person subject to the treatment. But there are approximations to this condition. For example, an income-maintenance program may be designed to cover each and every person or household whose income falls below a certain minimum. An evaluation of the program might involve finding out how many eligible persons are being missed for some reason or other. Or, a training program designed to produce computer programmers must at least graduate students who have the ability to pass minimum standards in computer programming.

The obverse of the above also holds. If a soft method of evaluation does not show that a program or treatment has had any effect, then it is not likely that a very precise method would show that it has had more than very slight effects. For example, if a Headstart program produced no improvement in the verbal ability of its subjects in a before-and-after type of research design, it is not likely that a controlled experiment would show anything different. The existence of complex and large interaction effects that suppress large differences between a group subject to a treatment and a statistically constructed control group seems highly unlikely.[22]

Of course, if a correlational or before-and-after design does show some program effects, then it is never clear whether selection biases or the program itself produced the effects shown. Thus, testing children who have gone to Headstart programs and comparing them to those who have not may indicate only that those whose parents sent them are providing a cognitively richer home environment.

These considerations lead to the following strategy: It is worthwhile to use soft methods as the first stage in a program of evaluation, discarding treatments that show no effects and retaining those with more favorable showings to be tested with more powerful designs of the controlled-experiment variety. Thus, if a training program shows no increment in learning on the part of its participants, then it is not worthwhile to go into a controlled experiment. Or, if an optional food-stamp plan does not appreciably increase the quality of household diets, compared with those of eligible persons who do not elect to participate, then it is not worthwhile to conduct further, more precise evaluational research.

Although *ex post facto* designs of a correlational variety have obvious holes in them through which may creep (or even gallop) the most insidious of biases, such designs may be extremely useful in the investigation of effects that are postulated to be the results of lengthy treatments. For example, if one is concerned with the effects on the occupational adjustment of Negroes of attendance at integrated schools, the comparisons between adult Negroes who have attended such schools with those who have attended segregated schools will indicate at least whether it is likely that such effects exist without having to wait for a cohort of Negroes to go through their schooling experience and reach the labor force. If, as one study has shown,[23] such correlations do in fact exist, it is still not clear whether Negroes who did go to integrated public schools as children were more highly motivated intellectually or whether it was the fact of attending integrated public schools that produced the effect.

A more dramatic example can be taken from the correlational studies of the association between smoking and lung cancer. Despite the fact that the association may be caused by factors common to both smoking and lung cancer, the evidence from *ex post facto* studies can hardly be ignored and certainly justifies the expenditure of considerable sums of money in before-and-after studies.[24]

Similarly, our study[25] of the effects of Catholic education on subsequent religious behavior and occupational attainment of adults can still be easily objected to on the grounds that self-selection biases could have produced the effects we have shown, even though we made every attempt to hold obviously relevant factors constant. Nevertheless, we have gained a great deal of knowledge concerning the order of effects that could be expected, were controlled experiments to be conducted. The net differences between Catholics who attended church schools and those who did not are so slight that we now know that controlled experiments assigning Catholics randomly to Catholic and public schools would not produce results that showed the schools to be enormously effective as devices for maintaining religiosity or promoting occupational success.

From these considerations a strategy for evaluation research emerges. The strategy involves two successive phases: First, a "reconnaissance" phase in which "soft" correlational, *ex post facto* or before-and-after designs are used to screen out those programs worth being investigated further. Second, an "experimental" phase in which powerful controlled experiment designs are used to evaluate the differential effectiveness of those programs that survive the first phase. In this connection, it is worthwhile to consider the use of social placebos to achieve more political acceptance for controlled experiments.

This is a strategy that is designed to provide hard knowledge in time enough to guide policy makers toward ever increasingly effective social action programs.

NOTES

1. An earlier version of this paper was given at the 1966 Meetings of the American Statistical Association. This paper was revised with the help of a grant from the Russell Sage Foundation, whose help is hereby gratefully acknowledged.

2. WPA clerical assistance made possible such studies as St. Clair Drake and Horace Cayton's *Black metropolis* (Chicago: University of Chicago Press, 1945) and Robert E. L. Faris and Warren Dunham's *Mental disorders in urban areas* (Chicago: University of Chicago Press, 1939), but social science contributions to our understanding of the Great Depression were confined mainly to a Social Science Research Council monograph series on the effects of the depression (for example, on the family and on migration) with little or no attention paid to the effects of ameliorative programs.

3. Karen Rosenbaum. A second chance for youth: A comparative study of federal youth programs in the 1930's and the 1960's. Educational Research Associates, 1966.

4. The writer was director of the National Opinion Research Center (NORC) at the University of Chicago between 1960 and 1967.

5. This is not to deny that such programs could have favorable cost-to-benefit ratios as Robert A. Levine's chapter, in James L. Sundquist, ed., *On fighting poverty* (New York: Basic Books, 1969), suggests may be the case for the Job Corps. It means primarily that a program like the Job Corps will have lower ratios than traditional approaches to training adolescents for the labor force.

6. The survey was conducted by Mr. Paul T. MacFarlane, a graduate student in the Department of Social Relations at Johns Hopkins University, whose help is gratefully acknowledged.

7. The remaining 829 had either not yet produced reports or had produced such skimpy reports (one- or two-page summaries) that they were not cataloged by the library.

8. Daniel Yankelovich. Detailed findings of a study to determine the effects of CAP programs on selected communities and their low income residents. Unpublished report, March 1967.

9. Kirshner Associates. Description and evaluation of the economic opportunity loan program. Unpublished report, February 1966.

10. See account in Chapter 9 [James L. Sundquist, ed. *On fighting poverty*. New York: Basic Books, 1969.]

11. See for example, Frances D. Horowitz and Howard M. Rosenfeld, Comparative studies of a group of Head Start and non-Head Start pre-school children (University of Kansas, January 1966).

12. This statement can only be taken to mean that controlled experiments are very rare in the total universe of OEO evaluation studies. Levine [see chapter in Sundquist] reports on a controlled experiment currently being undertaken to evaluate the effects of a negative income tax policy.

13. This interested reader can find a masterful exposition of the relative utilities of research designs in Donald T. Campbell and Julian C. Stanley, *Experimental and quasi-experimental designs for research* (Chicago: Rand McNally, 1963).

14. Reported in James A. Davis, *Stipends and spouses* (Chicago: University of Chicago Press, 1962).
15. In Chapter 9 [Sundquist], Levine notes that the Kirshner evaluations of the small-business-loan program is being ignored by Congress in favor of the benefits that might accrue to the small businessmen involved, even though they are not the target population (the poor) for whom the program was originally set up.
16. Even in the controversy over whether there is some causal link between smoking and lung cancer, both sides were able to muster experts of considerable stature.
17. Donald Ross. *Administration for adaptability*. New York: Metropolitan School Study Council, 1958.
18. There is, of course, the danger that a program that shows only marginal increments over a placebo treatment might be shown to be quite effective as compared to no treatment at all. To guard against the possibility and to maximize the information to be obtained in such social-action experiments, the placebo treatment should be conventional and of minimum cost. The reasoning behind this recommendation is that an experimental treatment to be worthwhile should do better than relatively inexpensive conventional treatments.
19. That these obstacles may be peculiar to the American political system and ethos can be seen in the fact that large-scale experimentation is possible in at least one other Western society. For several years now Sweden has had underway a large-scale experimental evaluation of the relative merits of comprehensive versus traditional high schools. The high-school population of Stockholm was divided in half, one going to a traditional high-school system and the other attending comprehensive high schools.
20. Another possible direction would be to set up generalized control groups, for example, a continuing study of poor youth that could be used as control groups for a wide variety of social-action programs. Levine indicates that such a program is presently underway at OEO which is setting up a panel of poor youths to serve as controls for youth programs.
21. An ingenious design was employed in the evaluation of a manpower-retraining program in which participants in the program were matched with their unemployed friends, the assumption being that the correlation between friends in important respects was high enough to eliminate much of the bias in self selection. Obviously, while this is an ingenious attempt, it is hard to evaluate the extent to which it has reduced self-selection biases.
22. Even though possible, complex interaction effects of this sort have been found to be extremely rare.
23. U. S. Civil Rights Commission. *Racial isolation in the public schools*, 1967.
24. Note that controlled experiments can hardly be done on this problem since we cannot experimentally control smoking habits of subjects. Indeed, there are very wide classes of topics to which common decency, if not more cogent human rights arguments, bars the use of human subjects.
25. Andrew M. Greeley and Peter H. Rossi. *The education of Catholic Americans.* Chicago: Aldine Press, 1966.

"What criteria serve to test the adequacy of programs in the field of mental health?" It is to this question that Leslie Phillips addresses the next article. He argues that psychopathology is a vague construct. The criteria of therapeutic effectiveness that traditionally have been used are too narrow in scope for adequate evaluation of mental health programs. A better criterion, says Phillips, is that of competence. A person's social competence can be evaluated in terms of interpersonal, technological, and socioeconomic activities and in terms of personal relationships. The criterion thus becomes appropriate for a wide range of social-action programs. He briefly reviews his research on competence and outlines some of the implications of the use of competence as a criterion.

the competence criterion for mental health programs[1]

Leslie Phillips

Mental health programs, which form one of the major social welfare movements of our times, are now in a period of rapid expansion. They already account for a large proportion of each state's budget and make use of substantial funds drawn from the federal treasury. The recent growth of these programs expresses a national commitment to improved mental health services for all citizens, along with augmented support for education, enlarged services for the mentally retarded, and the current campaign against the effects of poverty. Inevitably, these programs compete for large but not inexhaustible funds and for experienced personnel, who will always remain in short supply.

It is difficult to set any exact figure on the cost of all these services but currently several billion dollars annually are being expended on them nationally. The newly proposed system of community mental health centers will raise these expenditures substantially. Allocation of such large public sums to the fulfillment of any objective, however worthy, becomes a major social issue even for a country as wealthy as the United States. Because all these programs cannot be implemented without limit, their goals need the most careful consideration and must be articulated far more precisely than they have been to date. The intent of community mental health programs is in particular need of clarification. No one definition of mental health has found wide acceptance; there is no generally accepted theory as to the nature

[1]The position presented in this paper is based on work supported by the Dementia Praecox Research Project, Worcester State Hospital, Worcester, Mass., and a research grant (MH-06369) from the National Institute of Mental Health, United States Public Health Service.

Reprinted from the *Community Mental Health Journal*, 1967, **3**, 73-76, with the permission of Behavioral Publications, Inc. and the author.

of mental disorder; and there are no established criteria by which the effectiveness of mental health programs may be assessed.

This paper is directed to the last issue: What criteria shall serve to test
the adequacy of programs in the field of mental health? Freeman and
Sherwood (1965) have urged the development of an "impact model" by
which the quality of services is judged according to their success in bringing
about desired changes, i.e., having the desired impact. These authors
contrast their model with the more traditional emphasis on the extent and
quality of services rendered, in which "good service" is defined merely as that
which is offered in a professional manner by a qualified person who in turn is
supervised by a qualified supervisor. Yet, as Freeman and Sherwood observe,
services are only the means for the fulfillment of program goals; the ultimate
test of a program is not the procedures it invokes but the degree to which its
goals are achieved.

The "services-rendered" criterion is applied by nearly all those who set
policy for, or who carry out programs, in the field of mental health:
legislators and administrators at the state level, the courts, psychiatrists, and
other types of mental health professionals at the local level. Nevertheless,
they often differ drastically as to the yardstick by which these services are to
be measured. Administrators will judge hospital services by the cost per
occupied bed, while the courts will evaluate services according to whether
they can institutionalize for observation all those whose behavior is not
understood, such as that of alcoholics, drug addicts, or homosexuals. For
these public authorities, mental institutions exist to diagnose and house in
some humane fashion those persons whose behavior is deviant but not antisocial. In contrast, mental health professionals try to provide therapeutic services for their patients and call insistently for additional funds to pay for new
positions, programs, and buildings. In the provision and use of mental health
services, public authorities respond to social pressures, therapists to the
intrapsychic needs of their clients.

Latent in the services-rendered criterion is the impact criterion. All
those persons who set policy for mental health programs, as well as those
who administer them, are concerned with the value of these services and the
degree to which they fulfill their objectives. The courts and public administrators use an uncomplicated criterion of success. For the courts, satisfactory
services have been rendered when the offender is housed; administrators ask,
in addition, at what unit cost. The therapist's criterion by which services are
to be judged is far more complex. He is not satisfied with simply housing his
clients, nor is he particularly concerned with the cost of services. He is
committed to the proposition that therapy will lead to some desirable
(although not clearly specified) end.

It seems fair to represent psychiatry and its allied disciplines as
committed to the following propositions: (1) The primary goal of mental

health services is to diminish the impact of mental and emotional disorder on the psychological make-up of the individual client. (2) Relief from intra-psychic difficulties will have the consequence of enhancing his participation in the life of the community. (3) There is a need to increase the extent and intensity of psychiatric services available to the general public.

THE CRITERION OF THERAPEUTIC EFFICACY

Certain issues are raised by adoption of these propositions. The first problem is concerned with devising some criterion of therapeutic success. Its measure-ment is dependent on the clarity with which the pathological process itself is defined and measured. Unhappily, no generally accepted definition of psy-chopathology is available, and no adequate criterion for its classification and measurement has been devised. Clinicians vary in their assumptions as to the nature of disorder, treating it variously as a consequence of genetic dysfunc-tion, of psychological trauma, or of social disorganization. Clinicians often differ on the diagnosis of disorder and differ, too, in their judgments of its severity.

Further, there is a surprising dearth of studies on the effects of therapy. It has been shown that drugs can alleviate some of the more dramatic expres-sions of psychopathology, but there are no reports of full cures in psychiatric disorder based only on the use of drugs. The results of psychotherapeutic intervention are even more ambiguous. The evidence is ambiguous as to whether psychotherapy has significant impact on pathological forms of behavior (Eysenck, 1961; Rogers and Dymond, 1954), although many clients express a subjective sense of improvement in their condition. In the face of the enormous sums invested in mental health services over the last century and more, our knowledge of the effects of the various forms of therapeutic intervention is startlingly deficient. Relatively little attention has been shown for the need to evaluate the adequacy of the various types of therapy, perhaps because the efforts of professional staffs have concentrated on the provision of services rather than on any test of their efficacy.

Certain assumptions inhere in the use of therapeutic efficacy as the crite-rion by which mental health services are to be judged. First, it implies that the "patient" is the victim of some form of "illness." His role in the develop-ment of that illness is minimized, while his recovery is largely dependent on the skill of his therapist. This assumption determines a therapist-patient rela-tionship that demands active control by the practitioner and a state of passive cooperation on the part of the client.

Adoption of the criterion of therapeutic success as the test of mental health programs strongly reinforces the dominance of the medical discipline in this field. Even those nonmedical professionals who insist on their right to independent practice have largely adopted the framework of thought and even the vocabulary of medicine. They speak of mental health and illness, about their patients, of therapy, and prognosis.

To view mental disorder as a form of illness and to adopt a criterion of therapeutic efficacy underscores the uniqueness of mental health programs as a form of social action. This position fosters the current isolation of these programs from newly developing services in the fields of education, mental retardation, and poverty and reinforces the present public policy that provides separate funding for these programs. Yet the victims of poor education programs, retardation, mental disorder, and poverty are found clustered together in pockets of economic and cultural deprivation, and high rates of other forms of social pathology, such as drug and alcoholic addiction and delinquency and crime, also appear in these areas. Consequently, the wisdom of this policy is open to question.

THE CRITERION OF COMPETENCE

It is possible to devise a quite different criterion of success for mental health programs. This is the degree to which the person learns to resolve his life problems and to cope effectively with those expectations imposed by society according to his age and sex. A person's social competence (Phillips, 1968) can be evaluated in two areas of behavior: the impersonal world of technological and socioeconomic activities, in which the person acquires an education, develops work skills, and insures the well-being of himself and his dependents; and the world of personal relationships, which requires an acceptance of responsibility both for one's fate and that of others—whether of one's immediate dependents or or one's community. The social competence index has proved of significance in predicting the form and outcome of psychiatric disorder (Phillips, 1953; Phillips and Zigler, 1961; Zigler and Phillips, 1960; Zigler and Phillips, 1961b; Zigler and Phillips, 1962).

When the enhancement of competence becomes a primary program commitment, mental disorder itself may be viewed as only one of many forms of inappropriate response to deficient coping potential. Other possible inadequate responses to societal expectations include delinquency, alcoholism, prostitution, and poverty itself. In this sense, deviant behavior is not an illness that has attacked the individual but is an expression of the total person as he actively, although ineffectually, attempts to come to terms with his environment. Persons who behave inappropriately need help in order to develop means for effective participation in the life of the community. When "pathology" is viewed in this fashion, all social-action programs are directed at the development of individual social competence. This proposition serves to unify the objectives of the presently independent social-action programs and makes clear why government has an unambiguous responsibility for their maintenance. The development of social competence is as much the concern of society as is the education of its young or of new work skills among the unemployed.

EVALUATION OF PROGRAMS

Adoption of a competence rather than a therapeutic criterion transfers the locus of professional concern from the intrapsychic to the psychosocial sphere of client behavior. It demands a precise differentiation of the nature of competence and the development of objective criteria for its measurement. The writer and his colleagues have been engaged in this task for over a decade (Broverman, 1964; Broverman, Jordan and Phillips, 1960; Feffer and Phillips, 1953; Fine, Fulkerson, and Phillips, 1955; Fowler, 1957; Gerard & Phillips, 1953; Lane, 1955; Phillips, 1953; Phillips, 1962; Phillips, 1966; Phillips, 1968; Phillips and Cowitz, 1953; Phillips and Zigler, 1961; Smith and Phillips, 1959; Zigler and Phillips, 1960; Zigler and Phillips, 1961a; Zigler and Phillips, 1961b; Zigler and Phillips, 1962). It has been found related to performance under conditions of experimental stress (Feffer and Phillips, 1953; Gerard and Phillips, 1953) and achieved level of psychological development (Grace, 1956; Lane, 1955; Smith and Phillips, 1959). Others have related competence level to achievement motivation (Broverman, Jordan, and Phillips, 1960), the response to threat (Garmezy and Rodnick, 1959), and to various aspects of cognitive performance (Broverman, 1964).

Assessment of program impact requires the consideration of at least two aspects of program performance: its effectiveness and the efficiency with which it is carried out. In order to evaluate effectiveness, explicit program objectives must be spelled out in terms that are subject to measurement. In this light, the competence criterion is superior to the therapeutic criterion, for it is more amenable to direct, objective, and quantitative assessment. Program efficiency may be defined in terms of the cost of a given unit of successful achievement, for example, an increase in earning power measured in terms of additional dollars of income per year.

Adoption of the competence criterion as an alternative to any index of change in pathological state encourages the development of alternate forms of community mental health programs in addition to the present primary commitment to psychotherapeutic and pharmacological procedures. These programs should be free to compete in the market place and to be judged according to their relative contributions to community mental health, measured in terms of their efficacy and efficiency.

REFERENCES

Broverman, D.M. Generality and behavioral correlates of cognitive styles. *Journal of Consulting Psychology,* 1964, **28**, 487-500.

Broverman, D.M., Jordan, E.J. Jr. and Phillips, L. Achievement motivation in fantasy and behavior. *Journal of Abnormal and Social Psychology,* 1960, **60**, 374-378.

Eysenck, H.J. The effects of psychotherapy. H.J. Eysenck, ed., *Handbook of abnormal psychology.* New York: Basic Books, 1961. Pp. 697-725.

Feffer, M., and Phillips, L. Social attainment and performance under stress. *Journal of Personality,* 1953, **22**, 284-297.

Fine, H.J., Fulkerson, S.C., and Phillips L. Maladjustment and social attainment. *Journal of Abnormal and Social Psychology,* 1955, **50**, 33-35.

Fowler, R. Psychopathology and social adequacy: a Rorschach developmental study. Unpublished doctoral dissertation, Pennsylvania State University, 1957.

Freeman, H.E., and Sherwood, C.C. Research in large-scale intervention programs. *Journal of Social Issues,* 1965, **21**, 11-28.

Garmezy, N., and Rodnick, E. Premorbid adjustment and performance in schizophrenia. *Journal of Nervous and Mental Disorders,* 1959, **129**, 450-466.

Gerard, D.L., and Phillips, L. Relation of social attainment to psychological and adrenorcortical reactions to stress. *Archives of Neurological Psychiatry,* 1953, **69**, 350-354.

Grace, N.B. A developmental comparison of word usage with structural aspects of perception and social adjustment. Unpublished doctoral dissertation, Duke University, 1956.

Lane, J.E. Social effectiveness and developmental level. *Journal of Personality,* 1955, **23**, 274-284.

Phillips, L. Case history data and prognosis in schizophrenia. *Journal of Nervous and Mental Disorders,* 1953, **6**, 515-525.

Phillips, L.Social competence and the nature of psychopathology. A. Wellek, ed., *Proceedings of the Sixteenth International Congress of Psychology.* Amsterdam, The Netherlands: North-Holland Publishing Co., 1962. Pp.847-848.

Phillips, L. Social competence, the process-reactive distinction and the nature of mental disorder. P. Hoch and J. Zubin, eds., *Psychopathology of schizophrenia.* New York: Grune & Stratton, 1966. Pp. 471-481.

Phillips, L. The severe disorders. P. London and D. Rosenhan, eds., *Abnormal psychology.* New York: Holt, Rinehart and Winston, 1968.

Phillips, L., and Cowitz, B. Social attainment and reactions to stress. *Journal of Personality,* 1953, **22**, 270-283.

Phillips, L., and Zigler, E. Social competence: The action-thought parameter and vicariousness in normal and pathological behaviors. *Journal of Abnormal and Social Psychology,* 1961, **63**, 137-146.

Rogers, C., and Dymond, R. *Psychotherapy and personality change.* Chicago: University of Chicago Press, 1954.

Smith, L.C., Jr., and Phillips, L. Social effectiveness and developmental level in adolescence. *Journal of Personality,* 1959, **27**, 240-249.

Zigler,E., and Phillips, L. Social effectiveness and symptomatic behaviors. *Journal of Abnormal and Social Psychology*, 1960, **61**, 231-238.

Zigler, E., and Phillips, L. Case history data and psychiatric diagnosis. *Journal of Consulting Psychology*, 1961a, **25**, 458.

Zigler, E., and Phillips, L. Social competence and outcome in psychiatric disorder. *Journal of Abnormal and Social Psychology*, 196b, **63**, 264-271.

Zigler, E., and Phillips, L. Social competence and the process-reactive distinction in psychopathology. *Journal of Abnormal and Social Psychology*, 1962, **65**, 215-222.

The conceptual model presented earlier by Nagler and Cooper (Section four) is but one instance of the application of a systems analysis approach to the delivery of mental health services. In the paper that follows, Harold Halpert defines a system and a systems approach and demonstrates how systems analysis models may be applied to the delivery of mental health services. While still a rudimentary technique, or class of techniques, systems analysis is a tool of great potential worth for the community psychologist. Halpert explains how a systems approach can be used to answer a variety of questions that are central to the implementation and evaluation of mental health programs.

models for the application of systems analysis to the delivery of mental health services

Harold P. Halpert

Mental health service programs often have been developed on the basis of inadequately specified goals, and without sufficient consideration of the totality of need for helping services on the part of the target population. Evaluation of many such programs has been confined to measuring the quantity of service rendered, rather than the impact of the service on problem areas. A systems approach offers a logical basis for defining objectives in operational terms, and for planning programs and organizing services to meet changing needs.

What is a "systems approach?" It can perhaps be identified more readily by its absence than its presence. One or two negative examples should suffice. In the early 1940's, officials in an Eastern city called in a group of advisers to help them plan a housing project. They were told to build only small apartments, because the American family was getting smaller. This trend, of course, was soon reversed, and it never was a strong trend in the lower socioeconomic groups for whom the housing was designed. More recently, the same city again consulted housing advisers. This time they were told to build a project with nothing but three-bedroom apartments—the American family was getting larger. And so they built a project with only three-bedroom apartments. But the concentration of so many large families in one place has overtaxed the school facilities and the recreational facilities, to say nothing of the temper of the residents subjected to hordes of young children at close quarters. The planners altered one factor without considering its effects on other factors. A somewhat similar situation occurred during World War II when American military forces occupying some of the South

Paper presented at the 45th Annual Meeting of the American Orthopsychiatric Association, Chicago, 1968. Reprinted with the permission of the author.

Pacific islands hired young native workers at such high salaries that they upset the local economy and the local authority structure. The elders, who had kept the local society stable, could no longer command the respect of the community.

Lack of a systems approach amounts to tackling problems one at a time and making expedient solutions without regard to related consequences throughout the system. It is perhaps the answer to the Zen Buddhist *koan* (a riddle, contemplation of which is intended to promote *satori* or enlightenment) which asks: "What is the sound of one hand clapping?" The sound of one hand clapping is a striking metaphor for the failure to deal with all related elements of a given problem or system; it can become a loud sound in terms of social disruption. The systems approach attempts to overcome this failing. It tries to fit together the pieces of the "jigsaw puzzle," and to deal with all aspects of a given system as a totality.

What is a system? A system can be defined as a set of elements organized to perform a set of functions in order to achieve desired results. An element is a set of resources organized to perform a highly integrated subset of the desired system of functions. A systems approach is a logical way of examining and trying to solve problems. It attempts to "map the territory," to show interrelationships among elements in the system (or organization), and to identify operations basic to the mission of the organization. The systems approach stresses decision points and relations among various functions of the organization. It especially focuses attention on operations and functions for which information requirements are not well defined or are not being adequately met.

The systems approach involves the use of a whole family of systems engineering and operations research techniques for systems analysis, systems design, systems simulation, and testing.[1] This paper is confined to models related to delivery of mental health services, to systems analysis and design; it does not deal with simulation and testing.

The models attempt to show how a systems approach can be used to arrive at working answers to the following key questions in planning, organizing, and evaluating mental health service programs: (1) How can the goals of mental health programs be defined in quantifiable terms? (2) How does the currently organized network of services process individuals with problems, and how successfully do the services accomplish the stated goals? (3) What are the critical decision points in the caregiving system, and what kinds of

---

[1] The author suggests the inclusion of "a general caveat about the use of systems engineering and operations research techniques in mental health programming. Use of these techniques presupposes the ability to specify goals in objective, preferably quantifiable terms; to match relatively hard data on needs against resources, according to well scaled priorities; and to identify interrelationships among the various elements as they affect performance of system functions. The field of mental health has not yet developed these abilities beyond the beginning stages. The purpose of the article is to encourage further work along these lines."—Ed.

information are required to make decisions which will lead to accomplishment of specific program goals? (4) What methods can be used to develop a family-oriented information system for indicating specific user requirements? (5) How can a tracking system be established to follow individuals through the community service network? (6) Within a multiservice facility, what methods can be used to keep track of who did what to whom, and with what effect?

DEFINING THE PROBLEM

Model 1[2] approaches the task of defining and categorizing mental health and related problems in terms which will help the mental health agency to decide how large a territory of problems it will attempt to deal with, and what kinds of problems it will concentrate on. The model assumes that the community is the ultimate client of the program, and that the program (whether it is public, private, or voluntary) has been established to cope with difficulties that are of pressing concern to the majority of people in the community. Problems are grouped as being politically defined, socially or culturally defined, and individually defined. Within each category, problems are subgrouped as being direct mental health problems or related problems. (NOTE: This model does not attempt to be exhaustive in its listing of problems. Like many of the other models in this paper, it is presented as a method for systems analysis, rather than as a completed program planning tool.)

Some problems, like mental illness and mental retardation, appear in all three categories. Some, like hostile behavior, may be culturally defined as emotional problems, but, under some circumstances, constitute politically defined offenses. Some problems, like alcoholism and drunken driving, may oscillate between being mental health or related problems and, depending upon severity and environmental conditions, between being individually, culturally, or politically defined problems. The compulsive drinker who cannot hold down a job and support his family usually becomes a social problem; if he is caught driving while intoxicated, regardless of the degree of his social adjustment, he can be prosecuted for a criminal offense. The person suffering from an anxiety neurosis or going through an especially painful period of bereavement is categorized as having a mental health problem as defined by himself and/or his family. If the severely depressed person makes a suicidal attempt, he soon becomes recognized as a problem by the general community and by the local authorities.

[2]Model 1 derives in part from discussions of theoretical formulations with Dr. David J. Vail, Medical Director, and Dr. Arthur S. Funke, Director of the Mental Health Study and Planning Program, Medical Services Division, Minnesota Department of Public Welfare.

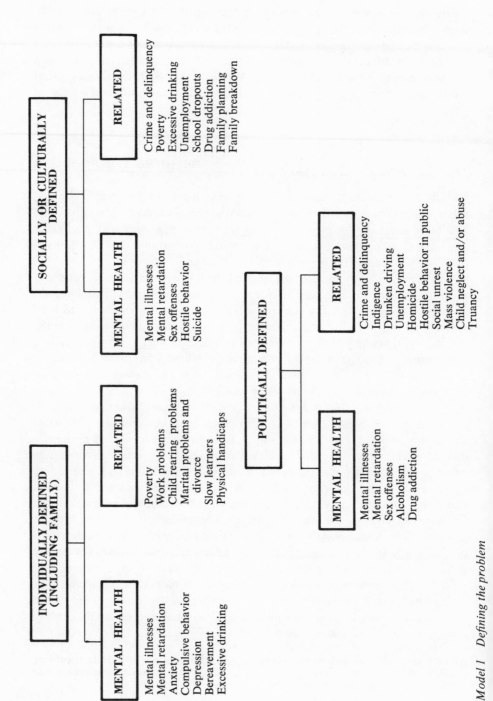

Model 1   Defining the problem

It is obvious that this model does not simplify the complex interrelationships of people with problems and those who try to do something about the problems. The model does attempt to expose and clarify some of these complexities, so that it may assist the mental health program in making a systematic appraisal of problem areas and setting specific goals and priorities.

ASSESSING THE RESOURCES

Model 2 deals with an assessment of the resources. It permits types of personnel and institutions that are available to provide services to be cross-referenced to types of intervention and/or services that may be required to deal with mental health and related problems.

Institutions and personnel are grouped into three categories: public agencies, private agencies, and independent professional workers. Types of intervention and services are subdivided into nine categories: acute emergency; diagnosis; referral; counseling; financial aid; treatment (outpatient, combination, or inpatient); incarceration (inmate or minimum security); care-giving for vulnerable groups, such as the very young, the old, the physically and mental impaired (institutional care, foster care, or home services); and habilitation and rehabilitation, including educational, vocational, physical, social, and recreational services, as well as probation and parole.

The model is essentially an inventory model, and can be used to assess the degree to which existing resources are available to fill various types of need. This model also can be used as a prototype for a model to track individuals through the local service network. (See Model 4.)

ASSESSING THE NEEDS

Model 3 is one example of an information system that may be used to develop data on need for services in terms of "user requirements." It is simply a diagrammatic representation of the flow of information in a county-wide data bank on current users of services, pooled and compiled on a family basis. To the extent that such a data bank is confined to information about current users, it assesses need in terms of the framework or structures in which services are provided as much as in terms of user requirements. It does have another advantage, however, for a different purpose. Pooled information can be made available to the staff of any one contributing agency, obviating the need for extensive and probably incomplete solicitation of information from other relevant agencies each time a new client applies for service.

INSTITUTIONS AND PERSONNEL   TYPES OF INTERVENTION

PUBLIC AGENCIES:	HANDLING ACUTE EMERGENCIES	DIAGNOSIS	REFERRAL	COUNSELING	FINANCIAL AID
Mental hospitals Institutions for handicapped M.H. centers and clinics Health agencies & departments School systems Welfare agencies Housing agencies Police Court system (including parole & probation) Correctional system Youth services Employment services Rehabilitation services Recreational services					
PRIVATE AGENCIES Hospitals M.H. centers and clinics Nursing homes Social service agencies Churches Employment services Rehabilitation services Recreational services					
INDEPENDENT PROFESSIONAL WORKERS: Psychiatrists Psychologists Social workers Nurses Physicians Lawyers Ministers Counselors					

Model 2   Assessing the resources

AND/OR SERVICES

TREATMENT			INCARCERATION		CAREGIVING FOR VULNERABLE GROUPS (young, old, physically and mentally impaired)			HABILITATION AND REHABILITATION (educational, vocational, physical, social & recreational, probation & parole)
O.P.	COMB.	INPAT.	INMATE	MINIMUM SECURITY	INST'NL CARE	FOSTER CARE	HOME SERVICES	

Other methods of assessing need should be mentioned here. These include epidemiological studies, health surveys, analysis of census data, and psychiatric and similar registers. A life crisis model also can be used, in which community needs for intervention at critical life junctures (birth, marriage, death, school crises, and the like) can be estimated on the basis of demographic data.

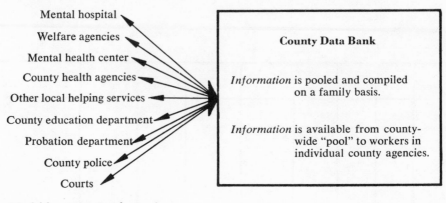

Mental hospital
Welfare agencies
Mental health center
County health agencies
Other local helping services
County education department
Probation department
County police
Courts

County Data Bank

Information is pooled and compiled on a family basis.

Information is available from county-wide "pool" to workers in individual county agencies.

Model 3   Assessing the needs

TRACKING THE INDIVIDUAL THROUGH THE CAREGIVING SYSTEM

Model 4[3] consists of a series of charts illustrating a method for determining the critical pathway of an individual through the caregiving system. These charts follow the individual in terms of services rendered and/or actions taken. The purpose is to show what happens to people at critical points, who makes the decisions about what kinds of service or care they should be given, and what kinds of decisions are made. The charts show, on the vertical axis, the agencies or individuals who might make the decisions or render the service. The horizontal axis lists five critical periods: emergency action, diagnosis and referral, treatment, rehabilitation, and follow-up. The charts can be adapted to show time intervals between these critical periods (and possible hiatuses in service) through the insertion of dates when each period begins and ends.

The mentally ill person's first encounter with the network may be the police, a minister, a physician, or an outpatient mental health facility. The decision as to where he will be sent for diagnosis and referral will depend on

[3]The original paper contained numerous instances of the utilization of Model 4. The two examples which are presented here are a result of an abridgment the author has made of the original material.—Ed.

the facilities available, the information available to the person called on for emergency action, the linkage or lack of linkage among community agencies, and other local factors. Thus, in some communities, police may hold the ill person in a local jail until he can be transferred to the mental hospital for diagnosis and referral. In other communities, diagnosis and referral are made by a court at a commitment hearing, and there is no mental health intervention until the treatment stage begins at the mental hospital. If emergency action is taken at a community based health facility (general hospital, mental health clinic or center), the likelihood is greater that diagnosis and treatment will occur in the community.

The alcoholic who is caught driving while intoxicated will be sent to a court for diagnosis and referral, with perhaps detours to a lawyer and a local jail on the way. The court may decide that he is to be treated at a correctional institution or placed on probation and treated in a mental health setting. Follow-up for the alcoholic may be in the legal rather than in the health sector of the caregiving system.

Similar charts can be used to track the pathway of the drug addict, the sex offender, the juvenile delinquent, the indigent, the victim of family breakdown, and others. This model can be used to identify the people who come for help, the places where they seek that help, and the kinds of problems for which they seek help. It spotlights the critical points at which information is required and the people who need that information. The model also can be used to ascertain why certain kinds of decisions are made and, if they are undesirable, to indicate how they may be changed. Changes can be effected by (1) providing better information, consultation, or other assistance to the decision-maker, and/or (2) introducing changes in the structure of the network so that someone else or some other agency makes the decision at one or more of the critical points. For example, if the mentally ill are being committed to the hospital without prior mental health intervention, it may be possible to arrange with the judge to refer them to a mental health center for care during the period of legal proceedings. Another alternative might be to transfer the diagnosis and referral decision from a legal to a health authority. From the over-all community point of view, such a change might be highly desirable even if it did not benefit the ill person. It would be removing a sizeable burden from an already overtaxed court system which is not particularly equipped to make this type of decision.

ANALYZING THE PRESENT CAREGIVING SYSTEM

Model 5 charts the flow of people with mental health and related problems to and through the web of services performed by different sources of help. The emphasis in these charts is on the linkages among agencies in the network,

PATHWAYS FOR THE MENTALLY ILL

Model 4   Tracking the individual through the system

PATHWAYS FOR CHILDREN AND ADOLESCENTS WITH PROBLEMS

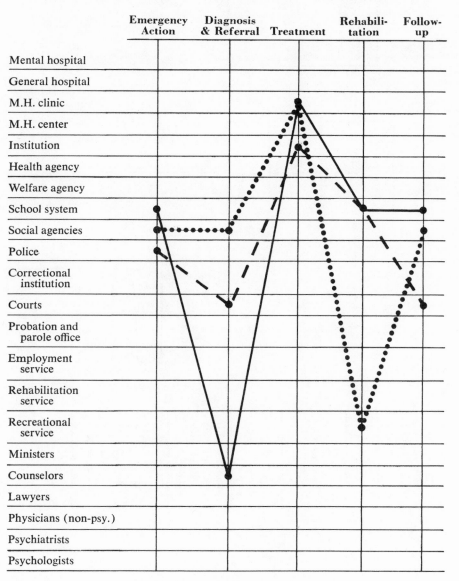

Model 4 Tracking the individual through the system

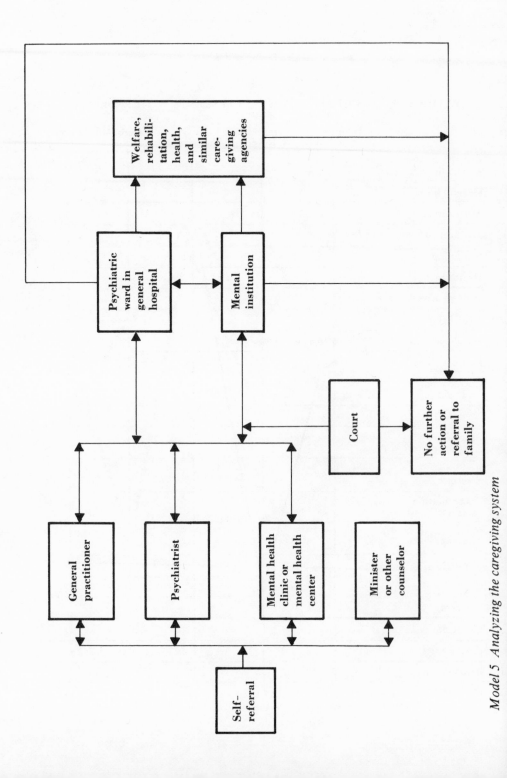

Model 5 Analyzing the caregiving system

and the channels along which people are processed. This model makes it easier to visualize the complex pathways and the many official and nonofficial agencies likely to be involved in providing help.

The first chart is a simplified diagram of pathways to mental health care, starting with self-referral. Model 5A shows another possible circuit in the system if family referral against the patient's wishes is involved. The system might start with school referral of children, with public intervention for severe acting-out behavior in public, or with any one of a number of other subsystems. A separate flow chart could be drawn to chart the interrelations of agencies included in the box labelled "Welfare, rehabilitation, health, and similar caregiving services" in Model 5.

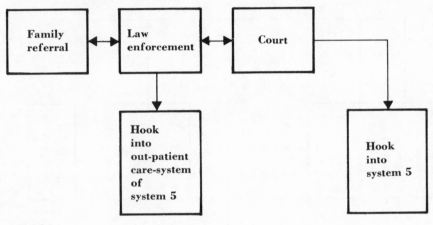

Model 5A

Similar charts can be drawn to analyze the flow of people through the network of agencies when intervention is initiated because of delinquency, adult crime, indigency, handicapping accidents, etc. Such charts make it easy to visualize existing interagency channels, to point up needed changes in those channels, and to indicate what the new pathways would look like. These flow charts are an essential prelude to use of computer simulation to study effects of changes in the system

LINKING THE ELEMENTS OF A MULTISERVICE FACILITY

Model 6[4] illustrates how the elements in a multiservice facility, such as a comprehensive community mental health center, are linked with one another in terms of people who come for help. It can be used to develop an interlocking system of information consisting of diagnosis at intake, admission and/or

[4] Parts of Model 6 were suggested by Dr. Alice Tobler, Director, Division of Planning, Maryland Department of Mental Hygiene.

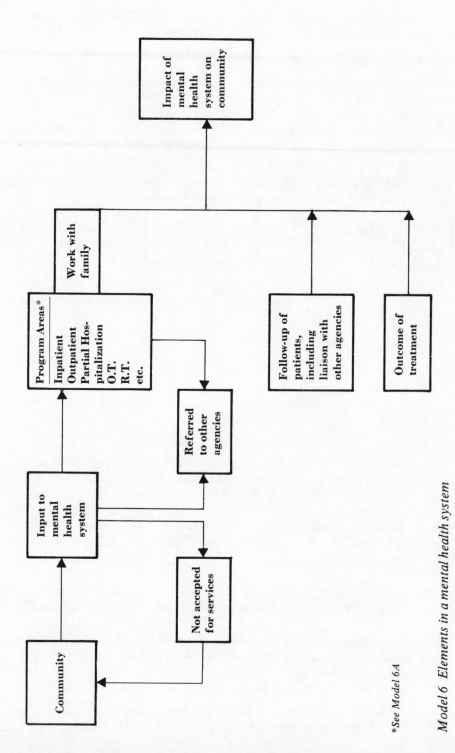

*See Model 6A

Model 6 Elements in a mental health system

referral, referral follow-up, flow and time within facility program areas, work with the family, prognosis at time of discharge, outcome, and follow-up. A system such as that suggested in Model 6 also may help the mental health agency to relate its activities and priorities to the desires, requirements, and expectations of other community agencies. Model 6A[5] charts the possible flow patterns within a mental health center's different facilities. Special problems will arise in maintaining records of this flow because some patients will straddle two or more categories: the outpatient may get treatment in the partial hospitalization unit for several days, the partial hospitalization patient may receive some of his treatment in the inpatient department or may receive therapy in the outpatient unit. Model 6B indicates how three separate data systems—one for the patient, one for the type of service, and one for each staff member—can be used to gather and record information on who did what to whom. In this model, mutually exclusive categories for patient status must be established, and patient status data kept separate from data about the services received.

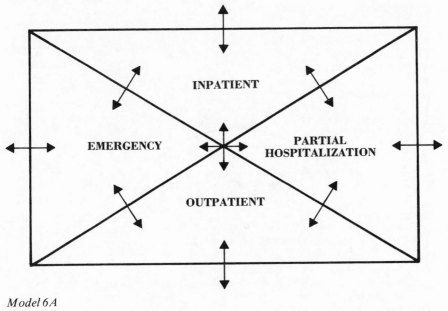

Model 6A

SUMMARY

This paper has attempted to show how systems analysis can be applied to the planning and delivery of mental health services. It stresses the kinds of critical issues that must be considered in organizing such services and evaluating

[5]Models 6A and 6B were developed by Dr. Philip H. Person, Chief, Special Area Studies Section, Biometry Branch, National Institute of Mental Health.

their effectiveness. The models provide a logical series of steps for gathering data, resolving key issues, and deciding on objectives and priorities. The models are merely a skeleton. Additional studies will be needed, particularly to assess needs. A considerable amount of flow-charting will be required to fully analyze the present caregiving system and to achieve a reasonably complete set of charts tracking the more common pathways of individuals through the caregiving system. Flow-charting the linkages between the mental health center and other community agencies will raise critical problems about coordination that may help clarify issues about agency objectives and priorities. The method described in this paper may appear to be no more than organized common sense, a logical approach to a set of problems. That is precisely what systems analysis is all about.

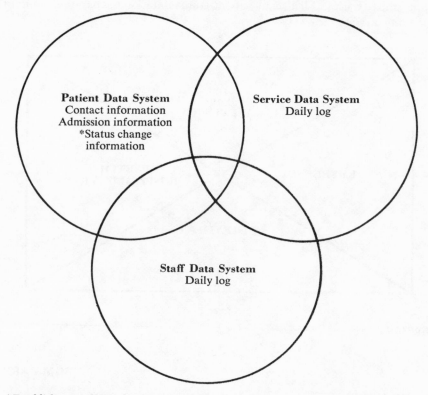

Establish mutually exclusive status categories; no patient can be in more than one category at any one time.

Model 6B

Beginning with a somewhat more formal definition of systems analysis, Levy, Herzog, and Slotkin discuss the uses of a systems approach in evaluating a statewide mental health program. They point out a number of factors that are important in systems evaluation, such as subsystem definition, the application of systems approach, differentiation between objective and outcome, classes of procedures, and practical issues. In addition, they identify several objective, routine indices that are related to community mental health and that can be systematically assessed over time. These ecological or aggregative systems variables are rates of extrusion, rates of antisocial acts, reduction in competence, and rates of social disorganization. Several subsidiary criteria, such as staff and client satisfaction are brought to our attention as well.

the evaluation of statewide mental health programs: a systems approach[1]

Leo Levy, Allen N. Herzog, and Elizabeth J. Slotkin

The current extensive interest in evaluative research in health and welfare contexts can in large part be traced to the concern of administrators and policy-makers in governmental agencies with justifying to themselves (and oftentimes to their politically motivated employers) that the sizeable expenditures of monies on program development and research are in some sense profitable. The determination of how to measure profitability is often a matter of considerable controversy. Economists prefer to measure program, agency or system effectiveness in terms of cost/benefit ratios; program-oriented mental health practitioners, on the other hand, prefer to measure profitability or program effectiveness in terms of health improvement at the individual patient level; finally, administrative program planners often prefer epidemiological measurement criteria, judging the effectiveness or profitability of a program in terms of its ability to reduce the incidence or prevalence of illness. This last type of measurement, much like the measurements of the economist, is measurement at the aggregative or ecological level in which achievements are defined in terms of agency rather than client objectives.

This attitude, characterized by concern with policy, objectives, decisions, costs, benefits, loss functions, systems, optimization, and so forth, can be contrasted sharply with the traditional model of the scientific researcher who the late Sir Ronald Fisher (1956) describes as having the "... duty to

[1]This paper was presented in a symposium entitled "Conceptual and Methodological Issues in the Evaluation of Community Mental Health Programs" at the 74th annual meeting of the American Psychological Association, September 2, 1966.

Reprinted from the *Community Mental Health Journal*, 1968, **4**, 340-349, with the permission of Behavioral Publications, Inc. and the authors.

form correct scientific conclusions, to summarize them and to communicate them to scientific colleagues" and not to be busy himself with the making of decisions to aid in the guidance of industry or in policy implementation.

Evaluative research in the environment of a state mental health department is in fact very much a matter of decision-making and cost-effectiveness determination. This is not to argue, of course, that it is not also a matter of scientific research in the traditional sense, but rather that such factors as time and cost crucially influence and limit our ability to design "ideal" experiments to assist us in making decisions concerning program development and resource allocation.

We have found that one of the first requirements of evaluation research in a state agency context has been the need to develop a conceptual model of the evaluation process so as to avoid being overwhelmed by the enormous variety of data that affect our activities. We have found that conceptualizing evaluation as one element in a systems process model is helpful in providing an overview of our total responsibilities. From this perspective, the evaluation procedure cannot be viewed as an isolated activity, but must be seen as an interdependent element in an interrelated group of activities concerned with the comparison of system achievements with system objectives in a dynamic environment. In a brief paper, it will not be possible to describe the systems process model in full detail but it will be useful to describe those parts of the model that can be illustrated in terms of tangible achievements.

WHAT'S INVOLVED IN EVALUATION

The activities involved in statewide mental health systems evaluation are of the following kinds: system and subsystem definition, system description, system measurement, system evaluation, system analysis, system design, system prediction, system control and system optimization. These activities may be viewed as being on a contiuum of complexity in which system evaluation—the continuous comparison and measurement of highly interdependent outcomes and objectives for purposes of making optimal decisions—operates at all levels of the process.

System definition is concerned with defining the boundaries of the system that we wish to study and eventually control and optimize. The total system we must define, measure and describe must be operationally specified in terms of the limits and constraints under which a state agency operates. These include the legal, budgetary, resource and demographic environmental constraints, as well as the constraints imposed by other competitive and cooperative health and welfare agencies.

Subsystem definition deals with the disaggregation of the total system into manageable parts, both for purposes of data collection and for systems analysis.

HOW THE SYSTEMS APPROACH WAS USED

An example of how we have utilized elements of this systems process model may help to clarify these remarks. In connection with implementing the requirements of the Federal Government's Community Mental Health Centers Construction Act, it was necessary to disaggregate the state into mental health planning areas that satisfied a number of constraints. These were a fixed population base, contiguity of areal units, relative homogeneity with respect to a large number of social and demographic characteristics, and easy accessibility to existing health services by the population. In solving this problem under the imposed constraints, we had to select an appropriate demographic unit to aggregate into larger population units, and to develop where needed, an objective (mathematical) optimization procedure for combining these elementary units. The selection of the units was an evaluation problem in that it required us to choose the best unit according to various operational criteria that would meet the overall objectives of the Department. A particularly difficult problem exists in Chicago because of the great variety of possibilities open to us. We eventually utilized a mathematical grouping procedure that satisfied the constraints and combined community areas (combinations of census tracts) so that they were maximally homogeneous with respect to a large number of ecological characteristics. We presently face the additional problem of evaluating to what extent this areal grouping will be satisfactory in the long run.

It should be noted that the problem of aggregation is especially peculiar to agency evaluation of programs in contrast to evaluation at the micro-level, as, for instance, in the evaluation of the effectiveness of psychotherapeutic procedures in clinical investigations in which the target population is defined as residing in a geographic area. For example, primary prevention programs are not aimed at particular individuals but at a population resident in a specified area. This makes it impossible to measure program effectiveness in terms of change indices measured on specific individuals over time, but instead forces us to utilize aggregative ecological measurements.

In solving this problem it can be seen that we used several of the system elements mentioned previously although in a highly specialized context. It was necessary to develop system descriptions of relevant variables, measurement procedures for defining these variables, systems analysis for interrelating the chosen variables, and systems optimization procedures for obtaining best solutions. Systems control and systems prediction were not applicable at this stage of our work. Systems design, on the other hand, was represented by the fact that in the procedures we developed we were guided by the informal design objective of the comprehensive community mental health centers model. This model can be seen as primarily a proposed systems design intended to provide a package of mental health services and programs at the community level. One major implicit objective of this approach is to reduce the patient population in the state hospitals as rapidly as possible.

So much then, for the conceptual systems approach. We aim ultimately towards total systems optimization and control but at present we are still working with fairly isolated subsystems rather than with the total system. In many cases, we have not progressed much beyond the level of system definition and description, although for some well-defined subsystems, we have achieved the measurement level. What this approach forces us to consider is the fact that we are dealing with a large number of interdependent subsystems and cautions us to consider at least conceptually, how changes in one part will affect other parts of the system. For example, it is fairly obvious that by providing state grant-in-aid to private facilities, we reduce the Department's ability to recruit personnel needed to operate its own subsystem programs. However, in terms of the community mental health model which guides us, this in the long run is expected to provide greater benefits than if we pursued more selfish ends. It has also provided us with a model for developing a statewide data base utilizing a very detailed facilities survey. This latter will permit us to evaluate the changing facility environment over time, and to measure the effectiveness of our resource use in providing greater and more varied services.

COMPARING OBJECTIVE WITH OUTCOME

In the foregoing remarks we have used the term "systems evaluation" in a fairly informal way on the assumption that it is a generally understood concept. We should now like to turn to the problem of providing a more careful explication of this notion. The question to be answered here is whether the qualifying adjective "evaluation" when attached to the noun "research" makes any useful distinction. Clearly, if it does not, then its only significance is emotive and not substantive. We should like to suggest that the distinguishing feature of "evaluation" at least in the context in which we use it, is the comparison of an operationally defined objective with an observed outcome. The purpose of this comparison is to make a decision among alternative actions that involve cost as well as effectiveness considerations. The determination of whether the objective and the outcome are coincident is a matter of inductive inference, and it is here that the techniques of inferential statistics and research design become highly relevant. Roughly what we are trying to say is that systems evaluation is not an isolated activity but an element in a systems process that is concerned with making an inference from the observation of a complex outcome as to whether an objective has been achieved. A decision resulting in an action is the product of this inference.

The crucial feature here is the comparison between objective and outcome and this involves the inferential strategy to be employed. In making decisions in an uncertain environment in which utilities are attached to outcomes with unknown probability distributions it is necessary to utilize whatever data are available to make such decisions even if this involves nothing more than informed guesswork.

CLASSES OF PROCEDURES

The inferential procedures we may utilize can roughly be divided into three classes: experimental, quasi-experimental, and nonexperimental. Experimental procedures that currently have a place of pride in our arsenal are characterized by: planned or homogeneous grouping of materials so as to eliminate the effect of background variables not part of the experiment; experimental design or patterning to avoid bias in making measurements; mechanical randomization so as to avoid bias among uncontrolled variables influencing the dependent variable; and replication so as to provide a measure of precision or experimental error. Randomization assures valid estimates of error and makes possible the application of statistical tests of significance. It should be noted, however, that the beneficial effects of randomization are obtained in the long run and not in a single isolated experiment—a situation rarely achievable in social experimentation in real situations.

Quasi-experimental inference is characterized by the fact that randomization is not possible but that some control over the treatment condition can be maintained. Campbell and Stanley (1963) have studied this problem in great detail and suggest a variety of designs that permit inferences from such situations with minimal bias. They distinguish between the internal validity of an experiment that asks the question: Did, in fact, the administered treatments make a difference in the outcome? And external validity that asks the question of generalizability: To what populations, settings, treatment variables and measurement variables can the noticed effect be generalized? Quasi-experiments are, perhaps, the only inferential paradigms applicable to the evaluation of impact programs such as community mental health and prevention programs, but even here it is often all but impossible to provide adequate treatment variable control.

Nonexperimental inference is concerned essentially with formulating and fitting models to observed data, no matter how observed, in which neither randomization or controlled treatment are possible. What is involved here is the development of models interrelating relevant variables in a conceptually meaningful way and then testing these models. It is one of the purposes of this paper to suggest that the use of quasi-experimental and nonexperimental inference modes are more appropriate to evaluation research than the traditional but often impractical experimental inference mode.

LOOKING AT PRACTICAL ISSUES

Having made some comments on theory and research methodology, we should like in the remainder of this paper to examine some practical issues. First, we want to examine the varied problems associated with estimating the true incidence and prevalence of mental illness; second, we should like to consider the problem of defining the significant kinds of ecological variables that might be associated with mental illness; and finally, we should like to describe the development of a procedure of program budgeting that we expect will permit us to determine program costs more accurately and so provide us with the ability to measure program costs. This, it is hoped will permit us to allocate our scarce resources more effectively and to evaluate institutional cost/effectiveness behavior. In connection with this last objective, we want to mention a number of aspects of system evaluation that are concerned with evaluating the support systems that are required in meeting our primary agency objectives.

From the long-run perspective our mission is seen as measuring the effects of treatment programs on the prevalence of mental illness in the state and the effect of prevention programs on the incidence of mental illness in the state. The methods available for determining whether these primary goals have been achieved must of necessity rely heavily on reported statistical indices concerning mentally ill people, and other ecological indices related to mental illness and treatment. The inferential procedures that can be employed are to a large extent quasi-experimental and nonexperimental methods associated with epidemiological and system models. Our problems in this area are well known and can be summarized very briefly.

Psychiatric conditions are ill-defined and our psychiatric nomenclature is highly unreliable. Exact counts of disturbed people are difficult to establish and very costly to estimate. The best examples of such estimates involve house-to-house surveys such as has been accomplished by the Leightons and associates in Nova Scotia (1963) and Srole and his associates in New York City (1962). A recent review of some 26 epidemiological surveys of this nature, done by Dohrenwend and Dohrenwend (1965) indicates a dilemma. Because of problems in the definition of what is a mentally ill person, such studies report findings that range from a small and insignificant fraction of the population afflicted with mental illness, up to the enormous figure reported by Srole that 80 percent of the population is in some degree psychiatrically impaired. One may legitimately question whether such prevalence studies are really economically worthwhile, in the light of the tremendous ambiguity surrounding the variables that we wish to measure. We might ask whether our basic problem is not to develop less ambiguous nomenclature.

Another kind of attempt to establish incidence and prevalence rates is based on the use of admission statistics to all psychiatric facilities. Such statistics can be collected at considerable expense in a fairly refined way by the use of a psychiatric case registry. Such registries have been developed in Maryland, Hawaii, Monroe County, New York and in a three-county area in North Carolina. The registry is immensely helpful to use in measuring the demand characteristics for psychiatric facilities and treatment. However, they do not answer the question of the actual incidence and prevalence in the population at risk, and one would be badly misled to accept admission statistics as representing a total count of disturbed persons. Such an error would lead us into the untenable position of having to say that every time a mental health facility opens up in a community, the incidence and/or prevalence of mental illness rises sharply. This is due to the peculiar tendency in the health field for demand to equal supply.

MEASURING PROGRAMS OVER TIME

Turning to another methodological problem, even if we could develop adequate measures of incidence and prevalence, we would still be confronted with a baffling kind of phenomenon. This has to do with the measurement of effectiveness of programs over time. If one establishes an incidence rate, for example, at one period of time, then institutes in a community, an explicitly formulated prevention program aimed specifically at that condition, and then measures of incidence are obtained periodically over a long period of time, changes may occur. As is well known, these changes may or may not be related to our prevention program. If a decrease in incidence occurs, one may say that it may have occurred anyway without the prevention program due to uncontrolled background factors, one of which may be that the population of the area has changed in terms of its demographic characteristics. In addition, other programs aimed at the same kind of morbid condition may have been developed concurrently with our own program and also affected the incidence rate. The very program that we introduce in its actual implementation may alter conditions in the community so that other agencies may, without any formalized statement of purpose, orient themselves toward the reduction of the incidence of the condition. This problem again emphasizes the need to approach the problem of program evaluation in terms of an overall systems model that takes account of as many related factors and programs as possible. One approach that has been suggested, particularly in delinquency studies, is to select a control and an experimental community and to measure not simply the change following the introduction of the program in the experimental community, but instead, the deviation from the predicted level of the variable under study in both experimental and control communities, since, without the program one would expect that the various uncontrolled factors would still continue to operate. This is in principle a quasi-experimental design since the subjects cannot be randomly allocated between communities. In addition, it should be noted also that the experimental unit here is a community and not the persons living in the community, thus providing relatively few degrees of freedom for error estimation. There is also a tendency for contaminating influences to feed back and affect the treatment variable.

ROUTINE INDICES

This latter problem suggests that as a statewide evaluation agency, we must carefully identify community units in the state. In addition, we must identify and describe all programs that are related to mental health in these communities. Having done this, we must then identify objective indices that are related to community mental health and systematically measure them over time. These are essentially what we have previously referred to as the ecological or aggregative systems variables. There are four general classes of indices that should be routinely examined. These are:

1. *Rates of extrusion.* A rate of extrusion is a basic index that tells us how many people are being disengaged from the normal community process forcibly and evacuated to noncommunity resources. This means admissions to state mental hospitals, persons sentenced to prison, persons sent to schools for the mentally retarded and to juvenile detention facilities. It is also of pertinence to measure the rates of admission to nursing homes for the elderly as these, too, are in effect an extrusion from the community. Our purpose here is quite simple. It is based on the assumption that mentally ill and retarded persons should be, for the most part, cared for in their communities of residence. Any mental health program that purports to be serving the community's needs should have an impact on the rates of extrusion into these various facilities.

2. *Rates of antisocial acts.* While offenses against the community are not synonymous with mental illness, they should be of concern to mental health professionals working in a community. Indices such as the commission of major crimes, particularly crimes against persons (rape, assault, murder), juvenile delinquent acts, numbers of battered babies reported, suicide rates, etc., may be considered the major responsibilities of other agencies. However, they are critically related to our mental health effort. We

think it could be safely asserted that an effective mental health program in a community would result in a progressive reduction of these categories of antisocial acts.

3. *Reduction in competence.* One of the goals of the mental health program is to maintain citizens in their community of residence, functioning at a high level of competence. Hence, statistics that indicate reduced competence in the community are of concern to mental health practitioners. These include rates of unemployment, divorce, school dropouts, welfare caseloads, outpatient clinic caseloads, including those being seen by private practitioners, social agency caseloads, rates of alcoholism and narcotic addiction.

4. *Rates of social disorganization.* Again, here one must accept the broadened definition of the responsibility of mental health workers in order to understand the inclusion of these kinds of rates as evaluative indices of a mental health program. The assumption that is explicitly made here is that good community mental health programs will make for organized and viable communities, and that the lack of them will promote social disorganization. While rates in this area such as number of racial incidents, extent of dilapidated housing, number of people in poverty, illegitimate birth rate, infant mortality and maternal mortality, are generally conceded to be the primary responsibility of other than mental health personnel, still, mental health programs must be evaluated in terms of how well they affect the statistics in these categories. Implicitly what we are saying is that the mental health program does not only offer services to disturbed persons but also offers consultation and facilitative advice to other primary caretaking agencies which may have a direct impact on these indices.

SUBSIDIARY CRITERIA

Although as mentioned previously, the evaluation of program effectiveness in reducing the incidence and prevalence of mental illness is our main objective, to achieve this remote goal, it is necessary also to consider the intermediate objectives and the support structure available to meet these objectives in our evaluation effort. This means that we must consider a number of subsidiary evaluation criteria as well. Among these are the following: (1) System Viability. Is the system or subsystem able to adapt to planned change and new demands; is it able to maintain its current level of operation; is it able to grow and develop without excessive external support? (2) Service Elements. Are the services provided adequate in quality and quantity and in the proper mix and variety to meet demands? (3) Satisfaction. Are the staff and clients satisfied with services provided and working conditions? (4) Resource Utilization. Are budgets, equipment and personnel utilized in such a manner as to meet agency objectives? (5) Management. Is there an adequate management control, information and planning system utilizing rational and economic means for allocating resources, monitoring achievements and meeting planned objectives on schedule?

PROGRAM BUDGETING

It is beyond the scope of this paper to describe in any greater detail the use of such intermediate evaluative procedures, but we should like to mention one tool we have been developing for evaluation purposes, namely, program budgeting. Essentially, program budgeting is a system in which expenditures rather than being classified in terms of inputs, are classified by objectives, and then subclassified by programs, subprograms, services, and activities in an hierarchical system. In developing this system we have defined five major departmental functions which are (1) primary prevention, (2) treatment and rehabilitation, (3) research and training, (4) plant maintenance and institutional services, and (5) administration. These are the major functions the Department must perform in order to achieve its three chief objectives which are (1) prevention of mental illness and treatment and rehabilitation of the mentally ill, (2) resource development through training and research, and (3) "good" management. The use of this technique for evaluation lies mainly in the possibility, which we are now exploring, of relating patient costs by program classification, which should permit us to determine cost per patient within program. Later we hope to relate such program costs to other indices of patient improvement to provide cost/effectiveness measurements of patient care. This approach is very similar to cost accounting procedures developed in many general hospitals, but it is oriented toward program objectives rather than toward service or responsibility centers cost allocation. We have made considerable progress in developing this procedure in that we have developed a chart of accounts, a coding system, and a computer-based procedure for processing the information for purposes of budget forecasting, operational control of expenditures, and between institutional comparisons. We have not as yet coded the patients by program elements which means that the system is currently primarily oriented toward evaluation of the budgetary management functions.

SUMMARY

In this paper we have tried to make a number of points which we believe are useful for discriminating between the kinds of evaluation processes a state evaluation division is concerned with, as contrasted with other research groups. Among the significant things we hope we have established are the following: (1) Evaluation is primarily for the purpose of making decisions about the cost/effectiveness with which administrative policies and objectives are achieved in a dynamic environment. (2) Since the problems we face in-volve considerations of very large bodies of data, it is necessary to take a systems approach in order to adequately grasp the interrelationships which affect our policy decisions. (3) The inferential procedures we use in evaluat-ing the outcomes of programs can rarely be experimental if we wish to react in sufficient time to provide guidance on policy matters. (4) There is a great need in evaluation procedures to consider not only the remote objective but also the intermediate objectives as well. And, finally, in developing adequate evaluation procedures, we must develop a variety of instruments and tech-niques both program-oriented and cost-oriented in order to make optimal decisions.

REFERENCES

Campbell, D. T., and Stanley, J. Experimental and quasi-experimental designs for research on teaching. N. L. Gage, ed., *Handbook of research on teaching.* Chicago: Rand McNally, 1963. Pp. 171-246.

Dohrenwend, B. P., and Dohrenwend, B. S. The problem of validity in field studies of psychological disorder. *Journal of Abnormal Psychology,* 1965, **70,** 52-62.

Fisher, R. A. *Statistical methods and scientific inference.* Edinburgh: Oliver and Boyd, 1956.

Leighton, D.C., et al. *The character of danger: Psychiatric symptoms in selected communities.* New York: Basic Books, 1963.

Srole, L., et al. *Mental health in the metropolis: The midtown Manhattan study.* New York: McGraw-Hill, 1962.

State of Illinois. Department of Mental Health, Division of Planning and Evaluation. The Illinois state plan for the construction of community mental health cen-ters, 1965-1967.

State of Illinois, Department of Mental Health. Program budgeting chart of accounts, 1966 (mimeo).

suggested additional readings

Carter, J. W., ed. *Research contributions from psychology to community mental health.* New York: Behavioral Publications, 1968.

Fairweather, G. W. *Methods for experimental social innovation.* New York: Wiley, 1967.

Phillips, L. *Human adaptation and its failures.* New York: Academic Press, 1968.

Suchman, E. A. *Evaluative research: Principles and practice in public service and social action programs.* New York: Russell Sage Foundation, 1967.

seven   the future

The Boston Conference, which formally heralded the arrival of community psychology, was a conference on training. It was mentioned previously that the development of a viable theory and a sound research base are two critical demands of community psychology and community mental health. There is one more: The training we provide for tomorrow's professionals will determine the extent to which the first two needs are met. It will determine also whether community psychology and community mental health ultimately will make significant contributions to human welfare, or whether they will fall by the wayside to be remembered as passing professional fads— a bandwagon that professionals were eager to board and eager to abandon.

The question of research and training in community psychology has not been ignored since the Boston Conference and, fortunately, the field is not "locked-in" to any one model of training. Training programs are even more varied than the kinds of community psychologists that Scribner identified (Section one). How do we go about training participant-conceptualizers? Only through constantly reevaluating our training programs will progress be made. The first article in this section offers some suggestions on training for research in community mental health.

As we await the establishment of a firm research underpinning for community psychology, as we evaluate training, and as theoretical formulations and reformulations are made, attention must be given also to the area of community psychology and community mental health practice. One issue at the Boston conference was a concern over activism. Bennett (Section one) reported: "It was not the province of the Conference to write a code of ethics for community psychology, but it was obvious that very subtle issues are at stake in distinguishing between professional expertness and value judgments in this unstructured area of community service." Scribner's discussion of the kinds of activities of community psychologists further highlighted this issue.

266

The social-movement psychologist does quite different things than the traditional psychologist. There is also a tendency to view the "social engineer" from a nonneutral point of view. Recently, many community psychologists have become interested in advocacy, in other words, active and political support and action on behalf of a client or constituency, a policy that raises some very interesting questions of value and ethics. The social work profession already has considered the professional implications of the advocate role (Ad Hoc Committee on Advocacy, National Association of Social Workers, Task Force on the Urban Crisis and Public Welfare Problems, 1969). Values and ethics in community psychology are as important as training to its development as a profession. And these facets of the development of the profession are as important as theory and research are to the development of the behavioral science components of community psychology. The final article in this collection suggests some of the ethical issues involved in community psychology.

The time for professional self-examination is here. The challenge is clear. With responsive action the behavioral sciences, social sciences, and helping professions can develop meaningful approaches to human problems.

REFERENCE

Ad Hoc Committee on Advocacy, National Association of Social Workers, Task Force on the Urban Crisis and Public Welfare Problems. The social worker as advocate: champion of social victims. *Social Work*, April 1969, 16-22.

Lenin Baler, in the following article, uses three concepts associated with the socialization process to discuss what training institutions can do to effectively prepare students for research in community mental health. He refers to "basic trust," "feelings of competence," and "sense of identity," and makes a number of suggestions related to training. Community practicum experiences, for example, are essential and should begin in undergraduate psychology training. Changes need also to be made with regard to classroom instruction, so that academia and the community be brought closer together.

training for research in community mental health[1]

Lenin A. Baler

Concerning research in the community mental health field, there would appear to be consensus on two points. First, the most urgent need is for basic and applied research on a wide scale. This assertion occurs in epidemic frequency in most official documents, conference reports, position papers, and symposia. It also typically appears in more muted form in the last paragraph of agency annual reports. Second, among the various specialties in mental health, psychology is expected, by virtue of its constitutionally defined self-image as both a science and a profession, to be ethically committed to doing research. To be sure, the relative ratio of research to practice is sensibly permitted to vary with the interest intensity and competence level of the individual psychologist, but university training programs have always operated on the assumption that the individual psychologist's direct and indirect contribution to research should be well above zero.

Now, if the community at large can confront the mental health professions with the challenge of enabling legislation and logistical support to launch a "bold, new approach" to the prevention and control of mental disorders, it would seem only fitting that psychologists accept the in-group challenge to train students so that they will be equipped with the requisite skills and motivation to make a contribution to community mental health research that will indeed be well above zero.

Manpower resources are such that students at all levels of training ought

[1]This article is a revision of "The Psychologist as Community Mental Health Research Specialist," a paper read at the Annual Meeting of the American Psychological Association, New York, 1966.

Reprinted from the *Community Mental Health Journal*, 1967, **3**, 250-253, with the permission of Behavioral Publications, Inc. and the author.

to be of some value in the research effort. It is certainly regrettable that the large number of talented psychology students who do not go beyond the bachelor's degree are lost to the manpower pool as potential research assistants and technicians frankly because their present undergraduate education has just about zero transfer value for community research tasks. Present doctoral training, in particular in clinical psychology, automatically produces, at least in the opinion of several observers, negative transfer value. Finally, staff members involved in postdoctoral community mental health specialist programs sometimes feel that it is too late and that as in psychotherapy few patients can really be "cured" in spite of best efforts!

The thesis of this paper is that training institutions need to socialize students early and continuously for the role of community mental health researcher.

One cannot, in fairness, identify a problem without proferring at least a few speculations as to the required remedy. Perhaps the simplest way of doing this is to organize the discussion around three concepts universally used when psychologists talk about the socialization process: basic trust, feelings of competence, and sense of identity.

BASIC TRUST

It is painful to note that psychologists who as professionals seek so earnestly to promote mental health in others by arguing the case for basic trust as nuclear to maturity in any social role have often failed to secure this "highest good" for themselves within their own training institutions. The reference here, of course, is to the long-endemic irrational and destructive clash between the so-called scientists and the practitioners within university psychology departments and between academic staff and community line workers. Probably few students, indeed, have failed to perceive this climate of distrust and consequently to suffer constraints upon their own full development as psychologists.

An articulate and thoroughly incisive analysis of this situation has recently been made by Chein (1966). He takes a close look at the problem as a social process, as the clash of two subcultures, and as a political conflict. One of the serious consequences of this basic distrust is the derogation of scholarship. In Chein's words, "blatant ignorance, stereotyping, and lack of comprehension become a sufficient basis for oracular pronouncements on the incompetence of the outermost out-group to make any significant contributions to psychology." Particularly disconcerting is that community mental health workers (whether in research or practice) currently constitute the most likely candidates for Chein's "outermost out-group" label.

The solution Chein proposes seems entirely reasonable. He says, "I am, thus, not pleading for a burial of differences. On the contrary, I am saying that we should open them up and bring them out from behind the fog of interpersonal and intergroup hostility. It is time for us to grow up and stop confusing our interpersonal and intergroup problems with the business of psychology." It needs only to be added that a similar solution is applicable to the divisiveness between psychologists and psychiatrists if they are to work really productively together in practice and research in the community mental health field.

If the present schism between the scientist and the practitioner continues unabated in the university, the university will remain a grossly inept socializing agent for training psychologists in community mental health. The academic scientist can produce much useful research even though he may escape into scientism. The clinical practitioner can contribute significantly to human welfare even though he may escape into clinicalism. In contrast, a line community mental health researcher cannot function with such a one-sided identity pattern; he must achieve an integrated identity as scientist-practitioner (Gelfand and Kelly, 1960). This is so because there is no such thing as community research apart from community practice. As long as psychologists are reared in a climate of distrust that demands schizophrenic adjustments to the scientist and practitioner roles, competent community mental health researchers will remain in very short supply.

FEELINGS OF COMPETENCE

One normally prefers to do what he feels competent to do. Psychologists as presently trained are all too frequently dramatically incompetent to undertake community research. Even senior psychologists enrolled in postdoctoral community mental health training programs often lack rudimentary practical knowledge of community organization, are totally inexperienced in operating in the real community in regard to sanction problems or collaboration with nonprofessionals, and find embryonic their mastery of relevant technical research skills, such as questionnaire construction, survey methodology, and the art of just plain naturalistic observation. This situation is rather appalling when one recalls that in the first lecture in introductory psychology the instructor is apt to write on the board the universally accepted formula "Behavior results from the interaction between the person and his environment." It is hard to understand how the study of the environment (in terms of the customary goals of description, prediction, and control) is subsequently so neglected conceptually in the curriculum and neglected experientially in field assignments. As pointed out earlier, adequate socialization for the role of community mental health research worker must begin early and occur continuously.

COMMUNITY PRACTICUM

Absolutely mandatory is the development of a series of graded community practicum experiences that begin as early as possible in undergraduate training in psychology. These can vary from simple homework exercises, tutorial supervision, clerkship, and extra assignments to summer apprenticeship and internship placement. What can be the objections to this? It will "water down" the intellectual quality of college work? Nonsense. It has every chance of doing just the opposite by enriching the student's awareness of the nature of reliable and valid data, the utility of theories and conceptual models for formulating hypotheses, and the operational complexity of research designs required to test such hypotheses. Another objection may be that the average undergraduate is not mature enough to carry out and to benefit from such assignments. Again, nonsense; look at what young people are able to do and learn as mental health volunteers, as Vista workers in the poverty program, as "big brothers and sisters" in delinquency control. The main requirement for success is that the community practicum be overtly and honestly valued by the faculty and integrated thoroughly into the formal classroom subject matter. Basic trust thus continues to be of overriding importance.

What are some specific examples of practicum experiences of potential value in the early socialization of psychologists as community mental health research workers? Space permits a sketchy listing of only five:

1. For a given community, obtain the U.S. census data for 1950 and 1960. What demographic and socioeconomic changes have occurred? Discuss the implications in terms of the need for mental health services of different types.

2. Administer a questionnaire that taps attitudes toward mental illness of members of the local police force. Discuss the results with reference to the need for a mental health in-service training program for the police.

3. In collaboration with the staff of the local high school, compute the over-all dropout rate over the past five years. See if the rate varies with some other variable, such as age or sex.

4. A certain health bill is coming up for legislative hearings. Attend these and observe what agencies present arguments pro and con. Follow up with individual interviews to ascertain agency goals and motivations behind the official position on the bill.

5. During the summer, volunteer to serve as an aide to a public health nurse. Accompany her on home visits. Keep a daily log and write a final report highlighting how her job involves mental health work directly and indirectly.

To summarize at this point, the contention here is that unless psychologists are socialized early in some fashion along the lines suggested above they will be unlikely to develop a serious interest in community mental health research during doctoral training or later in their career.

FORMAL CLASSROOM INSTRUCTION

The acquisition of feelings of competence as a community research worker requires not only the community practicum experience just discussed but also is dependent upon adequate classroom instruction in relevant research logic and methodology. That something is very much amiss here has been recognized by many. Recently Marvin Dunnette (1966) has cleverly pinpointed the details of the problem. Taking his cue from Berne (1964), Dunnette examines the games that psychologists play in the name of science but which lead "down the primrose path to nonscience" and to nonsense. One instance of Dunnette's slashing insight can be seen in his definition of folderol as "those practices characterized by . . . wasteful fiddle-faddle —including tendencies to be fixated on theories, methods, and points of view, conducting 'little' studies with great precision . . . asking unimportant or irrelevant questions . . . coining new names for old concepts. . . ."

Learning how to "play games" has its own reward, to be sure. The reward clearly is not, however, feelings of competence in skills relevant to community mental health line research. A solution is exceedingly difficult to come by, because the acquired love of gamesmanship perpetuates itself as each new generation of students passes through the university. A moral injunction "Let's stop playing games!" merely raises the suspicion that some fascinating new game is about to be played.

A few psychologists have managed to reject the "establishment" and happily have been socialized in the real world of social commitment and social action research. Part of the solution to the problem under discussion is somehow to get these individuals to accept appointments on the faculties of our academic institutions. Another part of the solution lies in getting some of the more promising university scientists out of the ivory tower to function, not as mere alienated consultants, but as line researchers on the community team. Maybe then students can learn the basic research skills they really need: the ability to accept without paralyzing anxiety the fact that nonexperimental data is unwieldy, the ability to see a correlation based on naturalistic observation, not as an object of disparagement, but as a challenge to explore further whether the relationship is direct, indirect, or simply spurious, the ability to undertake applied research without feeling that one is committing an unforgivable sin.

SENSE OF IDENTITY

The task of completing the socialization of the psychologist for the role of community mental health research worker falls necessarily to the community mental health field agency itself. It is here "on the firing line" that the sense of identity must be firmed up and spelled out. It is here where the action is that community research problems can most realistically be formulated. It is here where the newcomer must learn to get along with the other members of the multidisciplinary mental health team. It is here in the neighborhood around the agency that the community laboratory exists as the proper source of data and as the sounding board for action research. It is here, in short, where the acid test of self-worth as a community mental health research worker is given and scored and where the report card is issued.

The novice researcher must adjust to many problems, and he needs all the sense of trust his earlier training at the university has built into his role repertoire. He discovers quickly that he is not the central actor in the agency drama, that his colleagues are busy with incredibly heavy day-to-day workloads of service, that his administrators are preoccupied politically with winning program acceptance, that the community purse-holders are apt to regard research out of hand as mere frills, and that, on the surface at least, everyone accepts the worth of present services as face-valid and not requiring evaluative research.

Adaptation to this situation, interestingly enough, requires that the researcher use the practitioner skills acquired from earlier community practicum experiences to demonstrate that he feels competent to function as a researcher in such a way as to be of value to the agency and to the community. As Brooks (1965) states, the researcher can provide sensible ideas for experimenting with modifications in agency practice, collect and analyze demographic and other types of data necessary for agency planning, and assist in the planning process itself by helping the staff follow the steps in standard decision-making models. This type of cooperative behavior on the researcher's part is likely to lead automatically to agency sanction and encouragement to design and implement the basic research and program evaluative research that he is committed to as nuclear to his self-image. By way of contrast, if the researcher had come to the field agency without previously achieving a sense of trust and feelings of competence, he would almost certainly fail in turn to achieve an acceptable sense of identity.

REFERENCES

Berne, E. *Games people play.* New York: Grove Press, 1964.

Brooks, M. P. The community action program as a setting for applied research. *Journal of Social Issues*, 1965, **21**, 29-40.

Chein, I. Some sources of divisiveness among psychologists. *American Psychologist*, 1966, **21**, 333-342.

Dunnette, M. D. Fads, fashions, and folderol in psychology. *American Psychologist*, 1966, **21** 343-352.

Gelfand, S., and Kelly, J. G. The psychologist in community mental health: Scientist and professional. *American Psychologist*, 1960, **15**, 223-226.

The last paper in this section is an excerpt from an article on ethics by Stuart Golann. Golann reports that community psychologists feel the Ethical Standards of Psychologists *to be basically adequate for the community psychologist, but lacking in examples of applications to community situations. He poses four questions that represent the sorts of ethical issues raised in community activities. The question emerges: What should be the ethical standards of the community psychologist, participant-conceptualizer, and change agent?*

excerpt from:

emerging areas of ethical concern

Stuart E. Golann

The work of the community psychologist may not be as defined or understood as that of the psychotherapist (Bennett, 1965). The community psychologist attempts to substitute new strategies of intervention in place of preoccupation with selection of the method of treatment for direct services to patients (Golann, 1969; 1970). He may attempt to develop and test intervention strategies based on several explicit choices including the selection of the helper, the selection of the target or client group, planful consideration of the occasion or timing of the intervention, and the selection of the location where the services are to be offered. Examples, such as utilization of nonprofessional therapists, identification of risk factors within the population and related attempt at preventive intervention, or consultation with practitioners or planners with community systems, present possible useful innovations and may also present ethical challenges.

In a survey of the membership of the Division of Community Psychology it was asked if the *Ethical Standards of Psychologists* was adequate for the needs of the psychologist working in this relatively new area.[1] The respondents suggested that the standards were seen as adequate in a general way. But much more exemplification derived from community practice was desired, and the need for something like the APA *Casebook on Ethical Standards* (APA, 1967) specific to community psychology was expressed.

There are several important ethical issues that emerge from or are highlighted by developments in community psychology. The following four may be especially important.

[1] The survey was conducted by Milton Shore and the present author.

1. Is there a basic conflict between community-oriented attempts to prevent personality disorder and growing concern for human rights such as privacy and informed consent?

2. Is consent required from consultees, such as teachers or public health nurses, before an attempt is made to change their attitudes or feelings toward clients with whom they work?

3. What guidelines should be followed if a psychologist is actively participating in programs of social change within a field of conflicting values, either in our own rapidly changing areas or in foreign countries?

4. What guidelines are required to deal with problems that may arise in various types of studies when the needs and objectives of the research sponsor conflict with those of the investigator at some point in the research process (Orlans, 1967)?

In questions such as these, the interests of the community psychologist merge with those of all social scientists whose work is coming to have increasingly important public policy implications. The politics of science may strain the *Ethical Standards of Psychologists* quite severely, and has already stimulated efforts at codification of ethical practice by several of the Associations representing allied social sciences.

REFERENCES

American Psychological Association. *Casebook on ethical standards of psychologists.* Washington, D.. C.: Author,1967.

APA Committee on Ethical Standards for Psychology. Ethical Standards for psychology. *American Psychologist,* 1963, **18**, 56-60.

Bennett, C. C. Community psychology: Impressions of the Boston Conference on the education of psychologists for community mental health. *American Psychologist,* 1965, **20**, 832-835.

Golann, S. E. Community psychology and mental health: An analysis of strategies and a survey of training. I. Iscoe and C. D. Spielberger, eds., *Community psychology: Perspectives in training and research.* New York: Appleton-Century-Crofts, 1970.

Golann, S. E. *Coordinate index reference guide to community mental health.* New York: Behavioral Publications, 1969.

Orlans, H. Ethical problems in the relations of research sponsors and investigators. G. Sjaberg, ed., *Ethics, politics, and social research.* Cambridge, Mass.: Schenkman, 1967.

suggested additional readings

Iscoe, I., and Spielberger, C. D. *Community psychology: Perspectives in training and research.* New York: Appleton-Century-Crofts, 1970.

Spielberger, C. D. *Current topics in clinical and community psychology*: Vol. I. New York: Academic Press, 1969.

index